MISCELLANEOUS STUDIES IN THE HISTORY OF MUSIC
By O. G. T. Sonneck

Oscar George Theodore Sonneck, the first Chief of the Music Division of the Library of Congress, was a pioneer in the field of American musicology. He broke new ground, stimulated scholarly interest, and set standards in the discipline which have rarely been matched. Many of his books are still the most authoritative works on their subjects, providing historical and social commentary as well as invaluable musicological data. These *Miscellaneous Studies* treat historical subjects as diverse as "Early American Operas," "The New Mise en Scene of Mozart's Don Giovanni at Munich," "The First Edition of 'Hail, Columbia!'"; as well as discoursing on contemporary music research facilities in "Music in our Libraries." The essays, which originally appeared in early twentieth century periodicals, owe their origin to historical problems that confronted Sonneck in his constructive work at the Library of Congress. Their scholarly yet vital approach to musicology established a direction for subsequent serious American writing on musical topics.

MISCELLANEOUS STUDIES
IN THE
HISTORY OF MUSIC

Da Capo Press Music Reprint Series

GENERAL EDITOR

FREDERICK FREEDMAN

VASSAR COLLEGE

MISCELLANEOUS STUDIES
IN THE
HISTORY OF MUSIC

BY O.G. SONNECK

𝄞 DA CAPO PRESS • NEW YORK • 1968

A Da Capo Press Reprint Edition

This Da Capo Press edition of *Miscellaneous Studies in the History of Music* is an unabridged republication of the first edition published in New York in 1921 by The Macmillan Company.

Library of Congress Catalog Card Number 68-9192

MISCELLANEOUS STUDIES
IN THE
HISTORY OF MUSIC

MISCELLANEOUS STUDIES
IN THE
HISTORY OF MUSIC

BY

O. G. SONNECK

New York
THE MACMILLAN COMPANY
1921

COPYRIGHT, 1921,
BY THE MACMILLAN COMPANY.

Set up and electrotyped. Published August, 1921.

Press of
J. J. Little & Ives Company
New York, U. S. A.

PREFATORY NOTE

Unlike my book "Suum cuique" this collection is devoted almost exclusively to historical studies. The one essay that is not mainly historical has been included for the purpose of showing why it is still impossible in America to attempt historical research work of the kind that attracted me, in any but exceedingly few of our most famous libraries. This lack of essential study material, whether antiquarian or modern, whether literature or scores, has been keenly felt even by those students of musical history who specialize in subjects of a more general local, biographical or evolutional interest. It indicates a sad state of affairs and explains why American contributions to musical history of more than "popular" and limited pedagogical value are so scanty; why, in comparison with Europe, those engaged here in scholarly research or codification of research are so few and why these few men and women have such a disheartening outlet for their life-work.

Most of the essays in this volume were prepared from material available at the Library of Congress. Indeed, it is safe to say that whatever their intrinsic historical value may be, they could have been written nowhere in America except in Washington. They owe their origin mostly to minor historical problems that confronted me in my constructive work as Chief of the Music Division of the Library of Congress from 1902 to 1917.

The essays are reprinted here, by permission, practically as they appeared in various magazines at the time of writing. I have not attempted to incorporate the subsequent "finds" of other historians. Happily they were so few and affected my views so little as to justify publication of these essays in their original form without "rescoring." The expert will know anyhow where to look for controversial and more or less supplemental literature. For instance, those interested in the history of the *pasticcio* will turn to the writings of Lionel de la Laurencie for certain additional data.

As in the case of my books published by G. Schirmer, Inc., I am indebted to Dr. Theodore Baker for seeing this volume through the press. I am also indebted to him for having relieved me of the necessity of translating the first of the essays into English, and especially am I under obligations to him for his remarkably able translation of the rather difficult early Italian text of Il Lasca's *Descrizione.*

O. G. SONNECK.

CONTENTS

PAGE

THE NEW MISE EN SCÈNE OF MOZART'S DON GIOVANNI
AT MUNICH   1

EARLY AMERICAN OPERAS   16

LISZT'S HULDIGUNGS-MARSCH AND WEIMARS VOLKSLIED   93

CIAMPI'S "BERTOLDO, BERTOLDINO E CACASENNO" AND
FAVART'S "NINETTE À LA COUR." A CONTRIBUTION
TO THE HISTORY OF PASTICCIO   111

THE FIRST EDITION OF "HAIL, COLUMBIA!" . . .   180

GUILLAUME LEKEU   190

"CARACTACUS" NOT ARNE'S CARACTACUS   241

A DESCRIPTION OF ALESSANDRO STRIGGIO AND FRAN-
CESCO CORTECCIA'S INTERMEDI "PSYCHE AND AMOR,"
1565   269

MUSIC IN OUR LIBRARIES   287

A PREFACE   296

THE HISTORY OF MUSIC IN AMERICA. A FEW SUG-
GESTIONS   324

MISCELLANEOUS STUDIES IN THE HISTORY OF MUSIC

THE NEW MISE EN SCÈNE OF MOZART'S DON GIOVANNI AT MUNICH

(Originally written in German; published in an Italian translation by Luigi Torchi in the *Rivista Musicale Italiana,* 1896.)

WHEN tardy Spring at last arrives in Munich, only to throw herself with unseemly haste into the arms of Summer; when "Sezession" and "Glas-Palast" [1] reopen their doors;—then one may rest assured that Ernst Possart will also do his part to make the summer season interesting both for natives and foreigners. Nor, in truth, is this brought about solely for artistic reasons. The position of Intendant in Munich necessitates an extraordinary heedfulness for the main chance, the more so because, since the death of the genial Ludwig II, conditions less favorable for art have supervened. But so long as a satisfactory compromise between the two contrasting points of view is achieved, there is no need of overexciting oneself. Such achievement has nearly always been the good fortune, the secret, the desert, of Possart. He began with the remarkable Wagner Cycles, followed next year by a production of *The Marriage of Figaro* absolutely finished in style, and this year, as the event of the season, a revival of *Don Giovanni.*

[1] Art exhibitions, the latter being the more conservative.

1

The tribute of admiration and love which the whole
world now pays to Mozart's masterwork, was by no means
so universal at the outset.   During his lifetime Mozart
was more highly esteemed, by many, as a virtuoso than as
a composer, and precisely his most soulfelt work, *Don
Giovanni,* at first met more than once with inappreciative
opposition.   For example, Salieri's showy operas suited
the Viennese far better than works by the German master.
But both were outrivaled in favor by Dittersdorf.   It is
a most remarkable fact that the opera *Figaro's Hochzeit*
by this latter popular master drove Mozart's *Don Giovanni*
off the boards in Brünn.   And again, when Gazzaniga's
Don Giovanni was presented at the Haymarket Theatre
in London in 1794, and the conductor, Federici, interwove
numbers of his own and by Sarti and Guglielmi in the
action, Da Ponte—at that time the official poet of that
theatre—succeeded in having only the "Catalogo" Aria
from Mozart's opera inserted.   Whereas, in 1857, the
Florentines considered his opera to be "worthless, hyper-
borean music," and hissed it off the stage, Berlinese critical
opinion in 1790 was totally at variance with them: "In
his *Don Juan* Mozart attempted to write something
extraordinary, inimitably grand; this much is certain—
it is something extraordinary, but not inimitably grand!
Caprice, whimsey, pride, but not the heart, presided over
Don Juan's creation!" and more nonsense of like sort.
This foolish uncomprehension, which *Don Giovanni* met
with in still other places, would seem to prove how slight
was Mozart's recognition as an opera-composer.   And this,
in turn, was not the least factor in determining the fate
of the work.

We do know what arbitrary treatment theatre-directors
accord even to admirable, impeccable operas.   They warp
and wrest the dramatic construction wherever and however
they list.   Mozart's masterpiece was not spared this or-
deal.   On the contrary, it suffered more than any other
at the hands of expert bunglers.   The master himself was

obliged to inaugurate this evil custom. The rivalries sub-
sisting between the Viennese singers of both sexes influenced him—as is shown in his diary—to insert the so-
called "bookbinder" aria, "Ein Band der Freundschaft,"
for Don Octavio, for Zerlina and Leporello the duet "Bei
diesen kleinen Händchen," and for Elvira the aria "Mich
verlässt der Undankbare." He did so with a heavy heart;
but what did or do the virtuosos care whether the action
drags, or the characters are ill drawn, or an art-work is
stultified in any way, if only their voices are effectively
shown off? And liberties were soon taken with the very
name of the opera. The title "Il Dissoluto punito," or
"Il Don Giovanni," was quickly turned into "Don Juan,"
"Don Jean," "Der Herr Johann." The first-night play-
bill at Innsbruck announces (1800) "Don Juan oder das
steinerne Gastmahl"; the one at Laibach (Carniola) has
even (1815) "Don Juan's Abenteuer in Spanien oder das
steinerne Gastmahl." And the title in the translation by
the Dessau Musikdirektor Neefe is equally good: "Der
bestrafte Wollüstling oder der Krug geht solange
zu Wasser bis er bricht." After the custom then
prevailing, Neefe also Germanized the cast of characters;
Don Giovanni becomes "der Herr von Schwänkereich,"
Zerlina, "Röschen," Octavio is transformed into "der Herr
von Frischblut," and Leporello into "Fickfack," etc. To
be sure, these are mere trivialities, but they are characteristic of the manner in which matters of prime importance were treated. When, for instance, on the play-
bills and librettos the title read, instead of da Ponte's
"dramma giocoso" (i. e., jovial comedy;—Mozart's diary
even calls the work an opera buffa), as years went on,
"tragi-comic," "tragic," then "romantic," and finally
"grand" opera, this arbitrary generic terminology in itself
proves how totally the work was misapprehended. A grand
opera requires, first and foremost, imposing choral masses;
and so these were actually introduced, like the celebrated
Liberty Chorus in the finale of the first act, the unison

stretta, and others. In the original score there is no hint of all this. The stirring "Viva la libertà" is sung by a solo-quintet, led by Don Giovanni. It would certainly be tasteless and out of keeping to allow a rout of peasants, made tipsy in a nobleman's house, to sing a liberty chorus at the reception of noble guests. The unison chorus is also a graft, as remarked above, for the entire passage is conceived simply as an ensemble of the seven principal characters. In the original the chorus plays, withal, a very subordinate part; there are only two places where it participates in the action—in Scene 7 of Act I with the refrain "la la la la," and in the first finale.

From these disfigurements one may easily imagine how the whole book gradually became transformed. I do not so especially refer to the translations themselves; they were, from the start, inexact and lacking in taste, like almost all translations of opera-books.—Mozart appears to have had a premonition of this, for, according to trustworthy tradition, Mozart's son possessed a free, but felicitous, translation written by his father's own hand. But, unfortunately, it is preserved only in fragmentary form.—Not the translations are meant, but something different. The moment that the (sung) secco recitatives were changed, in the German representations, into spoken dialogue, the "revisers" and "adapters" had every opportunity to compress or expand these passages. Rochlitz, for instance, whose "arrangement" is still adopted in many quarters, found it necessary to enliven da Ponte's flow of ideas. He inserted grandiloquent phrases, gave the characters a different complexion, and even treated portions of the dialogue in the style of Schiller's "Räuber." This produces a very comical effect in the rococo environment. But the most wildly willful deeds were done by an adapter —probably Spiess—when he cold-bloodedly injected three personages into the action—a constable, a hermit, and a tradesman. All three—according to Freisauff—had scenes together with Don Giovanni. "These scenes, following the taste of the times, remind one forcibly of the puppet-show and the harlequinades which were in high favor with the Vienna populace, and whose only aim was evidently to amuse said populace with coarse and stupid jokes." The scene with the tradesman, placed before the last finale, maintained itself on most stages until about 1830; Don Giovanni, instead of paying his due notes, burns them up and has the tradesman thrown out by his lackeys. The scene with the hermit—before the scene in the churchyard—was performed seldomer; its dull point consisted in the twisting of the hermit's words by Leporello. Don Giovanni asks the hermit, "What do you live on?"—*Hermit:* "On roots (Wurzeln) and herbs (Kräutern)."—*Leporello:* "What? The fellow eats infantry (Fussvolk) and cavalry (Reiter)?"—The above-mentioned writer rightly follows this with the observation, "These three scenes could have been fathered only by the grotesquely perverted Viennese taste of that period. They sufficiently demonstrate how little appreciation was then to be found of the wonderful beauties contained in Mozart's masterwork."

Foreign countries had less to suffer from such mutilations, for the simple reason that performances in Italian were commoner there than in Germany. And one may readily imagine that now, in Germany, earnest protests against this outrage made themselves heard. The first step was the rehabilitation of the original score. This was done here and there already in the first half of the nineteenth century. For similar reasons a number of more conscientious and exact translations were made later, like those by Viol, Bitter, Gugler, Grandaur, Wolzogen, Kalbeck, Vaupel, and others. In 1883 there was even a meeting of a committee of German theatre-directors, under the chairmanship of Intendant-General von Perfall, whose aim was to reach an agreement concerning the text of

Don Giovanni. Their efforts were fruitless, "for to-day nearly every considerable theatre has its own arrangement of *Don Giovanni.*"

Professional experts, more especially Gugler, gradually turned their attention to an examination of the musical side. They compared the modern growths with the parent stock—the altered scores with the original score in the possession of Mme. Viardot-Garcia and with almost equally reliable copies from the eighteenth century. Theatre directors, in so far as they were still possessed of an artistic conscience, utilized all the results thus arrived at and organized adequate representations of the mutilated work. In a word, the last decades finally aroused themselves to do justice to Mozart and da Ponte.

Ernst Possart, for his part, expressed the views which guided him in this affair both in a speech and a pamphlet of similar content. This little essay is well worth reading, even though not wholly free from errors, and though the historical material placed at his disposal by professionals may not always have been rightly understood. It was his purpose, "to explain how important and desirable it appears to base the project for a revival of the opera on the original text and the original score." Furthermore, he wished "to convince his readers, that with regard to the dimensions of the auditorium, the strength of the orchestra, and the musical and poetical elements in their entirety, the first representations in Prague, which took place in October, 1787, under the master's personal direction, ought to serve as a model; and that the advanced modern technique of the stage should be employed only in connection with the external equipment, i. e., the scenic decorations and the costumes."

This idea is not novel, but it is correct. When *Don Giovanni,* by Mozart, is set before us, what we want is Mozart's own, and not an arbitrary substitute concocted by some stage-manager or conductor. But between theory and practice there is a long step to be taken.

As *Don Giovanni* was, from the outset, intended for Prague; as da Ponte wrote the poem in Italian and the German Mozart composed it for Italian performers, taking into consideration the constitution of the orchestra and the size of the theatre, with which he was familiar; moreover, as the intellectual horizon of present-day audiences, the taste and the whole trend of our time, in brief, the entire *milieu* is fundamentally different from that of the late eighteenth century, etc., we are confronted by irreconcilable antagonisms.

Whoever should succeed in suitably combining the greatest number of the elements originally given in a stylistically finished representation, would, to be sure, come nearest to a solution of the problem.

The actors themselves are irrevocably lost to us; what is left is only the original Italian libretto, the original score, and—the theatre in Prague. An artistic, conscientious production based on these three would assuredly afford the acme of artistic enjoyment. In fact, this has already been attempted. By the Prague Conservatory on May the 12th, 1842, in the *Landständisches Theater* and in the Italian language, the opera *Don Giovanni* was "presented precisely as Mozart had composed it, in Prague, for the Italian opera of his time." However, the representation seems to have been not "precisely" so. For the play-bill announces "Don Juan," and "grand opera," besides other caprices.

After all, Prague is far away; so what shall other cities do? They can have recourse only to the libretto and the score.

Even so, it would be a sheer impossibility to let a German company sing in Italian. Our throats and ears would energetically protest against it. Such, indeed, was the experience of Possart the consistent, when he made the attempt on beginning rehearsals for the new production. So nothing remained but the score and the stage-directions.

Now, it is understood that parts of the original score are missing. Furthermore, there are cuts in it, made by Mozart from necessity rather than choice. Besides, it is by no means proved that the employment of trombones in the Churchyard Duet and the Descent into Hell is owing to their introduction by an alien hand. It may be assumed with equal probability that Mozart was induced to make changes because the trombone players in Prague found the passages beyond their powers.

So in this particular we also encounter difficulties.

And then, if Mozart had to hear how (with few exceptions) our contemporary singers mishandle the Italian style of the eighteenth century, he would stop his ears.

Contrary opinions are likewise held concerning the numerical strength of the orchestra. It varies with the size of the hall in which it plays. A large auditorium requires a large orchestra, diminishing with the size of the hall. That Possart chose the cozy Residenztheater for the Don Giovanni evenings this season, is a point deserving the heartiest praise. The modern circus-halls with their swollen orchestras spell ruin for all delicate effects. To squeeze some eighty players into the orchestra of the Residenztheater would, of course, be a crude and perverse procedure. Mozart's orchestra, much more than that of our time, played the part of an accompaniment, and only seldom outrivals the voices in importance. But it does appear overdone and pedantic that Possart should have copied the strength of the Prague orchestra in 1787 —twenty-six pieces. Mozart appreciated the good will and efficient work of these men to the full; he even left a testimonial to the orchestra in his translation, where he renders Don Giovanni's query, "Che ti par del bel concerto?" and the response, "È conforme al vostro merto," as follows:

> "Don Giovanni: Herrlich spielen diese Leute!
> Leporello: Es sind Prager Musikanten."

"These men play finely."—"They are musicians from Prague."

This was certainly an amiable compliment. But it is evident from his letters that he longed for Vienna and its more opulent resources; for the Prague opera orchestra was, even in contemporary estimation, a very small one. The characteristic color of Mozart's instrumentation would not be vitiated in the least if the Munich Intendant chose to augment his orchestra by eight or ten string-players. Even then the strings would number only twenty-two, against twelve wind-instruments and a drummer. The Introduction, and the Descent into Hell, would gain decidedly thereby, and the rest would lose nothing.

It follows from the above, that we in Germany have nothing else to cling to for the institution of stylistically correct performances but the original musical score and the stage-directions. Everything beside is subject to limitations. To begin with, in making a German version of the libretto we encounter the old difficulty—a literal translation, if we would have it prosodic, is an absolute impossibility. In such cases, liberties are permitted, but these, in any event, must conform exactly to the sense of the original. It cannot be denied that this desideratum has been attained, on the whole, by the new translation (founded on Grandaur's) made with solicitous devotion by Hermann Levi. Yet even in this one, as in all the rest, we miss the requisite consistency. The so-called "popular" passages have not been thoroughly revised. We refer to those passages whose wording, however perverted or inexact, is held to be sanctioned by tradition. As long as the "champagne" nonsense is done away with, why not the following:

Reich mir die Hand, mein Leben, etc.—The *Là ci darem la mano,* etc., of the original bears a different meaning in connection with the context. And the wording of the lines at the very beginning, *Keine Ruh' bei Tag und Nacht,* etc. (*Notte e giorno faticar,* etc.), might be suppressed, although the poetic motif is, at bottom, better than da Ponte's own.

It was to be expected that Possart would elaborate the scenic side of the production with great refinement. In such matters he is regarded as a master. To be sure, it did not go off without certain daring details of performance. Although he, after Don Giovanni's descent into hell, let the palace crash into peals of thunder (as in *Le Prophète*), and thereupon brought on the original second finale (dragged to light by Possart for the occasion, and so dreadfully conventional and insipid that one would rather not see it)—although Possart let this finale take its course on the ruins of the palace, it shall not be reckoned among the "daring details." For this specimen of bad taste was happily discarded after three performances. The propitiatory and, as observed above, artistically depressing close now proceeds according to the directions in the libretto—without change of scene, without theatrical humbug. What I mean will be found in the answers to the questions, When and where does the action take place? They are exceedingly important, for on them the choice of costumes and decorations depends.

Both poem and music are conceived in the rococo style. But where the librettist's work is merely skillful routine, that of the composer discovers infinite depth. It goes so deep that the contrasts between the characters and the situations often seem too abruptly depicted, giving rise at times to a sense of uneasiness. Contrasted with the smooth verses, Mozart's music is far too soulfelt, far too dæmonic, to insure an harmonious reaction for his *Don Giovanni*. In truth, between poem and music there yawns an unbridgeable chasm. While Mozart, too, is of the rococo period as regards his means of expression, his inspiration spurns the environment of a predetermined epoch. His *Don Giovanni* fits as admirably into the fifteenth century as the eighteenth, or any succeeding time. This aloofness from time and space is the distinguishing mark of a genial, immortal work.

Otherwise the poem. In contrast with Mozart's music,

it may not be transplanted from the rococo soil. Da Ponte neither intended an excursion into history, nor sought to create the illusion of some imaginary time. In his poem lives the spirit of the waning eighteenth century—of the years before the French Revolution. Loose living prevailed, not because it afforded real pleasure, but only to deaden the dread of a frightful convulsion. The cry, "Après nous le déluge!" rose ever louder and more importunately, the nearer it was felt to approach. There was a revel in refined sensuality for the same reason that a murderer feels himself irresistibly drawn to the scene of his deed. In stage-performances a partiality was shown for reflecting the spirit of the times, whose weaknesses were parodied or scourged with ironic and sarcastic scorn, dallied and toyed with. And this same period was on an equally familiar footing with the most heedless materialism and with the mysteries of the spirit-world. A subject-matter like that of *Don Giovanni* was capable of producing a tremendous effect. This was rightly sensed by more than one librettist.

The year 1787 alone beheld the birth of four operas founded on that fable. (1) The one-act *Don Giovanni* by Gazzaniga (Venice); (2) the two-act *Il Nuovo Convitato di Pietra* (The New Guest of Stone) by F. Gardi (Venice); (3) the one-act farce *Il Convitato di Pietra,* by Fabrizj (Rome); and (4) Mozart's *Don Giovanni.* In all four lives the spirit of the eighteenth century.

Possart very clearly recognized this spirit, and had designs for all the characters made in rococo style for the rehearsals. But then he immediately changed his mind. "The monstrous, barrel-like hoopskirts of the ladies and the towering powdered perruques made a grotesque impression even in the sketches, while on the stage they would materially interfere with grace and plasticity of motion, and would impose most irksome restraints on outbursts of passion." He finally decided, like the organizers of the production at Prague in 1842, on laying

the scene in seventeenth-century Spain, which had been
left unscathed by the reactionary counter-reformation.
True, this was a liberty, but it afforded an acceptable
means of escape from the difficulty. That century offers,
in some details, an analogy to the eighteenth: "Here, too,
the nobleman is no longer the standard-bearer of the
nation, but only the member of a caste devoted to un-
bridled self-indulgence." And so Possart chose the costumes of the seventeenth century.—"And the magnificent
tableaux furnished by seventeenth-century Seville, provide
an harmonious background for these costumes."

However, Possart had a certain right to lay the scene
in Seville. The libretto itself designates the scene of
the action only as "a city in Spain." Furthermore, Gardi's
Convitato di Pietra likewise plays in Seville. But then,
the specific selection of this city, or the selection of any
specific city, is somewhat hazardous.

By Chrysander's investigations ("Vierteljahrsschrift
für Musikwissenschaft," Vol. IV) it has been definitely
established that da Ponte and Mozart were acquainted
with the *Don Giovanni* of the poet Bertati and the composer Gazzaniga, and made use of it. Mozart's borrowings
are negligible, whereas da Ponte's utilization of Bertati
must be branded as a barefaced plagiarism. Of course,
such poetic motives are to be excepted as are part and
parcel of the subject-matter of *Don Giovanni,* foremostly
the detail of the Guest of Stone. These are self-evidently
the common property of all versions. But most of the
others, and even the smallest and apparently most insignificant incidents, were similarly employed by da Ponte,
and by them we most clearly perceive the extent of his
borrowings. The fact that certain characters, like that
of Donna Anna, are not delineated like those in the model,
does not redeem da Ponte from the charge of plagiarism.
Much must necessarily be different in the construction of
a one-act play from that of a drama in two acts. Besides,
the happy conceits in this revised version would seem to

have come from Mozart. Da Ponte himself was manifestly troubled by a bad conscience. In his Memoirs he evades the issue of plagiarism—which a moment's comparison with Bertati convincingly proves—with the slippery facility of an eel;—he makes no mention of it whatever.

Ernst Possart is thoroughly familiar with these matters; he discusses them pertinently in his essay. He also appears to have familiarized himself with Bertati's book. For the detail of letting Donna Elvira (a lady of Burgos, deserted by Don Giovanni, as da Ponte, following the text of his model, remarks) enter "in a litter, with travelling impedimenta, followed by servants," though not found in da Ponte's version, is clearly set down in Scenes 4 and 5 of Bertati's. This renders it the more remarkable that Possart did not adopt the latter poet's stage-direction, first brought into general notice by da Ponte;—the scene is laid in a small town in *Aragon*. Observe the difference; Burgos is situated in Old Castile, that is, in northerly Spain, and Seville and Andalusia in the south, while Aragon lies next to France. The character of the scenery would assuredly have been altered, more particularly because the assertion that the Don-Giovanni legend is indissolubly bound up with Seville cannot be regarded as wholly well founded.

After all, these strictures are of slight moment; indeed, they are quite overborne by the praise extorted by the masterstroke of this season's production—the utilization of Lautenschläger's revolving stage. This invention consists —to employ Possart's own very skillful description—in superimposing on the bare stage floor a gigantic turntable. Upon the front half (or on a third or a quarter, or less, according to scenic requirements) is placed the first "set" of the piece to be played. The second "set," for the time being invisible from the auditorium, is put in position back to back with the first, on the rear side of the turntable. When the first scene is over, a motor revolves the

turntable so that the second "set" or scene replaces the
first. This latter is thereupon replaced by Scene 3, so
that when Scene 2 is finished the revolution of the turntable presents Scene 3 to the audience; and so forth.
These changes take place—of course with lights down on
the stage and in the auditorium—before the eyes of the
spectators. And this change of scene, which was accompanied by some noise in the first representations, besides
proceeding slowly, is now accomplished almost noiselessly
and with extreme rapidity. When the scene shifts frequently, as in *Don Giovanni,* the practical effect of this
clever invention is positively astounding. In theatrical
technics it unquestionably has a great future before it.
Neither is it bereft of artistic advantages: "We are no
longer limited to the four-cornered stage-setting with its
obligatory straight lines of decorations; diagonal settings
of picturesque effect will be evolved to delight the eye.
The dead uniformity of square rooms and halls will be
suppressed. The street scenes cut short by a flat back
drop will make way for well-composed and original pictures, and where formerly only painted canvases could
be employed, which were swiftly hoisted or lowered, we
can now make use of firmly set, plastic decorative objects
which materially enhance the naturalness of scenic effects."

Furthermore, the work of the Munich artists as a whole,
with their carefully considered and spirited conception,
being far and away beyond the ordinary, one cannot take
it amiss that Herr Possart views the crowning feat of
this season with very peculiar satisfaction—his revival of
Don Giovanni with revised book and music and new
scenic decorations.

It was in Munich that *Don Giovanni* was most despite-
fully used. In 1791 its performance was forbidden by
a narrow-minded board of censors "als ärgerlich für
allezeit" (as scandalous, and for all time), and was permitted only on "most gracious special command." This
year *Don Giovanni* celebrates its most brilliant representa-

tion—in Munich. Though even now it was not a wholly finished performance, this was owing less to a lack of good intention than to the weakness of certain isolated factors and to the impracticable character of the entire problem. We could acclaim Possart's success with joyful hearts—likewise the fact that Angelo Neumann has engaged the singers, the conductor, the revolving stage, the costumes, decorations, etc., i. e., the entire equipment, for the coming seasons in Paris and London—were there not a menace of serious dangers. Among the amazing contrasts in the musical life of Munich is the circumstance, that while Possart succeeds admirably with the revival of the works of earlier times, he is most unfortunate in his choice of new works. Not one of the novelties which he has brought out possesses genuine vitality. If only the Intendant's ambition is not diverted into an historic mania! If he only does not overwork his unrivalled specialty, the revival of early works in stylistic perfection, to the disadvantage of struggling and unrecognized talents! It is, of a surety, a difficult and honorable task to organize flawless productions of our classics, but far more difficult and honorable to recognize rising composers in their as yet unprinted scores, and to become their champion. Not until Possart has demonstrated that he combines this latter ability with the former, will he fulfill the highly responsible dual duty of a Munich Intendant in a worthy and absolutely commendable manner.

(Translated by Theodore Baker.)

EARLY AMERICAN OPERAS

(Sammelbände der I. M. G., 1904-5)

THIS monograph deals with English operas written during the eighteenth century by Americans, native or naturalized, in what are to-day the United States. Though Italian and French operas were introduced in the United States previously to the nineteenth century, a fact widely unknown, they exercised hardly any influence on our early operatic productions. These were imitations, as was our entire musical life, of English models.

Generally speaking, the history of English opera is a history of ballad operas, as in the broad sense of the term even Stanford's "Shamus O'Brien" belongs to this category. The efforts at musical dramas in which every word is sung, remained sporadic in Great Britain, especially after the tyrannical establishment of Italian opera. Whether the critical opposition was artificial or whether such real operas were foreign to the English character, would be out of place to decide here. At any rate, the attempts were sporadic and moreover professedly in the Italian manner, whereas the ballad operas were innumerable and professedly English in character. The theory that they developed out of the masques might be disputed, but they certainly originated quite independently from Italian influences, and it is erroneous to date their beginnings from the Beggar's Opera.

Whatever might be said to the contrary, the famous "Newgate pastoral" was among other things a veiled protest against Italian opera, and its novelty consisted mainly

16

in the employment of popular ballads, new and old, that is to say, more in appearance than in character. This, together with its political allusions and its literary cleverness, made the Beggar's Opera a formidable rival of the emasculated Italian operas, and encouraged British composers to continue their struggle for English opera. Very soon, however, the popular ballads gave way to original music, a fact which certainly goes far to prove that Dr. Pepusch's setting was considered a polemical experiment, if not the caprice of an antiquarian.

The literature of eighteenth-century ballad operas is abundantly rich, but it shows few stylistic variations. The differences between the older and newer works result from changes in literary and musical taste and from the greater or lesser talents of their authors. The main objection to the *genre* ever has been that the ballad operas are merely plays interspersed with music. The dramatic development is carried on in the spoken dialogue and the composer seldom found an opportunity to call the dramatic possibilities of his art into action, his collaboration being limited to lyrical effusions in soli or ensembles. In fact, a good many ballad operas would gain in interest if the music, however charming it might be, were not allowed to interrupt the plot. It is frequently difficult to see when a play stops to be a play interspersed with music and when it becomes a ballad opera. The distinction lies more or less *a priori* in the title chosen by the authors. For this reason the body of my essay will contain only works entitled operas, musical entertainments, etc., whereas the plays interspersed with music will be enumerated in an appendix, as also the "speaking" pantomimes, which often came nearer being operas than the ballad operas themselves.[1]

If English composers did not care or did not dare to

[1] This Appendix has not here been reprinted from the "Sammelbände." I may add that the whole subject of early American operatic music should be studied in conjunction with my books, "Early Opera in America," "Early Concert-Life in America" and "Bibliography of Early Secular American Music."

improve the genre stylistically, very much less the Colonials. They pinned their faith on their models and imitated them without the slightest effort to infuse new blood into their productions. In America the libretto remained of vastly greater importance than the music—to such an extent that the composer is hardly ever mentioned, unless in the theatrical advertisements. Quite in keeping with this fact is the other, that the librettos were often printed, whereas the music was not. Exceedingly few detached pieces were issued and of these I doubt whether more than a dozen or so have been preserved. This I beg to keep in mind if the data furnished in the following pages are more of a literary and chronological character than musical and if the reader, as would be natural, looks for musical illustrations.

JAMES RALPH'S "FASHIONABLE LADY," 1730

Among the victims of the "Dunciad" was one James Ralph, and to this day his literary reputation has fared ill through Pope's satire. As a member of the "Grub-street" fraternity Ralph certainly deserved his fate, for he was as unscrupulous as Pietro Aretino and ever willing to sell his pen to the highest bidder. But if the politicians took pains to secure or silence his opinion, the man must have been possessed of literary abilities. Indeed, Ralph's writings do not lack ideas, brilliancy, or forcefulness, and his "History of England during the Reigns of King William, Queen Ann and George I." is said to be a remarkable work. It was Ralph's misfortune that he tried to say clever things at any cost, and this journalistic tendency renders his writings unreadable to-day.

James Ralph died at Chiswick (England) on January 24, 1762. But where was he born? Benjamin Franklin narrates in his autobiography that he made the acquaintance of Ralph at Philadelphia, where he was "clerk to a merchant." The two young men soon became friends

and in 1724 together sailed for England to try their luck
in London.   According to Franklin, Ralph deserted wife
and children.   Consequently, he must have been born
about 1700; but where?   To this question there seems
to be no definite answer.   The authorities merely claim
that he was born "probably" in Pennsylvania.[1]   If they
were more positive, then the honor of being the first opera,
or rather opera libretto, written by an American born
in what are to-day the United States, would undoubtedly
belong to a performance of James Ralph.   I allude to

The Fashionable Lady; or Harlequin's Opera.   In the Manner
of a Rehearsal.   As it is Perform'd at the Theatre in Goodman's
Fields.   Written by Mr. Ralph.   [Ornament.]
     London.   Printed for J. Watts, at the Printing Office in Wild
Court near Lincolns-Inn Fields.   MDCCXXX.   [Price 1 s.
6 d.][2]

The opera is preceded by an adulatory dedication "To
His Grace the Duke of Manchester," signed "J. Ralph"
(3 pp.), by a table of the songs (2 pp.) and by the *dramatis
personœ* with the original cast (1 p.).

Men

Mr. Ballad	Mr. Penkethman
Mr. Meanwell	Mr. W. Giffard
Mr. Modely	Mr. Bullock
Mr. Drama	Mr. Lacey
Mr. Merit	Mr. W. Williams
Mr. Smooth	Mrs. Thomas
Captain Hackum	Mr. Huddy
Mr. Whim	Mr. Smith
Mr. Trifle	Mr. Collet
Voice, Harlequin's Man	Mr. Bardin.

[1] For an excellent sketch of Ralph's subsequent career see Stephens'
National Biography, where, however, Ralph's operatic career was overlooked.
[2] 8°. 94 pp. Library of Congress, Brown University, Peabody Institute,
Baltimore, New York Public Library (3 copies, as the assistant librarian
Mr. *Paltsits* had the kindness to inform me. He also notified me that one
of the copies has two pages of advertisements following the text. The latest
date mentioned on this list of books published is January 16, 1729/30). The
wording of the title renders it clear that the publication took place simultaneously with the performances of The Fashionable Lady, that is, in April,
1730.

Women

Mrs. Foible	Mrs. Mountford
Mrs. Sprightly	Mrs. Giffard
Prattle	Mrs. Palmer.

Mutes

Harlequin	Mr. Burney, jun.
Scaramouch	
Pierot	
Punch	
Pantaloon	
Colombine.	

Sir *Peevish-Terrible,* the Critick, Poets, Sailors, Gods, Goddesses, Witches, Dragons, Devils, etc.

That there must be some connection between The Fashionable Lady and the Beggar's Opera is evident; but though Ralph's work is enumerated in Grove's dictionary among the imitations of Gay-Pepusch's masterpiece, this is only partly correct. As in the Beggar's Opera, the dialogue is spoken and the songs are set to popular airs and ballads. But it certainly was not Ralph's serious intention to imitate the Beggar's Opera. On the contrary, he had in view to ridicule ballad operas with an occasional attack on the stilted Italian operas. He says in the dedication:

I must confess it appears no great compliment to present Your Grace with a Play, which has not the Sanction of either of the establish'd Theatres, to recommend it.

If this is not convincing, the following remarks, I hope, will prove my theory.

In the first edition of the "Dunciad" Pope did not mention our author by name. Nevertheless Ralph attacked, in a coarse parody of the Dunciad, entitled "Sawney," *Pope, Swift* and *Gay.* In the same year, 1728, he published under the pseudonym of "A. Primcock"

The Taste of the Town, or a Guide to all publick Diversions.
viz.

    I.   Of Musick, Operas and Plays. Their Original, Prog-
            ress and Improvement . . .
    II.   Of Poetry, Sacred and Profane.
   III.   Of Dancing, Religious and Dramatical.
   IV.   Of the Mimes, Pantomimes and Choruses of the
            Ancients . . .
    V.   Of Audiences . . .
   VI.   Of Masquerades . . .
  VII.   Of the Athletic Sports of the Ancients . . .

The Taste of the Town, though somewhat different in
scope, would be a worthy pendant to Marcello's *Teatro
alla moda,* had not Ralph's ambition to be a "Wit" led
him to caricature his own style. Still, the book is exceedingly interesting. It is a grotesque, almost clownish,
forerunner of "Oper und Drama" and certainly deserved
not to be overlooked as it has been by the historians of
opera and of English opera in particular. This by the
way; with reference to my theme, Ralph leaves no doubt
as to his aversion to ballad operas, though he does not
fully agree with the champions of Italian opera. Two
characteristic quotations will render this clear. He says
(on p. 11):

After the Restoration, we had at different Times several
Entertainments, which were then stiled *Drammatick Operas;*
which were indeed regular Stage plays larded with Pieces of
occasional Musick, vocal and instrumental, proper to the Fable,
and introduced either in the Beginning, Middle or End of an
Act, by single Voices, two or three Part Songs, and Chorus:
These were likewise embellished with Scenes, Machines, *French*
Dancing Masters, long Trains, and Plumes of Feathers . . .
This I look upon as the second age of Operas, as we then stiled
them; but I absolutely deny them that Title; that Term imply-
ing a regular compleat musical Entertainment, which they never
could arrive at, till they entirely came into a finished *Italian*
Plan; nor do we bestow the name of Opera on any Dramma, but
those where every Word is sung.

and on p. 16:

> *The Beggar's Opera* by robbing the Performers at *Pye-corner,*
> *Fleet-ditch, Moorfields* (and other Stations of this Metropolis,
> famed for travelling Sounds) of their undoubted Properties, has
> reinstated them in Wealth and Grandeur; and what shock'd
> most Ears, and set most Teeth on Edge, at turning the Corner
> of a Street, for half a Moment; when thrown into a regular
> Entertainment, charms for Hours.
>
> I must own they never appear'd to that Advantage in any
> musical Light as this Opera of the *Beggars;* Their rags of
> *Poetry* and Scraps of *Musick* joining so naturally, that in what-
> ever View we consider it as to Character or Circumstance, its
> Title is the most apropos Thought on Earth.

If Ralph entertained hopes of injuring the Beggar's
Opera with his parody, he failed, but he certainly succeeded in making his *Harle-uin's Opera* more grotesque
than a "Medley of fools at a Masquerade." Though a real
plot is missing, a thread clearly runs through all the cha-
otic nonsense: Drama versus ballad opera. Mr. Ballad
wants only "Highwaymen and Whores, Beggars and Rus-
ticks . . . they raise the loud laugh"; and Mr. Drama
remarks at the end of the play:

> . . . every little Creature now, who has ever scribbled a popu-
> lar Ballad, or an amorous Song, thinks himself capable of
> writing *English Opera* and charming the politest Audience.

Harlequin, in the few scenes he appears with his man
"Voice," has nothing to do but to dance and play the
fooling fool. He takes a special fancy to Captain
Hackum, and is finally imprisoned by Sir Peevish Ter-
rible, the Critic. Mrs. Foible with Mr. Merit and the
rest, too, do not act, but talk fashion and nonsense, and
their eccentricities are exposed by Messrs. Ballad, Modely,
Meanwell and Drama.

At times The Fashionable Lady reads as if three plays
were printed in one. An effect results, as intended by
Ralph, of absolute nonsense. The idea is carried out with
considerable wit. The dialogue is very fluent, even brilliant, but at the same time so coarse and obscene that the
play would be impossible on the modern stage. Compared

with The Fashionable Lady, the Beggar's Opera is a model
of decency.

It was consistent with the fundamental idea of Ralph's
parody that none but popular ballads, such as "A cobbler
there was" or "An old Woman poor and blind," were used
to lard the play. The entire work contains sixty-eight
"Airs," the first act 22, the second 22 and the third 24,
all tunes being notated in the text. Beyond this and the
fact that The Fashionable Lady was "performed at the
Theatre in Goodman's Fields," I have been unable to collect musical data. In particular, I do not know whom
Ralph engaged to write the accompaniments to the tunes.[1]

"The Fashionable Lady" was performed for the first
time on April 2, 1730, and acted nine times.[2] Surely, a
short career if we remember the persistency with which
other harlequinades appealed to the public taste. And
in this connection the opinion might be ventured that
"The Fashionable Lady" was not quite original with
Ralph. Possibly he took the idea, if not from French
and Italian sources, from the anonymous

Harlequin Hydaspes: or, the Greshamite. A Mock Opera As
it is performed at the Theatre in Lincoln's Inn Fields.
London: Printed and Sold by J. Roberts in Warwick Lane.
MDCCXIX (Price one Shilling).[3]

THE DISAPPOINTMENT, 1767

On April 6–13, 1767, appeared in the "Pennsylvania
Chronicle," Philadelphia, the following advertisement:

By Authority. By the American Company at the New
Theatre in Southwark on Monday next, being the 20th of April,
will be presented a new Comic Opera called *The Disappointment,*
or, the Force of Credulity.

[1] More data probably may be obtained in sources not available at the
Library of Congress.
[2] Compare "Some Account of the English Stage," v. 3, p. 277. I am
indebted to Mr. *Paltsits* for having directed my attention to this book.
[3] Copies of this libretto are at the New York Public Library and the
Library of Congress.

But the play was withdrawn in a hurry, the manager laconically informing the public in the "Pennsylvania Gazette" for Wednesday, April 16th, that

The disappointment (that was advertised for Monday) as it contains personal reflections, is unfit for the stage.

Evidently, the parties reflected on had brought pressure to bear on Mr. Douglass, who could not afford to lose the good will of influential people in a city where opposition to the theatre just then was very strong. However, those whose curiosity had been aroused by the withdrawal had ample and speedy opportunity for enjoying the personal reflections, as the opera was advertised in the "Pennsylvania Chronicle," Monday, April 20–27, as:

Just published and to be sold at Samuel Taylor's Bookbinder, at the Corner of Market and Water Streets, Price One Shilling and Sixpence . . .

That the libretto was not issued by the Philadelphia press appears from the title-page:

The Disappointment: or, the Force of Credulity. A new American Comic Opera of two Acts. By Andrew *Barton,* Esq. [verses.]
New York: Printed in the Year M,DCC,LXVII.[1]

Until James Ralph is positively proven not to have been born in America, The Disappointment will have to be considered the first American opera. If I devote a detailed description and discussion to the work it is on account of its unique position in the history of American music. The preface, important for several reasons, reads:

The Author's Preface To The Public.

The following local piece, intitled *The Disappointment, or the Force of Credulity* was originally wrote for my own, and the

[1] Collation: 12mo.; t. p. v. bl.; pref. pp. [III]–IV; prol.; dramatis personae V–VIII; text 9–56; epilogue [57]–58; errata p. 58.   Boston Public Library; Library of Congress; Library Company, Philadelphia; Pennsylvania Historical Society.   According to George Seilhamer's monumental "History of the American Theatre from 1749 to 1797", 3 vols. New York, 1896, the book recently sold at auction for $13.   It should bring more than that.

amusement of a few particular friends, who (unknown to me) were pleased to signify their approbation of it, in such a manner, that it soon engrossed the chief part of the conversation of all ranks of people; who expressed their desire to hear it and have it published.—Under these circumstances I was greatly at a loss how to proceed, I did not choose (as I saw no merit in it) to expose it to the criticism of criticks, to put it in the power of gentlemen skill'd in scholastic knowledge, to ridicule my ignorance, or condescend to the entreaties of those, who I thought had no more sense than myself, and who might (perhaps) have made it better than it really is. Conscious therefore of my own inability, I determined to excuse myself to all, and in this determination I persisted for some time, but at last, for my own safety, was obliged to capitulate and surrender on the following stipulations; First, the infrequency of dramatic compositions in America; Secondly, the torrent of solicitations from all quarters; Thirdly, the necessity of contributing to the entertainment of the city; Fourthly and lastly, to put a stop (if possible) to the foolish and pernicious practice of searching *after supposed hidden treasure.*

These terms, hard as they are, I have with reluctance been forced to submit to, I am therefore obliged in vindication of my conduct to assure the public that the story is founded on matter of fact, transacted near the city, not long since, and recent in the memory of thousands; for the truth of which assertion I appeal to numbers of my fellow citizens. But in order to give strangers, and those unacquainted with the story some idea of it, the following short history is thought necessary.—The scheme was planned by four humorous gentlemen, Hum, Parchment, Quadrant, and Rattletrap, to divert themselves and friends, and try what lengths of credulity and the love of money would carry men. In order to put their scheme into execution, they fram'd a plausible, well connected story of hidden treasure; and to gloss the matter, adapted sundry papers to their purpose, and pitch'd upon two suitable old fellows, Washball and Raccoon (as principal dupes) with others to try the success of their scheme; which had the desired effect!—The moral: the folly of an over credulity, and desire of money, and how apt men are (especially old men) to be unwarily drawn into schemes where there is but the least shadow of gain; and concludes with these observations, that mankind ought to be contented with their respective stations to follow their vocations with honesty and industry—the only sure way to gain riches.

I do not figure to myself the least advantage accruing from it, but the inward satisfaction of contributing my mite to stop the current of such folly. Such as it is, I submit to the public for their sanction or condemnation, and if any merit should appear in the performance, I shall not vainly attribute it to myself but give the credit of it to mere chance.

I am the Public's
most obedient,
most devoted and
most faithful
humble Servant
Andrew Barton.

The prologue flows in very much the same vein as the preface. But if the author claims that in The Disappointment "Our artless muse hath made her first essay", I fear modern historians will not agree with him, any more than Mr. *Douglass* did with the last lines of the prologue:

The subject's suited to our present times,
No person's touch'd, altho' she lash their crimes.
Nor gall or copp'ras tincture her design,
But gay good humor breathe in ev'ry line;
If you condemn her—she for censure stands;
But if applaud—then thund'ring clap your hands.

However thinly the personal reflections might have been veiled, we feel inclined to side with the author and to admit that his work breathes none but gay good humor through the medium of the

Dramatis Personae

Men

Hum Humorists
Parchment "
Quadrant "
Rattletrap, a supposed Conjurer
Raccoon, an old Debauchee
Washball, an avaricious old Barber Dupes
Trushoop, a Cooper "
M'Snip, a Taylor "
Meanwell, a Gentleman, in love with Washball's Niece
Topinlift, a Sailor
Spitfire, an Assistant to Rattletrap.

Women

Moll Placket, a Woman of the Town, in keeping by Raccoon
Mrs. Trushoop, Wife to Trushoop
Miss Lucy, Washball's Niece, in love with Meanwell
Collector, Blackbeard's Ghost, Taylors, Servants, etc.

If these names are ludicrous, very much more so the plot.[1] When the curtain rises Hum, Parchment and Quadrant are discovered seated around a table in a tavern, where they are drinking and discussing their theme. Raccoon, who "if he smells money, as great a coward as they say he is," will "venture to the gates of hell for it," is expected. Hum announces that he has contrived matters so that Raccoon shall make the discovery himself. Quadrant informs the others that he has drawn in both Trushoop and M'Snip. With his share of the treasures, Quadrant says, Trushoop "talks of building a chapel at his own expense and employing a score of priests to keep up a continual rotation of prayers for the repose of the souls of those poor fellows who buried it." As for M'Snip, he "intends to knock off business, go home to England and purchase a title."

Mr. Parchment prepared the papers, which were duly enclosed in a letter to Mr. Hum, purporting to come from his sister in England. One of these papers, that "looks as if it had been preserv'd in the temple of Apollo or in the tower of Babel," contains the "draught of the place where the treasure lies: together with the memorandum signed by all present at the time it was deposited." Quadrant thinks this droll enough and—we are in a comic opera—expresses his sentiments in a Song:

Air I

I am a brisk young lively lass
In all the town there's none like you,
When you're on mischief bent, sirs;

[1] Mr. Seilhamer's analysis of the plot (op. cit. v. I, pp. 180–4) being so witty and clear, I availed myself of it except where I considered corrections and additions necessary.

With pen and ink, one well can write,
What you do both invent, sirs, etc.

Rattletrap, whom Quadrant found "poreing over the
canto of Hudibras and Sydrophel in order to furnish himself with a set of hard words, which added to his knowledge in the mathematicks, will sufficiently gratify him
for a modern conjurer," enters singing

Air II

The Bloom of May

Behold you my magic phiz,
How solemn and grave I look;
Here, here, my good friends, here is
My brass bound magical book, etc.

His idea is to have a fifth person to act as a "demi-devil
or familiar spirit," and Hum proposes "an old artillery
. . . a snug dry dog" of his acquaintance.

When Raccoon enters, Hum steps out for a moment,
dropping the papers. Raccoon picks them up, looks over
them and crams them into his bosom. Hum returns lamenting the loss of his papers and declaring that the
drawer must have picked his pocket. The poor servant
is roughly handled and searched. At the beginning of
this scene Washball, Trushoop and M'Snip enter. Finally
Raccoon gives up the papers on condition that Hum lets
him in for a share. Parchment pretends to know nothing of the papers, and declares that if they contain any
scheme, plot, combination, rout, riot or unlawful assembly
—in fine anything against his most sacred Majesty,
George II., etc., etc.—he'll at once to the Attorney General
and lodge an information against every man in the company and hang every mother's son of them. Parchment
is finally convinced and then wishes he had been in such
a plot twenty years ago.

Hum pretends to have received a letter from his "loving
sister-in-law in England (who is heir to the famous Capt.

Blackbeard) inclosing sundry papers, such as plans, draughts and memorandums, of a great quantity of treasure, that was buried by the pirates." Parchment reads the particular account of the treasure:

Imprimis, in golden candlesticks, chalises, and crucifixes; 30 000 Portugal pieces; 20 000 Spanish pistoles; 470 000 pistereens; 73 bars of gold; a small box of diamonds; 60 000 pieces of eight; and 150 pounds of weight of gold dust.

This remarkable instrument is signed by Edward Teach, *alias* Blackbeard, captain; Moses Brimstone, first lieutenant; Judas Guzzlefire, gunner, and Jeffery Eatdevil, cook.

"By my saul," cries M'Snip, "I'll away we all me dranken joorneymen and kick the shapboard oot a the wandow."
"I'll shave no more," exclaims Washball,—"no, not I—I'll keep my hands out of the suds."
"Dis will make me cut de figure in life," says Raccoon, "and appear in de world de proper importance; and den I'll do someting for my poor ting," *alias* his mistress Moll Placket.

The conspirators obtain two pistoles each from the dupes and the scene ends with a solo by Parchment:

Air III

How blessed has my time been.

Now let us join hands and unite in this cause;
'Tis glorious gold, that shall gain us applause:
How blest now are we, with such treasure in store,
We'll clothe all the naked, and feed all the poor.
We'll clothe, etc.

In the second scene of the first act Trushoop finds himself locked out by his wife. The old reprobate, Raccoon, in the third carries a spit, pick-axe, and spade into Moll Placket's home and puts them under the bed. Moll calls him her "dear cooney" and he not only tells his "pet" and "dear ting" all about the treasure but promises her 500 a year for pin money when it is obtainable. Both have a song in this scene.

Raccoon:

Air IV

Yankee Doodle

O! how joyful shall I be
When I get de money,
I will bring it all to dee;
   O! my diddling honey! etc.
(Exit, singing the chorus, Yankee Doodle, etc.)

Moll:

Air V

Shambuy

Tho' I hate the old wretch, full as bad as Jack-Ketch,
My necessities tell me to please him;
I will ogle and whine, till I make the gold mine:
For that's the best method to ease him, etc.

The fourth is a street scene where Hum, Rattletrap and
Quadrant agree to assemble their dupes at the town tavern.
In the fifth, M'Snip, after turning his journeymen out
of the shop, sings with a Scotch accent

Air VI

The bonny Broom

I'se cut out political claith,
To patch and mend the state;
My bodkin and my thamble beith,
Combine to make me great, etc.

Follows a love-scene between Lucy and Meanwell. Lucy
tells her lover that her uncle Washball has ordered her
to discard him, and promised her a marriage portion of
10,000 if she marries agreeably to his wishes. Of course
this scene gives occasion to a duet.

Air VII

My fond Shepherds, etc.

Meanwell

My dear Lucy; you ravish my heart,
I am blest with such language as this;

> To my arms then, oh, come, we'll ne'er part
> And let's mutually seal with a kiss.

Lucy

> Ten thousand sweet kisses I'd give,
> O! be you but contented with me,
> Then for you my dear Meanwell I'll live,
> And as happy as constant I'll be.

As always in comic opera, Washball makes his appearance at the most inopportune moment and the love-scene ends like all such love-scenes—Meanwell is put out of the house.

The seventh scene discovers the humorists and dupes at the tavern discussing the details of their plan. In one point they all agree, that "the greatest exertion of . . . courage will be necessary," as they "have to engage with principalities and powers of darkness, with invisibles and demons, more powerful than the united legions of the most invincible monarchs on earth." But they become quite merry in prospect of the treasure and do a good deal of drinking, singing and boasting.

M'Snip has

Air VIII

Over the hills and far away.

> This money makes the coward brave,
> And freedom gives to ev'ry slave;
> My gude brod-sword I'll soon display,
> And drive those warlocks far away,
> And drive those warlocks, etc.
> And drive those warlocks, etc.
> My gude brod-sword I'll soon display,
> And drive those warlocks far away.

After "canoe" has been chosen as watchword, Trushoop sings:

Air IX

Chiling o Guirey

> By shaint Patrick, dear honeys, no longer let's stay
> But take laave together, and bundle away,
> To the plashe under ground, where the treasure's expos'd

And bring that to light, which shall ne'er be disclosed;
And when we have got it, my jewels, o hone!
For keeping it snug,—arra! let us alone,
We'll sing whillalew, at the sight of the palf,
And as for the sharing, laave that to myself.
Sing laral lal, etc.

The act ends with a drinking song by Rattletrap:

Air X

The Jolly Toper

The merchant roams from clime to climes
Regardless of his pleasure;
To hardships and fatigue resigns,
When in pursuit of treasure.
And, a digging, etc. (*they drink and fill.*)

The second act opens with a broad, coarse scene that
would be inadmissable nowadays between Topinlift, the
sailor, and Moll Placket, in which Topinlift sings (Air
XI): "No girl with Placket can compare" to the tune of
Nancy Dawson. Shortly afterwards Raccoon comes for
his spit, pick-axe and spade. Topinlift conceals himself
under the bed where the implements were placed, but to
prevent Raccoon from going there Moll pretends that she
is about to raise a familiar spirit, and the sailor makes
his escape as a ghost, knocking Raccoon over as he rushes
out. Raccoon when recovering from his shock thinks "he
look like de sailor," finds his tools, and walks out with

Air XII

The lass of Patie's mill.

Oh! when I get de welt, dat's bury'd by de mill;
Insur'd long-life and helt, and pleasure at my will.
What store of gold I'll bring my lovely pet to dee,
Den none but my poor ting shall share de same wid me.

Moll, after his departure, adds some peculiar reflections
of her own, partly in a monologue and partly in

Air XIII

Black joke and band so white
Sure gold is the fewel, that kindles the fire,
And serves for to fan up a woman's desire,
To a fumbling fool, that's decrepid and old, etc.

The next scene is the "Place of Action, near the Stone Bridge." Rattletrap, dressed in his magic *habit*, when all are assembled "draws the magic circle and pronounces words of incantation: Diapaculum interravo, testiculum stravaganza." The digging proceeds under similar incantations and astrological reflections of a most grotesque character; the convulsions of nature are rather unusual, and finally the ghost of the pirate appears and spits fire. Trushoop says the spook "looks like no slouch of a fellow"; Washball, thoroughly frightened, prays *Mea culpa,* and Raccoon, who now wishes he had lived a better life, asks him to pray in English, saying "dese spirits don't understand de Latin.' The ghost resists the search for the treasure, but in vain, and when the chest is finally secured Rattletrap jubilantly breaks forth into

Air XIV

Granby

Tho' my art some despise, I appear to your eyes,
For a proof of my magical knowledge;
Tho' the wisdom of schools, damn our art and our tools,
We can laugh at the fools of the college.
Chorus: We can, etc.

The second scene takes place in a room in Washball's house, where Lucy and Meanwell decide to elope. But though "the precious moments are swiftly passing" they find time to sing a duet:

Air XV

Kitty the Nonpareille

Lucy: My throbbing heart must now give way
To love, to honor, and obey.

Lo! Hymen's torch is lighted.
Lo! Hymen's, etc.

My heart! my all!—I do resign,
O! Meanwell!—Meanwell!—I'll be thine,
In wedlock's band united!
In wedlock's, etc.

Meanwell: Of Venus' charms, let poets write!
Diana chaste, or, Juno bright!
Of Kitty, Doll, or, Susey!
Of Kitty, etc.

The charms of all, are center'd here,
In Lucy!—charming Lucy dear!
Haste! haste! my lovely Lucy!
Haste, etc.

The third scene is a street-scene in front of the collector's house and begins with a monologue of Washball which leaves no doubt as to his being "an avaricious old barber." It begins:

I can't bear the toughts of dividing, not I . . . charity begins at home and he must be the greatest fool on earth that cheats himself. . . . I'll go and inform the collector; then I shall have one half to myself, the other will go to the king.

This he does in the fourth scene. The fifth opens in a room in Washball's house and discovers M'Snip, Trushoop and Raccoon, sitting on the chest, and old Gabriel, Washball's servant, standing by. When Washball enters with the collector, Hum takes the latter aside and tells him of the "scheme of diversion" whereupon the collector on some pretense retires. The chest is now opened and, of course, contains nothing but stones. The dupes look at one another confused, it dawning upon them that they have been fooled, and the "humorists" laugh and run off the stage. Poor Trushoop is the first to remember that he is the duped hero in a comic opera and he bewails his fate in

Air XVI

The Milking Pail.   (To be sung slow and with an Irish accent.)
> Arra what a fool was I; by my showl! I think I'll cry.
> When I spake of all thish, it encreases my blish;
> I will kill me bafare I die, etc.

But on the whole he takes it good-naturedly and begins to enjoy the joke as much as the humorists.

The piece ought to end with the opening of the chest, but it cannot, for Lucy and Meanwell have eloped and are to be forgiven by Washball.   They receive his blessing, after which he takes occasion to sing the doleful

Air XVII

> Ah! who is me, poor Walley cry'd.
> Ah! who is me, poor wretched I,
> With broken heart and downcast eyes;
> To ease my mind where shall I fly?
> A prey to knaves poor Washball dies.
> Let future generations take
> Example by my dismal fall.
> Nor gods of gold, nor idols make,
> To shun the fate of poor Washball.

He is full of resignation, invites the dupes for dinner, tells old Gabriel to call in the neighbors, to bring his fiddle and play for a dance.   He also requests Lucy and Meanwell to give them a song, which they do with

Air XVIII

> Jolly Bacchanalian.

Meanwell: Banish sorrow, welcome joy
>   . . . .
>   Banish care and be at rest,
>   Of a bad bargain make the best.
>   Banish care, etc.

Lucy: Room for joy, how blest am I
>   . . . .
>   Virgins all, example take;
>   Virtue love, for virtue's sake,

Constant be as turtle dove,
Let your theme be virtuous love.
Constant be, etc.

Enter Gabriel with his fiddle and the neighbors. They strike up a country dance called "Excuse me" and the whole ends with an epilogue in which Hum sings some popular refrains like: Down Derry Derry down, tantara-rara, tol de rol, lol de rol loddy—and in which all the characters, including Moll Placket and Topinlift, make their final bow to the audience.

Mr. Seilhamer claims The Disappointment to be "without merit as a dramatic composition" (op. cit. I, 184), but I disagree with him. I fear the coarseness of the play prevented him from being just. No doubt The Disappointment contains scenes which would to-day be quite unfit for public performance, but it must be added that this indecency is that of naïve brutality and not of a morbid suggestiveness, as in so many plays of our *fin de siècle* decadents.

Should these scenes undergo a skillful operation, a performance of The Disappointment would prove that it does contain a good deal of merit as a dramatic composition. To-day the personal reflections would neither make a performance impossible, nor would they—as a species of published gossip—facilitate a success of the work. It would have to stand on its intrinsic merits.

The fundamental idea is excellent and well adapted to dramatic treatment. The characters are cleverly contrasted, and the different dialects, not being used to exaggeration, give a delightful flavor to the whole. The dialogue is exceedingly fluent, and the plot is well developed. It falls short only on account of the conventional *finale* of the play, which was caused by the preceding love-scenes between Lucy and Meanwell, and they, too, conventional. The author possessed a surprisingly keen eye for what is effective on the stage. This, combined with much natural wit and humor, makes many scenes "irresistibly comic," as even Mr. Seilhamer had to admit. Take, for instance, the scene in which the poor devil of a waiter is accused of theft, abused and maltreated, the real culprit, that rascal Raccoon, not making the slightest effort to interfere, but quietly and as if unconcerned waiting for the storm to pass. Here are unusual opportunities for a clever comedian!

But even this scene is surpassed in theatrical clairvoyance, brilliancy and wit by the one at the place of action. It is masterly with all its fantastic and burlesque drollery. It is within the limits of dramatic probability and worthy of the pen of famous playwrights. All in all, The Disappointment deserves more attention than has been paid to it, and the fate of the farce vividly recalls that of Otto Niebergall's brilliant but also unduly neglected "Tatterich."

Turning to The Disappointment as a comic opera, we readily classify it as a ballad opera. Evidently the Beggar's Opera, then immensely enjoyed in the Colonies, was taken as a model. With this difference, however, that the American work is not overloaded with ballads, there being only eighteen of them in the opera. The introduction of Yankee Doodle is especially noteworthy, being probably the earliest reference to the tune in American literature, and liable to overthrow certain theories as to its history in the Colonies. That the airs have a right of dramatic existence cannot reasonably be maintained, but this ever has been and ever will be the weak point in ballad operas, Singspiele, vaudevilles and the like. The attempts at ensembles and choruses are exceedingly few and feeble. To improvise or to write "accompaniments" for "The Disappointment" cannot have been a very interesting task, and we hardly regret not to know the name of the musician whose duty it was to do so.

Thirty years after the first, a second edition of the opera, protected by copyright, appeared at Philadelphia under the title:

The Disappointment, or, the Force of Credulity. A new comic opera in three acts. By Andrew *Barton,* Esq. Second Edition, revised and corrected with large additions by the Author. [verses.]
Philadelphia. Printed for and sold by Francis Shallus, No. 40, Vinestreet. 1796.[1]

The preface and prologue show but unimportant alterations, whereas the expansion of the opera into three acts called for considerable changes. It is hardly necessary to dwell on them in detail. A rapid survey will be sufficient.

In the first place the dramatis personae have increased. Instead of four dupes we notice five, M'Snip having been superseded by "Buckram, a Taylor" and "Trowell, a Plaisterer," "Perrance, Servant to Trushoop," is also new. Furthermore we make the acquaintance of "Mrs. Trowell, Wife to Trowell" and "Dolly, Servant to Mrs. Trushoop."

The first scene opens as in the edition of 1767, but the dialogue is now preceded by a drinking song by Parchment:

Song I

Come now, my boys, let's jovial be,
The cash we'll soon disclose;
And spurn at sneaking poverty,
Tho' Gorgons dire! oppose.

In the middle of the scene Trushoop now addresses Washball with a very lengthy

Song IV

You seem in a flutter
And pray what's the matter, etc.

We further notice that all allusions to the government in Parchment's monologue have been revised. Instead of "His most sacred Majesty, George the Second" we now read "illustrious President of the United States." In the

[1] 12°. 94 p. Boston Public Library; Brown Univ.; Mass. Hist. Soc.; New York Public Library; Library of Congress; Pennsylvania Hist. Soc.; British Museum, etc.

third scene we witness Mrs. Trushoop's efforts to starve
her husband into fidelity.   Then follows the burlesque and
coarse meeting between Moll Placket, Topinlift and Raccoon.   In the fifth scene Mrs. Trushoop repents her treatment of Mr. Trushoop and endeavors to reconcile him by
ordering Dolly to

take the two market baskets, and go down into the cellar, and
fetch up everything there for master to eat and drink.

In the following scene Dolly and Ferrance, as servants
probably will do in all eternity, laugh at their master
and mistress, and the scene ends in harmony between Mr.
and Mrs. Trushoop.

The second act discovers Mrs. Trowell at work in her
parlor.   Mrs. Trushoop enters and we soon become familiar with her family troubles: that Mr. Trushoop has become a Free Mason, that he spends more time at the
Lodge than at home, that she revenges herself by almost
starving him to death, and that "he ought to be sent to the
Bastille and Burttong-bay in the bargain."   The moment
she is at the height of her rage Mrs. Trowell mentions
the "mistery" and how she "wheedled, coaxed, fonded,
hugg'd, squeez'd, caress'd and kiss'd her husband" till she
got the whole secret of the buried treasure out of him.
The change that overcomes Mrs. Trushoop's sentiments
for her now "dare Trushoop" is highly comical and she
hastens away to "make it up with him."

What was the seventh scene of the first act in the edition
of 1767 now follows with slight alterations as the second
of the second act, and the play proceeds on the same lines
as the original until the "Place of action" is reached,
which has become the opening scene of the third act.   The
last scenes have remained intact as far as the plot is concerned.   Finally, instead of an ensemble-epilogue, we notice one in the form of a monologue, without being told
by whom it shall be spoken.   It "shews" the moral lessons
contained in the opera and ends rather proudly thus:

Condemn or not—we satisfaction feel,
In thinking, we have caus'd a reformation,
Amongst the dupes of this our congregation.

Owing to the expansion of the play, of course, the numerical order of the "Songs," as they are now called, has not remained the same. If I further remark that the names of the tunes have been dropped, that the language is less coarse, that the changes in literary taste, political and social conditions between 1767 and 1796 were taken into consideration, I believe I have mentioned all that is necessary to indicate the difference between the two editions. If the author felt satisfied with his revision, not so the historian. While The Disappointment in its original form had been considered unfit for the stage on account of its personal reflections, it became impossible for performance in 1796 for very much stronger reasons: the expansion and revision weakened the plot, diluted the witty dialogue, and robbed the "opera" of its genuine and forceful, though brutal, spontaneity.

So far The Disappointment calls not for much critical acumen. However, the opera comes in for a full share of the mystery that surrounds the beginnings of art in the United States. We need but take an interest in the person of Andrew *Barton,* Esq., to be confronted with a threatening question mark.

"Evidently," says Mr. Seilhamer, "the name of Andrew Barton, Esq., on the title page is an assumed one, and in the Ridgway Library [1] copy the name of Colonel Thomas *Forrest,* of Germantown, is written in ink as the author." [2] A startling statement; the more so as it is not at all self-evident why the not very uncommon name of Barton should be a pseudonym. Had Mr. Seilhamer written "because" instead of "and" he would, at least, not have dismissed his readers without a reason for his theory. As the statement stands, his "evidently" appears merely to

[1] A branch of the Library Company of Philadelphia.
[2] Op. cit. I, 178.

be an argument *a posteriori.* The fact is, that Mr. Seil-hamer, like Messrs. Durang, Ford, Tyler and other historians, based the theory more or less on a few delightful passages in Watson's "Annals of Philadelphia." Had they informed us that they failed to find the name of Andrew Barton either in the Barton genealogies or in the city directories of Philadelphia and New York published before 1797, and that "in most of the English chronicles under the year 1511" the story is to be found of how Lord Charles Howard captured Sir Andrew Barton, "a Scotish rover on the sea"—we should be prone to abide by their decision.[1] Under the circumstances, however, a reëxamination of their mutual source is advisable.

Mr. Watson had this to say:[2]

Colonel Thomas *Forrest,* who died in 1828, at the age of 83, had been in his early days a youth of much frolic and fun, always well disposed to give time and application toward a joke. He found much to amuse himself in the credulity of some of the German families. I have heard him relate some of his anecdotes of the prestigious kind with much humor. When he was about 21 years of age, a tailor who was measuring him for a suit of clothes, happened to say, "Ah, Thomas, if you and I could only find some of the money of the sea robbers (the pirates), we might drive our coach for life!" The sincerity and simplicity with which he uttered this, caught the attention of young Forrest, and when he went home he began to devise some scheme to be amused with his credulity and superstition. There was a prevailing belief that the pirates had hidden many sums of money and much of treasure about the banks of the Delaware. Forrest got an old parchment, on which he wrote the dying statement of John Hendricks, executed at Tyburn for piracy, in which he stated that he had deposited a chest and pot of money at Cooper's Point in the Jerseys. This parchment he smoked and gave it the appearance of antiquity; and calling on his German tailor, he told him he had found it among his father's papers, who had got it in England from the prisoner, whom he visited in prison. This he showed to the tailor as a precious paper which he could by no means lend out his hands. This operated the desired effect.

[1] See the splendid ballad of Sir Andrew Barton in "A select collection of English songs," London, 1783.
[2] Op. cit. v. I, pp. 268–70.

Soon after the tailor called on Forrest with one Ambruster, a printer, whom he introduced as capable of "printing any spirit out of hell," by his knowledge of the black art. He asked to show him the parchment; he was delighted with it, and confidently said he could conjure Hendricks to give up the money. A time was appointed to meet in an upper room of a public house in Philadelphia, by night, and the innkeeper was let into the secret by Forrest. By the night appointed, they had prepared a closet, a communication with a room above their sitting room, so as to lower down by a pulley, the invoked ghost, who was represented by a young man entirely sewed up in a close white dress on which were printed black-eyed sockets, mouth, and bare ribs with dashes of black between them, the outside and inside of the legs and thighs blackened, so as to make white bones conspicuous there. About twelve persons met in all, seated around a table. Ambruster shofled and dealt out cards, on which were inscribed the names of the new Testament saints, telling them he should bring Hendricks to encompass the table, visible or invisible he could not tell. At the words "John Hendricks, du verfluchter, cum heraus," the pulley was heard to reel, the closet door to fly open, and John Hendricks with ghastly appearance to stand forth. The whole were dismayed and fled, save Forrest, the brave. After this, Ambruster, on whom they all depended, declared that he had by spells got permission to take up the money. A day was therefore appointed to visit the Jersey shore and to dig there by night. The parchment said it lay there between two great stones. Forrest, therefore, prepared two black men to be entirely naked except white petticoat breeches, and these were to jump each on the stone whenever they came to the pot, which had been previously put there. These frightened off the company for a little. When they next essayed they were assailed by cats tied two and two, to whose tails were spiral papers of gunpowder, which illuminated and whizzed, while the cats whawled. The pot was at length got up, and brought in great triumph to Philadelphia wharf: but oh, sad disaster! while helping it out of the boat, Forrest, who managed it, and was handing it up to the tailor, trod upon the gunnel and filled the boat, and holding on to the pot dragged the tailor into the river—it was lost! For years afterwards they reproached Forrest for that loss, and declared he had got the chest himself and was enriched thereby. He favored the conceit, until at last they actually sued him on a writ of treasure trove; but their lawyer was persuaded to give it up as idle. Some years afterwards Mr. Forrest wrote a very

humorous play (which I have seen printed),[1] which contained
many incidents of this kind of superstition. It gave such
offense to the parties represented, that it could not be exhibited
on the stage. I remember some lines in it, for it had much of
broken English and German English verses, to wit:

> My dearest wife, in all my life
> Ich neber was so frighten'd,
> De spirit come and I did run,
> 'Twas juste like tunder mit lightning.

A pretty story, but does it go to prove the authorship
of Colonel Thomas Forrest or De Forest, as he is sometimes called, of "The Disappointment"? [2]

If the Colonel wrote the libretto, so full of personal reflections as to be unfit for the stage, why should its plot
differ so widely from Mr. Watson's anecdote, particularly
as the incidents of the latter would lend themselves easily
and without many alterations, even as to the name of the
pirate, for the plot of a farce? Then again, Mr. Watson
says that Thomas Forrest fooled the tailor "when he was
about 21 years of age" and that he wrote the play *"some
years afterwards."* How is this? The Colonel died in
1828 at the age of 83. Consequently he was born in
1745. Adding to this date 21 years we gain the year
1766. The Disappointment was *published* (!!) only one
year later, in April, 1767.—I confess, a strange contradiction! But this is not all. Says Mr. Watson: "I remember some lines.

> My dearest wife, in all my life
> Ich neber was so frighten'd,
> De spirit come and I did run,
> 'Twas juste like tunder mit lightning.

He must have had a peculiar memory, for *these lines appear in neither edition of The Disappointment.*

[1] A copy is now in the Athenæum, called "The Disappointment, or Force
of Credulity, 2d edition, 1796." (This is Watson's Footnote.)
[2] I lay no stress on the suspicious footnote: the second edition is mentioned, but not the first!

The inference is plain. It would be incompatible with historical reasoning to accept Forrest's traditional authorship unchallenged. But Mr. Seilhamer claims that "in the Ridgway Library copy the name of Colonel Thomas Forrest, of Germantown, is written in ink as the author." This is a fact. We indeed read, following the verses on the title-page, the ink memorandum "by Col. Thomas Forrest of Germantown."

As this gentleman became a colonel in the later part of the War for Independence, the memorandum cannot have been added until, let us say, about 1779—twelve years after the book was published. It might just as well have been added many years later, perhaps by somebody who read Watson's Annals! Furthermore, is it not strange that, though a second edition of the opera appeared after thirty years, no other and more convincing allusions to Forrest's authorship should have been preserved, not to mention the fact that this gentleman did not himself come forward with such a claim when secrecy was no longer a virtue?

But let us examine the Ridgway copy more closely! It is full of manuscript corrections and additions, such as only the author himself can have made. Now the handwriting of these corrections differs from that of the memorandum on the title-page. Consequently it was not Thomas Forrest who attributed the book to himself in after years, and therefore the ink memorandum is by no means authoritative. Finally, how if the half faded sign, that follows this ink memorandum, should have been intended as a question mark, as it looked to me when I examined the copy Mr. Seilhamer mentions?

This historian ends his chapter on "The Disappointment" with the words: "there is no reason to doubt, . . . that the author was Colonel Forrest." We are obliged to contradict him. It seems to me that there are reasons enough to doubt that gentleman's authorship. In fact, Thomas Forrest is not the only competitor for the possible pseudonym of Andrew Barton, Esq.; and Mr. Seilhamer, like others, though predisposed in favor of the Colonel, was cautious enough to mention that "by some" (who?) the authorship of the opera was attributed to *Joseph Leacock,* who was a jeweler and a silversmith in Philadelphia at the time, and by others to *John Leacock,* "who became Coroner after the Revolution."

We may dispose of Joseph, by saying that he seems to have been among the dead when, in 1796, the second edition of The Disappointment, revised and corrected by the author, was issued. On the other hand, Coroner John Leacock figures in the Philadelphia directories even later.

If Andrew Barton, Esq., is to be considered a pseudonym, it seems to me that John Leacock, claimed also (by Mr. Hildeburn) to have written the tragi-comedy of "The Fall of British Tyranny," should not be cast aside so cheerfully in favor of Thomas Forrest. However, the simplest and most satisfactory theory will be to attribute The Disappointment to the pen of one Andrew Barton, Esq., until this name has *convincingly* been proved to be a pseudonym.

1780–1790

1781: The Temple of Minerva. 1782: The Blockheads. 1787: May Day in Town. 1790: The Reconciliation.

After the publication of The Disappointment in 1767 we do not come across American operas until the war for Independence drew to its end.[1] In my monograph on Francis Hopkinson [2] as the first native American poet-composer I described at some length his Temple of Minerva, performed in 1781, and it is hardly necessary to repeat here the history of this curious "Oratorial entertainment," as the newspapers called it. It was a politi-

[1] In 1778 was published at Philadelphia the comic opera "The Political Duenna," but as this piece was not written by an American, it is unnecessary to describe it.

[2] Extracts were published in Sammelbände V, p. 119–154. The book itself was published in 1905 under the title of "Francis Hopkinson and James Lyon."

cal, allegorical, semi-operatic sketch in two scenes, in which the Genius of America, the Genius of France, the High-priest of Minerva and the Goddess herself unite in saying and singing pleasant things of the French-American alliance. I also stated that it ended with the usual glorification of George Washington, that Hopkinson's music is not extant, and that the Temple of Minerva made part of a concert given on the 11th of December, 1781, by the minister of France in honor of "his excellency general Washington and his lady, the lady of general Greene, and a very polite circle of gentlemen and ladies."

In the following year a mysterious work left the press, entitled:

The Blockheads, or, Fortunate Contractor. An opera in two acts. As it was performed at New York.
New York printed. London, reprinted for S. Kearsley, 1782.

I have not seen the libretto and can only say that Mr. Wegelin [1] attributes it to the pen of Mrs. Mercy Warren, the author of two other political plays. The Blockheads is said to have been written as a counterfarce to General Burgoyne's Blockade of Boston, performed by his military Thespians in January, 1776, at Boston.[2]

Somewhat firmer ground is gained with Royall Tyler's "May Day in Town, or New York in an Uproar." This

"comic opera in 2 acts (never performed), written by the author of 'The Contrast' . . . The Music compiled from the most eminent Masters. With an Overture and Accompaniments.
The Songs of the Opera to be sold on the Evening of Performance."

was advertised in the "New York Daily Advertiser," May 17, 1787, for performance on the following evening. It was given for the benefit of the much admired actor Thomas Wignell, who in 1793 with Alexander Reinagle became manager of the "New Theatre" at Philadelphia.

[1] Oscar Wegelin: Early American Plays, 1714—1830. Dunlap Society publications. New series. No. 10. New York, 1900.
[2] Seilhamer, op. cit. II, 20.

The opera seems not to have been received favorably, for only one performance is on record. Mr. Seilhamer (II, 215) ably calls it "a skit on what has lasted in New York to our day—the much dreaded May-movings." By whom the music was compiled from the most eminent masters I have been unable to ascertain.

A very much more pretentious opera was Peter Markoe's "Reconciliation." The libretto was advertised as "this day . . . published" in the "Federal Gazette," Philadelphia, on May 24, 1790. The title reads:

The *Reconciliation;* or the Triumph of Nature. A comic opera, in two acts by Peter Markoe. [verses.]
Philadelphia: Printed and sold by Prichard & Hall, in Market Street between Front and Second streets, MDCCXC.[1]

As was the case with Andrew Barton's Disappointment, Peter Markoe's opera was accepted by the manager of the American Company but not performed. Of this the author informs us with some bitterness in the dedication

"To his Excellency Thomas Mifflin, Esq., President of the State of Pennsylvania; and to the Honorable Thomas M'Kean, Esq., Chief Justice of the said State; this *Comic Opera* approved of by them in their official Capacity according to Law; but withdrawn from the Managers of the Theater, after it had remained in their hands more than four Months; is . . . inscribed . . ."

The author also relieved us of the necessity of investigating the source of his plot. He remarks in the preface:

A revisal and correction of "Erastus," literally translated by a native of Germany, lately arrived in Pennsylvania, gave rise to the following piece.
The happy simplicity of the German original, written in one act by the celebrated Gesner, [*sic*] suggested an enlargement of the plan. A new character is added, songs are introduced, and the dialogue so modeled, as to be rendered (it is presumed) pleasing to an American ear. Those who understand the Ger-

[1] 8vo.; pp. III ded.; V–VI pref.; VIII Dram. pers.; 9–48. Text. Brown Univ.; Library of Congress; Library Company of Philadelphia.

man and the English languages will, on comparing the two pieces, readily perceive the difference between them . . .

Though this task of comparison would be simple, I prefer to avail myself of the "impartial review" of Markoe's [1] libretto, as it appeared in the "Universal Asylum," Philadelphia, July, 1790 (pp. 46–47). Being practically the earliest critical analysis of an American opera, a literal quotation cannot fail to arouse some interest. It reads:

The Reconciliation: or the Triumph of Nature: a comic opera, in two Acts. By Peter Markoe. Published in Philadelphia.

This little performance is founded on Erastus, a dramatic piece in one act, written by Gessner. The plan is said to be enlarged, so as to differ considerably from the German production. The plot is perfectly simple. Wilson by marrying Amelia has displeased his father. Neglected by him, and forsaken by his friends, he retired from the world, into an obscure retreat, with his wife and son, a man and maid-servant. Here they remained twelve years struggling with all the evils of poverty, but supporting themselves under their afflictions with the consciousness of innocence. Old Wilson, during a violent illness, became sensible of his unjust and cruel treatment of his children, and determined to find them out. While passing over the mountains, with this intent he is met by honest Simon, Wilson's servant, who, not knowing him, obliges him to deliver him half of his money, conceiving it more consistent with justice to rob a man of superfluous wealth, than to suffer a family to starve. The money he offers to Wilson, and tells him that he received it for him from an unknown friend. But the incoherence of his tale leads Wilson to suspect the truth of it and he at length makes a confession of the robbery. Wilson convinces him of the iniquity of his conduct, and obliges him to set out to find the man whom he has robbed, and to restore the money to him. As he is preparing to do this old Wilson enters to enquire the road, and upon seeing Simon is much alarmed. But his fears are soon removed by Wilson's assurances. By means of a letter the old man drops from his pocket, Simon

[1] Peter Markoe was born in Santa Cruz (St. Croix) in 1735 and died at Philadelphia in 1792. He was educated at Trinity College, Dublin; read law in London and settled in Philadelphia in 1783. His "Miscellaneous Poems" were printed in 1787.

discovers him to be his master's father; a reconciliation takes place, and all parties are happy.

Such a story appears calculated for the pathetic, rather than the humorous. Accordingly we find the former abounding, and the latter very scantily dispersed. The sentiments are in general fine. The moral inculcated throughout the whole is a confidence in the ways of Providence, and an adherence to probity and rectitude.

The characters are uniformly supported. Wilson is an amiable virtuous man, who in the midst of his afflictions and concern for his wife and child, and all the distresses which have been heaped upon him, suffers not his integrity to be lessened. Amelia is an admirable pattern of conjugal affection, and firm reliance upon the justice of Heaven. This gives to her, in the greatest misfortunes, a tranquillity of soul, with which she endeavours to inspire her husband; nor are her attempts fruitless. Their son William, unconnected with the world, talks with the most childish simplicity, at the same time manifesting a virtuous charitable disposition. Simon is a faithful, affectionate servant, who prefers the service of his old master, to a more profitable place, and retires with him into the mountains. He is made sometimes to utter sentiments which seem superior to the station in which he is placed. Debby is an honest, plain woman. She and her Simon have some little quarrels, but all matters are at last composed between them.—Old Wilson manifests sincere contrition for his harsh conduct towards his son.

The songs are in general good. Some of them appear to us to possess real excellence; particularly the 2d, 3d, 6th and 7th. What effect this piece would have upon the stage we cannot say. It appears to us, however, that the want of humour, of variety in the dialogue, and the length of some of the soliloquies, render it less fit for the stage than for the closet.

There is no occasion to disagree with the *confrère* of olden times except where he touches the musical side of the Reconciliation. If the impartial reviewer attributes real excellence to the songs mentioned—*de gustibus non est disputandam.* For instance, Wilson sings:

Air II

Tune, The Birks of Indermay.

Why sleeps the thunder in the skies,
When guilty men to grandeur rise?—

> Or why should innocence bewail
> Distress, in bleak misfortune's vale?
> Just are the dark decrees of heaven,
> Since short the date to either given,
> Vice earns unnecessary dread and shame,
> While endless joys are virtue's claim.

These may be good ethics but they are poor musical lyrics. Such stilted poetry may do in the philosophical abortions of Wagnerian epigones, but certainly not in comic ballad operas. Especially not if they be fashioned after those of the older type, that is, those in which the songs are sung to popular tunes. Of the seven "airs" used as solos or duets and which precede the finale the first is the least objectionable from the standpoint of ballad opera, though certainly not from that of poetry. It runs thus to the tune of "My Jockey is the blythest lad":

> How happy once were Debby's days!
>   Ah! days of sweet content!
> The hearth rejoic'd her with its blaze
>   The jack alertly went.
> Since Simon leaves his love to weep
>   No comfort can she know;
> The jack eternally may sleep;
>   And Debby's cake is dough, etc.

Still it cannot be denied that Peter Markoe possessed a faint conception of operatic effect. He concludes his opera after the reconciliation has taken place with what we may call a feeble attempt at a finale:

Duet.

Tune, Guardian Angels, etc.

Wilson.

Nature! to thy throne thus bending
Hear a son—

Amelia.

A daughter too!

Both.

Grief no more our bosoms rending,
Brighter prospects now we view.

Wilson.

Let him, Heaven! thy favours share.

Amelia.

Make him thy peculiar care!

Both.

And in Death's awful hour
On him the blessings pour,
Who thus preserves a faithful pair.

William.

Tune, The Babes in the Wood.
Dear Grand-papa! indeed, indeed!
    I love you passing well.
To you with joy I'll sing and read,
    And pretty stories tell.
I mean to copy all your ways,
    Instructed by mamma;
That wond'ring crouds the youth may praise
    Who loves his Grand-papa.

Deborah.

Tune, Good morning to your Night-cap.
If she may be so bold, Sir,
    Poor Debby takes upon her,
Although you are not old, Sir,
    To tend and nurse your honor.
With happy art I'll play my part,
With soup and sago cheer your heart;
    For you I'll pray,
    And bid each day
Good morning to your night-cap.

Simon.

Tune, the same as the last.
Since now our cares are over
    I sue for Debby's favor;

No more I'll play the rover
    But stick to her for ever.
    To you—and you
    My thanks are due;
Your worship claims my service too.
    For you I'll pray,
    And bid each day,
Good morning to your night-cap.

Wilson, senior.

Tune, How happy a life does a miller possess.
Affection! continue to warm ev'ry breast;
Henceforth I shall hail thee the welcome guest.
To nature if just, we most evils defy;
It charms us on earth and conducts to the sky.
If fond of our friends and our kindred we prove.
Our country may safely depend on our love.
Then may true affection each bosom possess!
'Tis the parent of union; the source of success!

Chorus.

If fond of our friends and kindred we prove, etc.

Evidently Peter Markoe's libretto was considered quite
an achievement in some quarters, for not only did the
Universal Asylum review the opera "impartialy," but it
published in June, 1790, in addition to the words of two
airs both words and music of Air VI to the tune of "In
Infamy" (Wilson. Act II, Scene 5). This interest taken
by the editor in Peter Markoe should be appreciated,
as it enables us to submit at last, if nothing better, at
least an excerpt from the operatic literature of the United
States during the eighteenth century.[1] It is the following:

Air in the Reconciliation; A Comic Opera, by Peter
Markoe.

[1] To avoid confusion I remark that the 'Reconsaliation' (sic). The
Words by a Gentleman of Philadelphia. Music by J. Gehot, in the first
number of Young's Vocal and Instrumental Miscellany has nothing to do
with the opera as performed. Gehot, the violinist, member of the "opera
house, Hanover square," London, did not come to the United States before
1792, and the collection mentioned was published in 1793.

Truth, from thy radiant throne look down On man's be - wil - der'd

race;   Teach us, how - e'er mis - for - tune frown, That

want is... no dis - grace,........... That want is

no dis - grace.   Teach us, since guilt a -

lone is woe, To smile at weak dis - tress.   The

Pow'r who man af - flicts, be - low, Is prompt a - bove to

bless,................ is.... prompt a - bove: to bless.

1793–1794.

1793: Capocchio and Dorinna; Needs must; Old woman of
eighty-three; 1794 Tammany.

Until the last decade of the eighteenth century Hallam and Henry's "American Company" controlled
theatrical matters entirely in our country. Being without serious competitors, this company deteriorated about
1790. Finally it was dissolved. This dissolution
marked a new era in our theatrical life. A rivalry sprang
up between Hallam and Henry, and Thomas Wignell
and Alexander Reinagle, to import English actors and
singers of high standing. Henry reorganized his company under the name of the "Old American Company,"
with headquarters at New York; Wignell and Reinagle
selected Philadelphia, where in 1793 they built the Chest-
nut Street Theatre, for many years the wonder of the
United States. Though the two companies were about
equally matched as to histrionic and musical talent, they
differed in one respect. Without neglecting opera the Old
American Company took more to drama, whereas Wignell
and Reinagle decided to lay stress on opera. This rivalry
of the two companies filled our operatic life with new
blood. By far the majority of popular English operas
received a hearing in our country and often in a manner
to command respect.

The weak spot in the performances of former years had
been the orchestra. Here, too, a remarkable change took
place after the conclusion of the War for Independence.
To the many adventurous persons who flocked to the new-
born United States musicians contributed a proportionate

percentage. Though these musical emigrants did not, as a rule, represent the highest order of their profession, yet not a few, like Alexander Reinagle, William Brown, Benjamin Carr, Raynor Taylor, James Hewitt and others, were able men. Furthermore, when the revolutions in France and the West Indies broke out, the number of skillful musicians was increased by many who sought refuge in the United States. They added to the English and German a distinctly French element, represented by such artists as Gehot and Victor Pelissier. While this influx of musical talent was due mostly to political causes, the above-mentioned progress in theatrical matters contributed towards the improvement of our orchestras, as the managers of the rival companies took pains to enlarge and improve their "bands." Ready to pay good salaries, they had little difficulty in securing musicians who, with justifiable pride, would advertise upon their arrival in the New World that they had played, for instance, under Haydn.

As a matter of course, all this had its effect on the literature of American opera. Musicians, even the meanest, will insist on reaching for the laurels of composers, and whether the managers needed new accompaniments to older works or new settings to accepted operatic novelties, they could now count upon their own forces to supply the demand. For a while the activity in these spheres of "Kapellmeister-Musik" assumed, relatively speaking, formidable proportions until suddenly checked by various obstacles.

For the years 1791 to 1793 I am not aware of any work to be called an American opera as defined in the introduction. True, Raynor Taylor [1] advertised

---

[1] Taylor, Raynor, born [1747] in England, died at Philadelphia, Aug. 17, 1825.—According to John R. Parker (Musical Biography, Boston, 1825, pp. 179–180) Taylor entered, at an early age, the king's singing school as one of the boys of the Chapel Royal. After leaving the school, he was for many years established at Chelmesford, Essex county, as organist and teacher. From there he was called to be the composer and director of the music to the Sadler's Wells Theater. Taylor was a ballad composer of standing before he, in Oct., 1792, appeared in Baltimore as "Music Pro-

for performance at Annapolis on January 20, 1793,[1] his

> Mock Italian Opera, called *Capocchio and Dorinna* . . . Dressed in Character . . . Consisting of Recitative, Airs and Duets . . . the whole of the music original and composed by Mr. Taylor.

but this vaudeville-parody, like his

> "comic burletta never performed, called *Old Woman of eighty-three*"

announced for performance *ibidem* on February 28,[2] cannot be considered as operas. The nearest approach to this kind of entertainment in 1793 was a musical trifle, called "Needs Must, or the Ballad Singers." It had its first performance at New York on December 23d and served as a vehicle for the reappearance of the popular Mrs. Pownall who, having broken her leg during the first few weeks of the season, when she again came before the public was still on crutches.[3] For "Needs Must" Mrs. Anne Julia Hatton, a sister of Mrs. Siddons, and wife of Wm. Hatton, a musical instrument maker at New York, furnished the plot, which was slight, and wrote one of the songs. The whole of the dialogue was the work of Mrs. Pownall. The only example of the songs in "Needs Must" that has come down to us is the following:

fessor, Organist and Teacher of Music in general, lately arrived from London." He was appointed in the same year organist at St. Anne's in Annapolis, but receiving no fixed salary he preferred to settle in Philadelphia. Here he was for many years organist at St. Peter's and, in 1820, influential in founding the Musical Fund Society. His compositions are numerous, and mostly of a secular character. As a specialty he cultivated burlesque olios or "extravaganzas" which came dangerously near being music-hall skits. He strikingly illustrates the fact that the American public of the eighteenth century was not horrified by secular tendencies in an organist, outside of the church walls. Besides Taylor it was B. Carr and Alexander Reinagle who worked most for the progress of music at Philadelphia about 1800. He was famous for his improvisations. His more important works were never published.

[1] "Maryland Gazette," January 14, 1793.
[2] "Maryland Gazette," Feb. 21.
[3] Mrs. Pownall, who arrived in the United States during the winter of 1793–4, was identical with the celebrated Mrs. Wrighten. Comp. Seilhamer, v. III; for the remarks on Needs Must, see this author or his source, Dunlap's History of the American Theatre.

To her enraptured fancy flies
Whose image fills the heart;
Swells on the beam of her dear eyes
Whose smiles ecstatic joy impart, etc.

More important as an attempt at opera was Mrs.
Hatton's "Tammany, or the Indian Chief." [1] A serious
opera, "the music composed by James Hewitt," [2] and first
performed at the John Street Theatre, New York, on
March 3, 1794. The performance was thus advertised in
the "New York Daily Advertiser" for the same day:

This evening . . . An opera (a new piece) never before per-
formed, written by a lady of this city, called *Tammany,* or the
Indian Chief.
>   The Prologue by Mr. Hodgkinson
>   The Epilogue by Mr. Martin.
The overture and accompaniments composed by Mr. Hewitt
with new scenery, dresses and decorations.[3]
In Act 3rd a Procession, by the Company. And an Italian
Dance, by Messrs. Durang and Miller.

Soon after her arrival at New York during the winter
of 1793–94 Mrs. Hatton began to wield her pen as the
bard of American Democracy. Party spirit ran high in
those years, the Federalists and Anti-Federalists opposing
each other with the same fervor as Republicans and Dem-
ocrats of to-day. Mrs. Hatton catered to the Anti-Federalists, whose "platform" among other political issues strongly

---

[1] Comp. Wegelin, op. cit.

[2] Hewitt, James, violinist, composer, music publisher.—Came to New
York in 1792 with Gehot, Bergman, Young and Philips as "Professors of
music, from the operahouse, Hanoversquare, and professional concerts
under the direction of Haydn, Pleyel, etc. London." Hewitt managed
excellent "Subscription Concerts" at New York during the following year
and was very active as virtuoso and "leader of the band" of the Old
Americans. He held an undisputed position as leading musician of New
York, and his social standing was excellent. In 1797 or late in 1796 he
seems to have purchased the New York branch of B. Carr's Musical Repository. Though he can be traced back to 1794 as publisher it was not until
1798 that he became important in that capacity. Hewitt's career extends
far into the nineteenth century. He was born in 1770 and died in 1827.
Quite a number of his compositions are extant, scattered in our libraries,
though mostly his less important works.

[3] The new scenery was painted by Charles Ciceri, and (to use the words
of Dunlap) "they were gaudy and unnatural, but had a brilliancy of colour-
ing, red and yellow being abundant."

favored the French revolution. The Tammany Society, then almost as powerful as it is now, belonged to the same party. Under the circumstances Mrs. Hatton could easily win the far-reaching protection of the society for an opera based on the legend of its patron. She hesitated not to do so, and, as a matter of course, the opera was praised by the Anti-Federalists and condemned by their political opponents. For instance, when the work was revived in the following year, the critic of the "New York Magazine" indignantly queried on March 13th:

Why is that wretched thing Tammany again brought forward? Messrs. Hallam and Henry, we are told, used to excuse themselves for getting it up, by saying that it was sent them by the Tammany Society, and that they were afraid of disobliging so respectable a body of critics, who, having appointed a committee to report on the merits of this piece, had determined it to be one of the finest things of its kind ever seen.

The opera actually seems to have been received with "unbounded applause" on the first night, but even the report of this success in the "Daily Advertiser" did not pass unchallenged, and William Dunlap, he too a Federalist, with evident satisfaction quotes in his History of the American Theatre several sarcastic communications to that paper. He calls Tammany "literally a melange of bombast" and finally remarks:

. . . a more severe and well written communication takes notice of the *ruse* made use of to collect an audience for the support of the piece by circulating a report that a party had been made up to hiss it; and goes on to describe the audience assembled as made up of "the poorer class of mechanics and clerks" and of bankrupts who ought to be content with the mischief they had already done, and who might be much better employed than in disturbing a theatre.

The disturbance alluded to was an attack upon James Hewitt, the leader in the orchestra, for not being ready with a popular air when called upon.

From all this it might be seen that Tammany was not treated with indifference. However, the interest did not last, as is the case with most plays applauded for reasons not artistic. The opera enjoyed three performances at New York and two at Philadelphia in 1794, one upon its revival at New York in 1795, and one at Boston in 1796, where the eminent singer and actor John Hodgkinson selected it for his benefit performance.[1]

It would be an easy task for us later-day critics, not hampered by the political jealousies of yore, to disclose the real merits of the case by an examination of the book and the music. But neither seems to have been published. Only "books with the words of the songs" were "sold at the doors" at the second and third performances,[2] and nothing appears to have become of the

Proposals for printing by Subscription, the Overture with the Songs, Choruses, etc., etc., to Tammany as composed and adapted to the Pianoforte by Mr. Hewitt.

The price to subscribers 12 s. each copy, 4 s. to be paid at the time of subscribing, and one dollar on delivery of the book, to non-subscribers it will be two dollars. Subscriptions received by James Harrison, No. 108 Maiden-lane.[3]

By reading the prologue, the cast, and

"The Songs of Tammany, or the Indian Chief. A Serious Opera. By Ann Julia Hatton. To be had at the Printing Office of John Harrison, No. 3 Peck Slip and of Mr. Faulkner at the Box Office of the Theatre (Price One Shilling) 1794."[4]

we may, at least, gain a vague idea of the plot.

The prologue was written by a young poet named Richard Bingham Davis, and published in a volume of his poems at New York in 1807. It reads in part as follows:

Secure the Indian roved his native soil,
Secure enjoy'd the produce of his toil,

[1] Comp. the lists of productions for these years in Seilhamer and in my book "Early Opera in America."
[2] Comp. "Daily Advertiser" for March 5 and 7. On March 5 the public was also "respectfully acquainted that two of the Songs will be omitted as unnecessary to the conduct or interest of the piece."
[3] Comp. "New York Daily Advertiser" for March 29, 1794.
[4] Collation: 12mo. 16 pp. New York Historical Society; 2 copies, one lacking title-page.

Nor knew, nor feared a haughty master's pow'r
To force his labors, or his gains devour.
And when the slaves of Europe here unfurl'd
The bloody standard of their servile world,
When heaven, to curse them more, first deign'd to bless
Their base attempts with undeserved success,
He knew the sweets of liberty to prize,
And lost on earth he sought her in the skies;
Scorned life divested of its noblest good,
And seal'd the cause of freedom with his blood.

Manifestly the historically correct but poetically absurd lines present the plot in an ethno-ethical nutshell. After this prelude came the fugue, with the following subjects:

Tammany	Mr. Hodgkinson
Columbus	Mr. Hallam
Perez	Mr. King
Ferdinand	Mr. Martin
Wegaw	Mr. Prigmore
Indian Dancers	Mr. Durang, Mr. Miller
Manana	Mrs. Hodgkinson
Zulla	Mrs. Hamilton [1]

Reading between the lines of the "Songs" we observe this: Tammany and Manana are in love; Ferdinand tries to separate them and finally carries Manana off by force. Tammany comes to her rescue, but the Spaniards burn him up in his cabin with his beloved squaw. Truly, a serious opera, but not enough so to exclude the comic element, which is represented by Wegaw. Beyond this nothing definite appears between the lines of the songs. The musical structure is simple and was evidently made to order for Mrs. Hodgkinson, as Manana sings most of the airs.

The first act contained four, and all for Manana. There seems to have followed an ensemble scene in which the refrain of a chorus of Indians is taken up first by Zulla, then by Manana, with an additional monologue. The act ends with the same refrain. The second act contains an

[1] Cast copied from Seilhamer, v. III, p. 84.

Air for Wegaw, a Song for Ferdinand, two more airs for
Manana and a final chorus. In the third act Tammany
at last, in Air I, shows his power of song. Manana follows with two airs, and the act ends with a regular operatic finale. It consists of a duet between Tammany and
Manana before they are burned up in their cabin, and a
chorus of "Indian Priests." After the catastrophe is
reached, follows a chorus of "Indians and Spaniards" in
praise of "valiant, good and brave" Tammany, and a
chorus of women in praise of "chaste" Manana. The
whole ends with a chorus drawing the moral *facit*.

A few examples may show that Mrs. Hatton possessed
some power of characterization and that her songs called
for an operatic setting very much more than those of
Peter Markoe. For instance, after Ferdinand carries
Manana off Tammany sings:

> Fury swells my aching soul,
> Boils and maddens in my veins;
> Fierce contending passions roll
> Where Manana's image reigns.
> Hark! her shrill cries thro' the dark woods resound!
> She struggles in lust's cruel arms,
> My bleeding bosom, my ears how they wound
> And fill ev'ry pulse with alarms.
> Come, revenge! my spirit inspire,
> Breathe on my soul thy frantic fire,
> O'er each nerve thy impulse roll,
> Breathe thy spirit on my soul, etc.

Quite different from these somewhat bombastic strains
is Wegaw's hymn in praise of the "fire-water:

> For deep cups of this liquor I swear,
>   Have made foolish Wegaw quite wise;
> And faith now, I can tell to a hair
>   What's doing above in the skies.
> The sun is a deep thinking fellow,
>   He drys up the dews of the night,
> Lest old father Time should get mellow,
>   And so become slow in his flight.

The moon she looks drinking, 'tis plain,
  She governs the tides of each flood,
And oft takes a sip from the main;
  You may know by her changeable mood.
Thou dear tippling orb give me drink,
  Large lakes full of glorious rum.
My head turns, I'm swimming I think,
  Sweet Rhema! Why look you so glum?

This is really not bad for a drinking song, and we only hope that Mrs. Hatton herself enjoyed the charms of Bacchus in a more womanly manner.

To these specimens, though they are sufficient to illustrate Mrs. Hatton's art, I add the duet between Tammany and Manana for a particular reason:

Tammany.   Altered from the old Indian Song.

The sun sets in night and the stars shun the day
But glory unfading can never decay,
You white men deceivers your smiles are in vain;
The son of Alkmoonac, shall ne'er wear your chain.

Manana

To the land where our fathers are gone we will go,
Where grief never enters but pleasures still flow,
Death comes like a friend: he relieves us from pain,
Thy children, Alkmoonac, shall ne'er wear their chain.

Both

Farewell then ye woods which have witness'd our flame,
Let time on his wings bear our record of fame,
Together we die for our spirits disdain,
Ye white children of Europe your rankling chain.

The reason for quoting this certainly not very poetical duet is this. In Royall Tyler's comedy, "The Contrast," published at Philadelphia in 1790, *Maria* sings almost identical words in the second scene of the first act. Had they been original with Tyler, Mrs. Hatton certainly would not have remarked "altered from the *old* Indian song." This remark of hers was evidently overlooked

by the Dunlap Society when it reprinted "The Contrast" in
1887 together with "Alkmoonok. The Death Song of
the Cherokee Indians" by way of illustration. The
curious little piece deserves a second reprint in this monograph on early American operas, as there can be no
doubt that the air had also been used in Mrs. Hatton's
opera.

ALKMOONOK.[1]

The Death Song of the Cherokee Indians.
New York.   Printed & sold by G. Gilfert.   No. 177 Broadway.
Likewise to be had at P. A. Von Hagen, Musicstore No. 3
Cornhill, Boston.

The Sun sets at night and the Stars shun the day; But

Glo - ry re-mains when the light fades a-way. Be-gin, ye tor-

[1] Mr. Thomas McKee says on p. X of the introduction to the reprint:
"The illustration to the song of Alkmoonok, is from music published contemporaneously with the play. This song had long the popularity of a
national air and was familiar in every drawing room in the early part of
the century."—But the New York directories render it impossible that the
song was published contemporaneously with the play (1790), for Gilfert's
address above given appears only between the years 1798–1801. Furthermore, P. A. Von Hagen resided, according to the Boston directories, at
No. 3 Cornhill, Boston, not earlier than 1800 (or possibly 1799, as a
directory for this year was not issued). Therefore, the date of publication
was probably 1800.

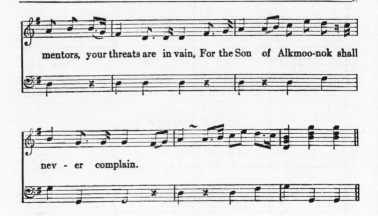

mentors, your threats are in vain, For the Son of Alkmoo-nok shall

nev - er complain.

1795-1796

1795: Sicilian Romance; 1796: The Recruit; The Archers; Edwin and Angelina.[1]

In 1794 Mrs. Siddon's Sicilian Romance with William Reeve's music was received with great favor at London. Always eager to acquaint their public with successful novelties, Messrs. Wignell and Reinagle introduced the work to Philadelphians on May 6, 1795. As a rule Alexander Reinagle[2] contented himself with writing new accompani-

[1] The "Little Yankee Sailor" of 1795 was a "musical farce" with music borrowed from Shield, Hook, Dibdin, Taylor, etc.

[2] Reinagle, Alexander. Pianist, theatrical manager, composer.—According to John R. Parker (Euterpiad, 1822), Reinagle was born [1756] in Portsmouth, England, and commenced his early career in Scotland, where he received instruction in both the theory and practice of music from Raynor Taylor. He came to New York in 1786, calling himself "Member of the Society of Musicians in London." His proposals to settle in New York not meeting with sufficient encouragement, he went to Philadelphia after giving proof of his abilities to the New Yorkers in an excellent concert. In Philadelphia his talents were readily appreciated, and he became music teacher in the best families. He conducted and performed in numerous concerts, besides presiding at the harpsichord in opera, in several cities, especially in Baltimore, before he and Wignell founded the New Theatre at Philadelphia in 1793. This enterprise was in every respect remarkable, but too great a preference was given to opera, and the commercial success was not in keeping with the artistic. Reinagle developed an astonishing activity as composer and arranger during these years. He died at Baltimore on September 21, 1809. "During the latter years of his life, he was ardently engaged in composing music to parts of Milton's Paradise Lost. which he did not live to complete. It was intended to be

ments and occasionally a new overture to such importations, but in this case he reset the entire libretto for reasons unknown to us. The "Daily American Advertiser" announced on May 5, 1795, that for Mrs. Morris's benefit would be given on the following evening:

. . . a Musical Dramatic Tale, in 2 acts, called The Sicilian Romance, or, the Apparition of the Cliffs. Now performing at Covent Garden in London with unbounded applause. The music composed by Mr. Reinagle.

Merely alluding to an unimportant "Musical Interlude" called "The Recruit" and performed at Charleston, S. C., in 1796, the book of which was written by the actor John D. Turnbull, we now have to concentrate our attention on two operas, whose librettos were both published in 1796: *The Archers,* frequently but erroneously called the first American opera, and *Edwin and Angelina.*

The book to The Archers was written by William Dunlap,[1] and the music by Benjamin Carr.[2] The opera was advertised for first performance at the John Street Theatre,

performed in the oratorio style, except that instead of recitatives, the best speakers were to be engaged in reciting the intermediate passages." [Parker.] The L. of C. possesses some really fine sonatas of his in autograph.

[1] Dunlap, William, 1766–1839. The well-known painter (pupil of Benjamin West), playwright (70 original plays and translations), theatrical manager, historian, founder and vice-president of the National Academy of Design, etc.

[2] Carr, Benjamin, [1769]–1831. This prolific composer was a member of the London "Concert of Antient Music" before he, in 1793, emigrated to the United States. He is first mentioned in the Philadelphia papers of the same year as partner of "B. Carr & Co., music printers and importers." When opening a branch of his "Musical Repository" at New York in 1794 he probably removed his residence from Philadelphia to New York. Late in 1796 or early in 1797 he seems to have sold the New York branch to James Hewitt.—Carr was a favorite of the American public as a ballad singer, and tried the operatic stage with some success. But his career as organist, pianist, concert manager, publisher and composer was of by far greater importance for the development of musical life in Philadelphia. In fact, he is equaled by very few in that respect.—His compositions, both sacred and secular, are very numerous, but scattered. The New York Public Library, for instance, possesses a miscellaneous collection of sacred music in Carr's handwriting and full of original compositions by him, a fact that has escaped attention. Carr tried almost every branch of composition with success. He was a thoroughly trained musician of the old school. His works are distinguished by a pleasing softness of lines. He also wrote a few theoretical treatises.—The Musical Fund Society, of which he was a founder (1820), erected a monument to his memory after his death in Philadelphia on May 24, 1831.

New York, in the "American Daily Advertiser," 1796,
April 16th, as follows:

> On Monday Evening the 18th of April will be presented
> a new Dramatic Piece, in 3 Acts, called *The Archers,*
> Founded on the story of William Tell. Interspersed with Songs,
> Choruses, etc. . . .

The opera was repeated "by particular Desire and the last
time of performing it this Season" on April 22nd,[1] and
revived on November 25th, 1796, for one performance.[2]
During the following year it was twice given at Boston,
the second time with an advertisement to the effect that
it had been performed in New York "several nights, with
unbounded applause."[3]   The Archers then seems to have
fallen into oblivion.

For want of other contemporaneous criticisms I quote
what Dunlap had to say on his own behalf in the American
Theatre (1832, pp. 147, 149):

> The story of William Tell and the struggle for Helvetic
> liberty was . . . moulded into dramatic form . . . and with
> songs, choruses, etc., was called an opera . . . Mr. Carr, for
> whom the principal singing part was allotted, composed the
> music. Comic parts were introduced with some effect.
> Schiller's play on the same subject did not then exist . . . The
> writer of the American play gave it a very bad title, "The
> Archers." . . .
> On the 18th of April, 1796, the opera of The Archers was
> performed for the first time, and received with great applause.
> The music by Carr was pleasing and well got up; Hodgkinson
> and Mrs. Melmoth were forcible in Tell and wife. The comic
> parts told well with Hallam and Mrs. Hodgkinson, although
> Conrad ought to have been given to Jefferson. The piece was
> repeatedly played, and was printed immediately.

The title-page reads:

> *The Archers* or Mountaineers of Switzerland; an opera, in
> three acts as performed by the Old American Company, in New

---

[1] Comp. "American Daily Advertiser," April 22, 1796.
[2] Comp. "American Minerva," November 25, 1796.   This third performance escaped Mr. Seilhamer's attention, and it must be said that his antag-
onism to William Dunlap induced him to treat of The Archers too super-
ficially.
[3] Comp. "Columbian Centinel," Boston, October 7, 1797.

York. To which is subjoined a brief historical account of Switzerland, from the dissolution of the Roman Empire to the final establishment of the Helvetic Confederacy by the battle of Sempach.

New York. Printed by T. & J. Sword, No. 99 Pearl Street— 1796—[1]

The history of the libretto is thus given in the preface:

In the summer of the year 1794, a dramatic performance, published in London, was left with me, called Helvetic Liberty. I was requested to adapt it to our stage. After several perusals I gave it up, as incorrigible; but pleased with the subject, I recurred to the history of Switzerland, and composed the piece now presented to the public.

Any person, who has the curiosity to compare the two pieces, will observe that I have adopted three of the imaginary characters, from Helvetic Liberty,—the Burgomaster, Lieutenant, and Rhodolpha: I believe they are, however, strictly my own. The other similarities are the necessary consequences of being both founded on the same historic fact. . . .

The principal liberty taken with history is, that I have concentrated some of the actions of these heroic mountaineers; making time submit to the laws of the Drama. But the reader will not have that sublime pleasure invaded, which is felt in the contemplation of virtuous characters; Tell, Furst, Melchthal, Staffach, and Winkelried, are not the children of poetic fiction. . . .

New York, April 10th, 1796.   W. Dunlap.

After the prologue ("We tell a tale of Liberty to-night . . .") follow the

Characters.

William Tell, Burgher of Altdorf, Canton of Uri }	Mr. Hodgkinson
Walter Furst, of Uri	Mr. Johnson
Werner Staffach, of Schwyz	Mr. Hallam, jun.
Arnold Melchthal, of Unterwalden	Mr. Tyler
Gesler, Austrian Governor of Uri	Mr. Cleveland
Lieutenant to Gesler	Mr. Jefferson
Burgomaster of Altdorf	Mr. Prigmore
Conrad, a seller of wooden ware in Altdorf	Mr. Hallam
Leopold, Duke of Austria	Mr. King

[1] Collation: 8vo. pref. pp. (V)–VI; prol. (VII)–VIII; text 78 pp.; hist. account pp. 81—94 (1). Boston Public Library; Brown University; Library of Congress; Library Company of Philadelphia; New York Historical Society; New York Public Library; Pennsylvania Historical Society.

Bowmen	Messrs. Lee, Durang, etc.
Pikemen	Messrs. Munto, Tomkins, etc.
Burghers	Messrs. Des Moulins, Wools, etc.
Portia, Tell's wife	Mrs. Melmoth
Rhodolpha, Walter Furst's daughter	Miss Broadhurst
Cecily, a basket woman	Mrs. Hodgkinson
Boy, Tell's son	Miss Harding
Maidens of Uri	Madame Gardie, Madame Val, Miss Brett, etc.

Scene lies in the City of Altdorf and its Environs. Time, part of two days.

A fair example of the strength and high standard of the Old American Company!

Having the right of priority over Schiller's Wilhelm Tell, The Archers shall be treated here with especial consideration. A synopsis will also help to disclose the differences in plot, spirit and *genre* between the work of the so-called Father of the American Stage and the German master-poet.

The first scene of the first act "shows" a Street in Altdorf. Enter Cecily crying "Baskets for Sale" or rather soliciting trade with a song. She is met by "Conrad with a Jackass loaded with Wooden Bowls, Dishes, Ladles, etc." Conrad is a jolly sort of fellow from beginning to end of the opera, as may be seen from his entrance-song:

> Here are bowls by the dozen, and spoons by the gross,
> And a ladle or two in the bargain I'll toss.
> Here are ladles for soup and ladles for pap,
> To feed little Cob as he lies in your lap.
> By, by, by, by,
> Come, buy . . . etc.

In the following dialogue we hear of the troubles of the peasantry and of their preparations for overthrowing Gesler's tyrannical government. But the couple is not very much interested in politics and prefers to make love in a duet. Their happiness comes to a sudden end "when

enter Lieutenant and Guard, Drums, etc.   Some pressed
men bound—Citizens following—Conrad attempts to steal
off" but is seized by the guards and made a prisoner.
This calls for a Trio between Conrad, Cecily and the
Lieutenant.   The latter is anything but "honest and sound
at the heart," as Cecily sings of her Conrad, for his entreaties are cynically outspoken.

In the second scene we discover William Tell adjusting
his arms, "his little son trying to draw his sword."   They
are joined by Portia, and in a highly patriotic dialogue
we are informed in detail of Gesler's violations of char-
tered rights.   Finally we are entertained with a song by
Tell, the following lines of which will prove him to have
been a greater marksman than Dunlap a poet.

> Forever lives the patriot's fame,
> Forever useful is his name,
>   Inspiring virtuous deeds.
> How glorious 'tis in spite of time
> In spite of death, to live sublime;
>   While age to age succeeds.

The scene shifts and "bowmen are discovered preparing
their arms by the Side of a Piece of Water; on the other
Side of which is seen the sublime Hills, hanging Rocks,
and various appropriate Beauties of the Lake of Uri."
After a chorus by the bowmen, enter Walter Furst and
Arnold Melchthal.   Horns sound at a distance, are recognized as those of Schwyz and answered by the bowmen of Uri with the "song of Uri."   Enter Werner Staffach at the head of warriors.   They march down the stage
and range opposite (we are in opera) the bowmen of Uri,
singing

> To the war horn's loud and solemn blast,
>   Floating on the affrighted air,
> Obedient Schweitzers hither haste,
>   The fight with Uri's sons to share.

Of course, the "Ruetli Schwur" follows, Dunlap spelling
the word *Gruti,* and it is here where he "concentrated

some of the action of these heroic mountaineers" by avail-
ing himself of Arnold Winkelried and the Battle of Sempach—an anachronism of eighty years, to make "time
submit to the laws of the Drama."

The operatic illusion becomes complete when "enter
Rhodolpha, equip'd as a Huntress." She requests and
receives her father's permission to fight with the men for
the liberty of her country. The act could end here to
the satisfaction of everybody, but a finale is needed. It
is furnished by Melchthal and Rhodolpha in a duet and by
the "Chorus of the whole."

The second act opens "in front of the castle of Altdorf.
A pole is seen with a Hat on it. Enter Lieutenant with
Guards, among whom is Conrad, armed as a Cuirassier,
his Armour much too large for him and apparently very
heavy." The Lieutenant leads him to a spot near the
castle, with orders to force every passer-by to bow to the
governor's hat. Exit Lieutenant after a clever duet with
Conrad, who continues his buffooneries. He not even in-
terrupts them when Gesler and Lieutenant enter with deep-
laid plans against the burghers of Altdorf in general and
"saucy Tell" in particular. Having informed the audience of their intention to hang Tell, they leave, whereupon enters Rhodolpha. We are now entertained with a
rather burlesque episode between her and Conrad. The
play again becomes serious for a while after the appearance of the burgomaster, who bows to the hat. A skillfully contrasted dialogue follows between him

"traitor! no, no, . . . one of Switzerland's best friends"

(as he calls himself) and Rhodolpha. Finally, aiming at
the burgomaster with her weapon, she forces him to kneel
down and bow to her, "the representative of Liberty."
From a melodramatic standpoint this is very effective and
would please an American audience to-day as much as it
probably did one hundred years ago. The scene, however,

is weakened by a rather tawdry song of Rhodolpha and by additional buffooneries of Conrad.

The next scene carries us to the town-hall of Altdorf. Its interest is concentrated in a fine monologue of Tell, who incites his fellow-citizens to speedy action. He is surprised and disarmed, whereupon we are carried back to the castle, the pole, etc., and—Conrad in *Morpheus'* arms. Enter Burgomaster, Tell, and Lieutenant. Traitor and patriot are contrasted in a pathetic manner, but the effect is destroyed by what follows: a low-comedy scene between Conrad and Cecily. For instance, Cecily sings a song, tickling at its refrains her sleeping lover's nose. Finally, Conrad "gets out of the cuirass and dresses up Cecily."

The fourth scene carries us to the governor's palace, where Gesler gives orders to execute Tell immediately, though Portia pathetically cries for mercy. The news that the Austrians "have stop'd; amaz'd" and that Leopold of Austria has taken supreme command, forces Gesler to defer the execution. He resolves to free Tell under the condition that "he must somewhat do to please us." Of course, we now expect to be witnesses of how Tell shoots the apple from his son's head. Strange to say, Dunlap contents himself with merely letting Gesler stipulate this feat as the *conditio sine qua non,* and with contrasting Gesler's devilishly cruel designs with Portia's pathetic outcries.

The next scene shows "the Mountains, a Waterfall and a distant View of a part of the Lake." Enter Walter, then Melchthal and bowmen, rejoicing in the news of the emperor's death. After a rather bombastic song of Melchthal, those present are joined by Werner, Rhodolpha, pikemen, and maidens bringing the belated news that "Gesler hath seiz'd on Tell, and threatens death." All this occasions a trio between Rhodolpha, Melchthal and first bowman "altered from Goldsmith":

> Dear is the homely cot, and dear the shed
>   To which the soul conforms;
> And dear to us the hill, whose snow-crowned head
>   Uplifts us to the storms, etc.

With the quoted lines as chorus-refrain, the curtain falls, the interruption of the apple-scene being an obvious technical blunder.

Its development is taken up in the first scene of the third act, on lines and at times in words almost literally the same as in Schiller's drama. The second scene presents "The mountains. Violent Storm, Wind, Rain and Thunder." After the storm has abated, enter Melchthal with this song:

> Hark! from the mountain's awful head,
> To stranger's hearts inspiring dread,
> The genius of our hills in thunder speaks!
>   Switzers, to arms! to arms! arise!
>   To arms! each hollow cave replies
> To arms! to arms! from every echo breaks.

Then enters Rhodolpha, followed by her female archers. We listen to a song by her and are then notified by Werner Staffach—how weak is this all compared with the corresponding scenes in Schiller—:

> the tyrant Gesler's slain
> . . . .
> 'Twas Tell that slew him—here upon the lake.

Hardly has he narrated how Tell escaped, when the hero arrives. He is greeted with:

Song

Rhodolpha

> He comes! he comes! the victor comes,
> Who conquers in his country's cause, etc.

Chorus

> He comes! he comes! etc.

Arnold

Not so the bloodstain'd hero, he
Who murders but to gain a name, etc.

Chorus

He comes! etc.

Tell is chosen commander in chief.   He distributes his
orders.   Exeunt all except Rhodolpha and Arnold, who
remain true to the traditions of opera by singing a duet
before hastening away.

The third scene is of an essentially comic character.   It
plays in the Castle of Altdorf, where Conrad is tried as
a deserter.   But he seems to know that nothing will happen to him, for he is extremely merry, though the guards
prepare to shoot him.   They are prevented from doing so
by Rhodolpha and her Amazons, who have attacked and
stormed the castle (as Melchthal has the kindness to inform the public).   After some funny lines by Conrad
and a song by Cecily, the scene closes with a *glee* between
Rhodolpha, Arnold and Cecily.

Scenes fourth and fifth represent the *finale* of the work
on "the Field of Battle, surrounded by Mountains."   It
is a regular stage skirmish void of dramatic interest.   Leopold is slain by Tell, Conrad has a few jokes in store,
and with much noise of sounding horns and trumpets "an
almost bloodless victory" is won by the Swiss.   Tell ad-
vances and delivers a patriotic speech with a song:

When heaven pours blessings all around
O! May mankind be grateful found, etc.

Arnold Melchthal follows with

Ye youths, to Melchthal look and learn;—
It's blest reward to see Virtue earn, etc.

Rhodolpha with

If foreign foes our land invade,
Like me, may each undaunted maid
A patriot heart display, etc.

Cecily with

> Now war is o'er, and Conrad mine,
> I'll make my baskets, neat and fine, etc.

Chorus of the whole:

> When heaven pours blessings all around, etc.

and curtain.

Necessarily, the American and German plays have much in common, "being both founded on the same historic fact," as Dunlap puts it in his preface. That Schiller's drama surpasses The Archers in dramatic logic, vigor, purity of style and poetic beauty goes without saying, for Dunlap was not a master-poet, but merely a dramatically gifted stage-manager. However, it would be unjust to deny The Archers some forcible monologues and skillfully contrasted scenes in which the mongrel form of opera is well kept in mind. It would also be unjust to condemn Dunlap wherever his version differs from Schiller's, merely because it differs. We generally grow so familiar with the structure of a masterpiece that a different version appears to be a failure, though it may possess its independent merits. For instance, no esthetic objection can be raised against Dunlap's endeavors to picture Tell as an active "politician" or to keep Tell's wife more in the foreground than Schiller did.

Dunlap falls short less in such details than in his arid lyrics and in the general aspect of the play. The Tell story is bound to be the theme for a serious drama, and no theme is less appropriate for a comic opera, as the story contains no comic elements whatever. If, therefore, an author stoops to make of it a comic opera, he will be forced to use violence. This Dunlap has done, and this combination of heterogenous elements has been futile, the more so as the comic scenes decidedly smack of low comedy. At times Conrad and not Tell seems to be the hero. In fact, The Archers could greatly be improved if

WHY HUNTRESS WHY

Sung by Mr Tyler in the Opera of the Archers at the New York Theatre and by Mr John
Darley at the Concerts in Philadelphia

Compofed by B: Carr

Publifhed at the requeft of feveral Subfcribers

(33)

- lued by thy friends   If thou shouldst

fall the death of all our foes . If thou shouldst fall the death of all our foes can

never make a - mends   then huntrefs why   wilt thou thy life expofe .

Ah! think what pangs thy Father ftill muft feel
What pangs muft Arnold know
When thourt expofd unto the biting fteel
Shall rufh amid the foe
Then huntrefs why &c

Conrad and Cecily were omitted. Of course, then the main reason for calling the work a *comic* opera would disappear and the part which music has in the play would be further reduced.

Perhaps it would have been better to omit music entirely, with the exception of some patriotic choruses and the storm music between scenes 1 and 2 of the third act, since nearly all the songs, duets and trios are wholly undramatic. They retard the solution of the problem and contain but repetitions of the contents of the spoken monologues and dialogues in the form of musical lyrics. Still, we must not censure Dunlap too severely. Others, and greater than he, sinned against good taste by forcing serious themes into the straitjacket of comic opera.

This had to be pointed out, as the origin of the peculiarly spectacular and nonsensical character of the American (so-called) comic operas of to-day—veritable operettinaccias, to murder the Italian language—must partly be traced back to the beginnings of operatic life in America. The remark will go a good way towards a reasonable explanation of why so far the birth of genuine American opera has been so tardy, for American comic opera is, at its best, a deeply rooted national evil.

Of Carr's music to Dunlap's Archers hardly anything can be said, as it seems to be lost. However, I was fortunate enough to discover, in No. 7 of Carr's Musical Miscellany, the number having been copyrighted in 1813, a

Rondo from the Overture to the opera of the Archers or Mountaineers of Switzerland and composed by B. Carr. Arranged for the Piano Forte.

A reprint of this extremely scarce piece[1] will be found in the Sammelbände, 1904-05. That it in no way pre-

[1] The only copy I personally knew of at the time of writing this essay was in the possession of the Hopkinson family of Philadelphia. Since then I acquired a copy for the Library of Congress and also of the song "Why, Huntress, Why" (in B. Carr's "Musical Journal," *ca.* 1800), a facsimile of which was first published in my book "Early Opera in America," G. Schirmer, 1915. Both the New York Public Library and the Library of Congress possess this rare piece.

sents an overture programmatic of the Tell idea will be
seen at the first glance. It is a simple rondo, the themes
of which may or may not have been used in the opera. If
the songs, etc., were as dainty as this rondo, we surely must
regret their loss.

Edwin and Angelina.

Allusion was made to the prevailing idea that The Archers was the first American opera. It was not, for at least

Edwin and Angelina, or the Banditti, an opera, in three acts.
New York. Printed by T. & J. Swords, No. 99 Pearlstreet.
1797.

possesses the claim of priority.[1] The libretto was written
by Elihu Hubbard Smith, a physician, graduate of Yale,
who was born at Litchfield, Conn., in 1771 and died of
yellow fever at New York in 1798. The preface, as all
good prefaces should, gives the history of this opera, and
a strange history it is.

. . . The principal scenes of the following Drama were composed in March, 1791, as an exercise to beguile the weariness
of a short period of involuntary leisure; and without any view
to theatrical representation. From that time, till the month
of October, 1793, they lay neglected, and almost forgotten.
An accident then bringing them to recollection, several short
scenes were added, agreeable to my original design; and the
whole adapted to the Stage. The piece was presented to the
then Managers of the Old American Company, for their accept-
ance, the December following; but the peculiar situation of the
theatre prevented any attention to this application, till June,
1794; when on a change in the management, it was accepted.
An interval of six months, and a further acquaintance with the
Stage, had convinced me that the piece might undergo alterations, with advantage. These were undertaken, immediately:
the loss of a comic character, which was now rejected, was supplied by two new additional scenes; additional songs were com-

[1] Collation : 8vo. t. p. V. bl. ; p. (3) ded. signed E. H. Smith "To Reuben
and Abigail Smith, Connecticut. My Dear Parents . . ."; pp. (5)–6
pref.; p. 7 dramatis personae ; pp. 8–72 text.—Boston Public Library ;
Brown University ; Library Company of Philadelphia ; Massachusetts Historical Society ; New York Historical Society.

posed; and a Drama of two acts, in prose, was converted into the Opera, in its present form, in the course of the succeeding month. The inherent defects of the plan were such as could not be remedied, without bestowing on the subject a degree of attention incompatible with professional engagements; and, which I, therefore thought myself justified in withholding. But should this performance meet the same generous indulgence, in private, with which it was received in public, I shall neither attempt to disarm Criticism of her severity, nor be ashamed of this feeble effort to contribute to the rational amusement of my fellow-citizens.

New York, Feb. 15, 1797.

P.S. It may not be improper to observe (though the reader can scarcely be supposed uninformed, in this particular) that the first, second, third, fifth, and sixth songs, in the third act of the following Drama, are from Goldsmith; and all except the first, from the Ballad of "Edwin and Angelina." I have taken the liberty to make a slight alteration in the second, to accommodate it more perfectly to my purpose; and it will be obvious that, in the principal scene between Edwin and Angelina, I have availed myself of the sentiments, and, as far as possible, of the very expressions of the Author.

The performance alluded to took place at New York on December 19, 1796. The work was advertised in the "American Minerva" for the same day as:

"never performed . . . With songs, partly from Goldsmith, partly original. Music by Pelissier." [1]

From the libretto the cast appears to have been this:

Sifrid	Mr. Hodgkinson
Edwin	Mr. Tylor
Ethelbert	Mr. Martin
Walter	Mr. Crosby
Edred	Mr. Munto
Houg	Mr. Miller
Banditti	
Angelina	Mrs. Hodgkinson

[1] Pelissier, Victor, performer on the French horn and composer.—First mentioned on Philadelpia concert programs in 1792 as "first French horn of the Theatre in Cape François." After residing in Philadelphia for one year he moved to New York as principal hornplayer in the orchestra of the Old American Company. His name is frequently met with on New York concert programs, and most of the arrangements and compositions for the Old American Company were written either by him or James Hewitt. Pelissier resided in New York for many years.

If Victor Pelissier's music, which seems not to be extant,[1] was as defective as Elihu Hubbard Smith's libretto, the managers were justified in according Edwin and Angelina but one performance.

The "scene lies in a forest, in the northern extremity of England, and in a Cavern, and the entrance of a Hermitage, in the Forest. Time, that of the Representation." Earl Ethelbert, wealthy, and reputed generous, and Sifrid, of noble birth but poor, were born in the same city.

> . . . . While young,
> Distinction proud was neither known nor felt:
> But Ethelbert, arrived to manhood,
> . . . . . grew vain, debauch'd,
> Selfish and mercenary, false and cruel.

After the death of his father, Ethelbert took possession of the estate and

> . . . in place exalted, he no more,
> His former friend recogniz'd.

Sifrid, deeply wounded, left him and became tenant to a neighboring lord. There he saw, loved and was loved by Emma, the daughter of a simple husbandman like himself. Ethelbert strove to gain, betray and corrupt Emma; and, as she was constant, finally

> . . . . with armed force
> At night, he bore her captive to his tower.

In vain; she remained "inflexible to faithlessness or shame." Ethelbert then imprisoned Sifrid and caused a report to be spread that he had died, hoping "by long attention to o'ercome her hate." Several years pass. Sifrid forces his escape and flees. Convinced that the worst has happened and that the earl killed Emma, he

---

[1] Since writing this study, I acquired for the Library of Congress Pelissier's "Columbian Melodies. A monthly publication consisting of a variety of songs and pieces for the pianoforte composed by Victor Pelissier," Philadelphia, 1811. This extremely rare collection contains "Few are the joys" and "The Bird when summer" from his "Edwin and Angelina."

becomes an outlaw and finally chieftain of bandits.   But
Emma is still alive and still loves Sifrid.   In the meantime, Ethelbert "sinks a slave" of Angelina's beauty.   She
is also loved by Edwin, a poor knight.   Angelina loves not
Ethelbert but Edwin, though for a while her affection
is subdued by "arrogance of wealth" and "false pride
of birth."   Edwin, "murdered" by her disdain, flees
and becomes a hermit in the same forest where Sifrid
is chieftain of bandits.

Angelina, tortured by remorse, seeks to find Edwin.
Ethelbert follows her to the forest, but again she rejects
his love.   In this very moment they are attacked by the
bandits.   Angelina escapes, but Ethelbert is captured.
On recognizing him, Sifrid at first contemplates cruel re-
venge.   He abandons all bloodthirsty designs after hearing
from Ethelbert that Emma is still living and still true to
his memory.   The band then receives orders to scour the
forest through for Angelina, who has found shelter in
Edwin's hermitage.   At first the lovers do not recognize
each other.   After some tearful scenes they do and embrace in perfect harmony.

Alas!   Sifrid, Ethelbert, and the robbers rush into the
hut.   Ethelbert is naturally very much surprised and bewildered to find Angelina in a hermit's arms, and commands him to release her, which Edwin, of course, refuses
to do.   Provoked by his firmness Ethelbert exclaims:

> I would not harm that reverend form, or dash,
> Against the earth, thy sacred heart;
> But, wert thou young, thy life should answer me,
> For thy insolence, old man.

Whereupon Edwin throws off his disguise and draws his
sword.

> Ethelbert (in great surprise): Edwin!
> Edwin (fiercely advancing): Edwin, Lord!
> Ethelbert (with great emotion): The saviour of my life!
>   The murderer of my love!

The scene ends in happiness, after an explanation how, when and where Edwin saved Ethelbert's life. But some difficulties remain to be removed. Sifrid is anxious to hasten back to Emma. His words to the bandits

> . . . . My friends! Hear all,
> To my fond arms, Earl Ethelbert restores
> The woman of my love; unto my care
> My fields paternal, and my earliest home

are met with an outburst of indignation by these gentlemen, who are not very anxious to reform. Gradually, however, their hearts soften, and the *finale* brings universal happiness and perfect harmony.

This plot, though simple, is full of improbabilities. And these improbabilities render the developments complicated, as the author has not carried out the dramatic idea with sufficient clearness and logic. It is, for instance, illogical that Ethelbert should recognize Edwin and not *vice versa* as well, which would have saved the public a good deal of guesswork and surprise, greater than that of Ethelbert on recognizing Edwin. In fact, the main defect of the play lies in the by far too many surprises that are sprung on the audience.

The language is "exalted" and "sublime" as in so many efforts of this era of "Sturm und Drang," Ossian, and "Die Räuber." The characters with their mixture of hyper-romantic sentimentality and stage villainy probably appealed to the public of those days, but they are woefully schematic. To dwell on Edwin and Angelina as an "opera" is hardly necessary after the confessions of the author in his preface. It is sufficient to state that the leading men and leading ladies all come in for their share of the dozen lyrics which protract the dramatic agony, and that the whole winds up in an elaborate but commonplace *finale*.

1797-1800

1797: Ariadne Abandoned; The Iron Chest; The Adopted Child; The Savoyard; The Launch. 1798: The Purse; Americania and Elutheria. 1799: Sterne's Maria; Fourth of July; Rudolph. 1800: Castle of Otranto; Robin Hood; The Spanish Castle; The Wild-goose Chase.

In 1797 a form of operatic entertainment was introduced in New York for which I believe the Americans to be peculiarly gifted: the melodrama. On April 22nd, the much admired Mrs. Melmoth advertised for her benefit on Wednesday the 26th in the New York Daily Advertiser:

The evening's entertainment will conclude with a piece, in one act, never performed in America, called *Ariadne Abandoned By Theseus, in The Isle of Naxos.*
Between the different passages spoken by the actors, will be Full Orchestra Music, expressive of each situation and passion. The music composed and managed by Pelissier.

This advertisement is about all I have been able to find regarding Ariadne Abandoned. It probably was an imitation of Benda's work, but neither this nor how the public received the melodrama, could I ascertain. At any rate, when John Hodgkinson invaded Boston during the same year, Ariadne was performed there on July 31st as a "Tragic Piece in one act" and again with Pelissier's music.[1]

The next American opera carries us to Baltimore, where on June 2, 1797,[2] was to be performed

. . . a favorite new play, interspersed with songs, called *The Iron Chest.*
Written by George Colman, the younger, founded on the celebrated novel of Caleb Williams, and performed at the theatres in London, with unbounded applause.
The music and accompaniments by Mr. R. Taylor.

[1] Comp. "Columbian Centinel," July 29, 1797.
[2] Comp. "Federal Gazette," June 2, 1797.

In England this Play, interspersed with songs, was styled
an opera. It had its first performance as such with Ste-
phen Storace's music in London in 1796, and it is for this
reason that I included The Iron Chest with Reinagle's
music in the body of my monograph instead of in the
appendix.[1]

Our managers have ever been eager to import the successful London novelties. A case in point is Samuel Birch's
Adopted Child.   First performed with Thomas Atwood's
music at Drury Lane in 1795, it was introduced to a
New York audience as early as May, 1796, and continued
to meet with the applause of different American audiences.
As a rule it was given with Atwood's music, but in Boston,
for some reason or other, the managers of the Haymarket
Theatre decided to perform "for the last time," on June
5, 1797,[2]

"The Musical Drama of the Adopted Child" with "the music
entirely new and composed by Mr. V. Hagen." [3]

Though an advertisement to that effect escaped my attention, it is almost safe to say that the preceding performances, too, were given with Van Hagen's setting.   When
the first took place I do not know; certainly between
January and the middle of March, 1797, since the second

[1] To repeat it, the appendix is not here reprinted from the "Sammelbände."
[2] Comp. "Columbian Centinel," June 3, 1797.
[3] This Mr. V. Hagen probably was P. A. Van Hagen, senior; organist,
violinist, composer.—P. A. Van Hagen, jun., came to Charleston, S. C., in
1774.   He called himself in advertisements "Organist and Director of the
City's Concert in Rotterdam.   Lately arrived from London," and gave
lessons on the organ, harpsichord, pianoforte, violin, violoncello, and viola.
He was probably identical with the violinist of the same name who
appeared at New York in 1789, having changed the "jun." into "sen." in
distinction from his son P. A. Van Hagen.   In the following year he called
himself "Organist, Carilloneur, and Director of the City Concert, at
Zutphen."   During the following years he resided in New York, from
1793–1796 as principal arranger of the Old City Concerts.   After his
removal to Boston, during the fall of 1796, J. C. Moller became his successor.   At Boston Van Hagen was for a while leader in the New Theatre
orchestra.   In his advertisements as music teacher he did not fail to call
himself "Organist in four of the principal churches in Holland" with an
"experience during 27 years as an Instructor."   With his son he seems to
have opened a music-store in 1798, but the firm probably was dissolved
late in the same year or early in the next.   Of his year of death I am
not certain; possibly he died about 1800.

was advertised for March 15th.   I have still less information to offer as regards a musical farce, performed at
Wignell and Reinagle's theatre in Philadelphia on July
12, 1797.   I glean from a theatrical advertisement in
Porcupine's Gazette for the same day the following title
and cast:

. . . a musical farce, in two acts (never performed) called The
Savoyard; or the Repentant Seducer.   (The music composed by
Mr. Reinagle.)

Jacques	Mr. Moreton
Belton	Mr. Fox
Front	Mr. Harwood
Simond	Mr. Warren
Father Bertrand	Mr. L'Estrange
Benjamin	Master H. Warrell
Banditti	Messrs. Francis, Warrell and Blissett
Countess	Mrs. Francis
Nanette	Mrs. Oldmixon
Claudine	Mrs. Warrell

The plays written during the years immediately following the War for Independence frequently had a patriotic or political background.   Though their literary
merit was very doubtful, their success with the public was
assured if they employed sufficient bombast, stage-battles
and patriotic tableaux to appeal to the pride of our new-
born nation.   To this category belonged John Hodgkinson's "The *Launch,* or, Huzza for the Constitution."
Again we are indebted to the old newspapers for the few
items relating to this piece.   The first was a preliminary
"puff" published in the "Columbian Centinel," Boston, on
Wednesday, September 13, 1797.

Theatrical

We hear that Mr. Hodgkinson has written a musical Drama,
entitled "The Launch," in celebration of the naval fête of
Wednesday next;—on which evening it will be performed, concluding with a splendid representation of the frigate Constitution breasting the curled surge.
The piece is said to contain a great diversity of national

character, and incidental Song. The idea is novel—the occasion happy.

On the day of the first performance the same paper went into further particulars concerning the

Musical Piece, in one act, never yet performed, called The Launch; or Huzza for the Constitution. Written by John Hodgkinson. The whole will conclude with a striking Representation of Launching the New Frigate Constitution. Boats passing and repassing on the Water. View of the River of Charlestown, and the neighboring country—taken directly from Jeffry and Russel's Wharf. The scenery principally executed by Mr. Jefferson.

Ned Grog	Mr. Hodgkinson
Constant	Mr. Tyler
Old Lexington	Mr. Johnson
Old Bunker	Mr. Munto
Jack Hawlyard (with a hornpipe)	Mr. Jefferson
Tom Bowling	Mr. Lee
Sam Forecastle	Mr. Leonard
Irishman	Mr. Fawcatt
Scotchman	Mr. Miller
and Nathan	Mr. Martia
Mrs. Lexington	Mr. Brett
and Mary	Miss Brett

Readers familiar with American history will notice patriotic allusions even in the nomenclature of this spectacular piece so generously called a "musical drama" in the "Columbian Centinel." As far as the music is concerned the "great variety of incidental song" stamped The Launch an operatic *pasticcio,* since we read in the advertisement of the fourth performance on November 21, 1797:

The Musick selected from the best Composers, with new Orchestra parts by *Pelisier.*

During the years 1798 and 1799 surprisingly few operas were written in the United States and these few would hardly deserve more than a passing account even if we were in a position to offer a minute description of them.

In his monograph on early American plays Mr. Wegelin mentions:

American Tars (The Purse). Played in the Park Theatre, New York, January 29, 1798.

Mr. Wegelin has not given the title quite correctly, as it should be "The Purse, or, American Tars," and a perusal of the "City Gazette" of Charleston, S. C., would have convinced him that the piece was given there under that title a year earlier than in New York, on February 8, 1797. It evidently was an Americanized version of William Reeve's opera "The Purse, or, the Benevolent Tars" (libretto by Cross), which was introduced in the United States in 1795 with great success. But if such versions *in usum delphini* were to be enumerated, I fear Mr. Wegelin's list would have to be considered very incomplete, as few English plays and operas of the day were not subjected to similar mutilations to suit the American public.

On the other hand, a work escaped Mr. Wegelin's attention that certainly should have found a place in his monograph. It was performed on February, 1798, at Charleston, S. C., and called

a new Musical and Allegorical Masque, never yet printed or performed, entitled *Americania and Elutheria; or, a new Tale of the Genii.*

Neither the author nor the composer are mentioned in the "City Gazette" from which I gleaned the title, but a sketch of the plot is printed, preceded by the following cast:

Jelemmo and Arianthus, Great winged Spirits, attendants on Americania	Mr. Cleveland and Mr. Downie
Offa, Chief of the Alleganian Satyri	Mr. Jones
Musidorus, the Alleganian Hermit, the only Mortal in the Masque	Mr. Whitlock

Horbla, Chief of the Dancing Spirits	Mr. Placide
Damonello, Lucifero, Horrendum, and Zulpho, Dancing Satyrs	Messrs. Hughes, Tubbs, J. Jones and M'Kenzie
Americania, Genius of America, a great Spirit, residing since the creation on the summit of the Allegani	Mrs. Cleveland
Vesperia, a winged Spirit, chief attendant on Americania	Mrs. Tubbs
Hybla, chief of the Hemmadriads or Wood Nymphs, and principal Dancer	Mrs. Placide
Tintoretto, Luciabella, Juberaia, Ariella and Tempe, dancing Nymphs	Mrs. Hughes, Mrs. Edgar, Miss Arnold, etc.
Elutheria, Goddess of Liberty, who flies to the arms of Americania for protection	Mrs. Whitlock.

Sketch of the Plot

Hybla, a Mountain Nymph, desirous to see a mortal, implores Offa, a Satyr, to procure that pleasure. Offa deludes an old Hermit up to the Summit of the Allegani Mountain, to a great Rock, inhabited by Genii or Aerial Spirits, the chief of whom, called Americania, understanding that the old Hermit is ignorant of the American Revolution, commands her domestics to perform an *Allegorical Masque* for his Information.

In Act first—A grand Dance of Nymphs and Satyrs, who will form a group of the most whimsical kind.

In Act second—A meeting taken place between Elutheria, the Goddess of Liberty, and Americania, who descend on Clouds on opposite sides.

A *Pas de Deux,* between the Satyr Horbla and the Nymph Hybla. The whole to conclude with a General Dance of the Nymphs and Satyrs, a Pas de Deux, by a young Master and Lady; and a Pas de Trois, by Mrs. Placide, Mr. Placide and Mr. Tubbs.

Turning to the year 1799, at least three works are on record that may be called American operas. In the first place:

An opera, in 2 acts, never performed here, called *Sterne's Maria,* or, the Vintage. In the course of the opera the following new scenery will be displayed. Opening scene—A Sunsetting, with a representation of the vineyards of France, and the manner of gathering in the Vintage.

Entrance to a French inn. Concluding Scene—Landscape and rising Sun.

This was the advertisement of the first performance on Jan. 14, 1799, as it appeared in the "New York Daily Advertiser" for Jan. 12th.[1] The book came from the fertile pen of William Dunlap, and as the author has a few lines to say on his play in the History of the American Theatre (pp. 259–260), they may follow for want of other information:

On the 14th of January, 1799, the manager of the New York theatre brought out an opera written by himself, founded on the story of Maris, and called "Sterne's Maria, or the Vintage." The music was composed by Victor Pelessier, and the piece pleased and was pleasing, but not sufficiently attractive or popular to keep the stage after the original performers in it were removed by those fluctuations common in theatrical establishments. Sterne's Maria was thus cast: Sir Henry Metland, Mr. Hallam, junr.; Yorick, Mr. Cooper; Pierre (an old man, father of Maria), Mr. Hogg; Henry (Maria's lover), Mr. Tyler; La Fleur, Mr. Jefferson; Landlords, Peasants, etc. Maria, Miss E. Westray; Nanette, Mrs. Oldmixon; Lilla, Mrs. Seymour. It is not necessary to observe to those acquainted with any part of American theatrical history, that the music of the piece was confined to Messrs. Tyler and Jefferson among the males. The females were all singers; Mrs. Oldmixon the superior. The opening chorus in the vineyard at sunset, and preparations for the peasant's dance.

Sterne's words were kept for Yorick, with little variation, and the story of Maria told in his language. La Fleur is the lover of Nanette, and gives . . . account of taking leave of his drum and his military life.

Again it was Victor Pelissier who furnished the music to a "musical drama," which, by the way, further illus-

[1] Mr. Wegelin incorrectly gives January 11th as the date of performance.

trates how spectacular theatricals were gradually encroaching upon legitimate drama on the American stage.[1]

At the Park Theatre in New York was performed on July 4, 1799, as appears from the "Daily Advertiser,"

a splendid, allegorical, musical Drama, never exhibited, called:
The Fourth of July; or, Temple of American Independence. In which will be displayed (among other scenery, professedly intended to exceed any exhibition yet presented by the Theatre) a view of the lower part of Broadway, Battery, Harbor, and Shipping taken on the spot.
After the shipping shall have saluted, a military Procession in perspective will take place, consisting of all the uniform Companies of the City, Horse, Artillery and Infantry in their respective plans, according to the order of the March.
The whole to conclude with an inside view of the *Temple of Independence* as exhibited on the Birthday of Gen. Washington. Scenery and Machinery by Mr. Ciceri—Music by Mr. Pelessier.

In addition, a melodrama should be mentioned for the year 1799, of which I found neither the date of first performance nor the name of the composer. It was written by the actor John D. Turnbull, and Mr. Wegelin gives the title of the libretto that appeared, he says, in several editions as follows:

Rudolph; or the Robbers of Calabria. A Melodrama in three Acts, as performed at the Boston Theatre.
18mo., pp. 141. Boston 1799.

If we except the "celebrated Musical Romance" of the

Castle of Atranto. Altered from the Sicilian Romance. Music and Accompaniments by Pelissier.

as first performed on November 7, 1800, at New York, and

The much admired Comic Opera of *Robin Hood,* or Sherwood Forest. Compressed in two Acts . . . The Music composed by Mr. Hewitt.

[1] In Pelissier's "Columbian Melodies," 1811, will be found his settings of "I laugh, I sing," "Hope, gentle hope," and "Ah! why on Quebec's bloody plain" for "Sterne's Maria." A copy of this extremely rare collection is in the Library of Congress.

as performed for the first time, also at New York, on December 24, 1800, the few novelties at the close of the eighteenth century were due to William Dunlap's pen.

Says the author in his History of the American Theatre:

> On the 5th of December [1800] an opera, the music put together by James Hewitt, and the dialogue by the manager, was performed, not approved of, repeated once, and forgotten. It was called the *"Knight of the Guadalquivir."*

Dunlap, when compiling his history, undoubtedly relied to a great extent upon his memory, and it is not surprising that he should have forgotten the original title of one of his numerous plays in which he himself did not discover literary merits. The "New York Daily Advertiser" thus advertised on December 5th the first performance of the opera with an abundant display of dons and señoritas in the cast and the inevitable Irishman in their midst:

> . . . a Comic Opera (never performed here), called *The Spanish Castle,* or, the Knight of the Guadalquivir. With new scenery and Dresses never before exhibited.

Characters.

Montalvan	Mr. Fennel
Sebastian	Mr. Hallam
Algiziras	Mr. Martin
Florenzo	Mr. Fox
Juan	Mr. Hallam, jun.
Anselmo	Mr. Tyler
Manuel	Mr. Powell
Hugo	Mr. Crosby
Pedro	Mr. Hogg
Pero	Mr. Jefferson
O'Tipple	Mr. Hodgkinson

Officers, Soldiers, etc., by Gentlemen of the Company.

Women

Olivia	Mrs. Hodgkinson
Henerica	Miss Brett
Lisetta	Miss Harding

The Music by Mr. Hewitt.

William Dunlap fared somewhat better with a libretto
that was only to a limited extent his own, being hardly
more than a translation of a farce by Kotzebue, the idol
of the theatre-going public of those days.   Again we must
refer to Dunlap's own words (op. cit., pp. 272, 275):

> In August, 1799, the yellow fever again appeared in New
> York. The manager of the theatre [Dunlap himself] resided
> at Perth Amboy, his native place, and was employed in trans-
> lating Kotzebue's comedy of "False Shame" and turning the
> farce of "Der Wildfang" into an opera, which he called the
> "Wild-goose Chase," a title which some wiseacres thought was
> intended as a translation of the German appellation. . . . As
> translated and metamorphosed into an opera . . . the Wild-
> goose Chase was performed on the 24th of January, and con-
> tinued a favorite as long as Hodgkinson continued to play the
> young baron.

Strange to say, Dunlap had his version of the "Wild-
fang" printed, not as an opera libretto, but as

> *The Wild-Goose Chase.* A Play in four Acts; with Songs,
> from the German of Augustus von Kotzebue; with Notes,
> marking the Variations from the Original.

The "play," as preserved (for instance) at the Boston and
New York Public Libraries, informs us that the music
was "composed by Mr. *Hewitt,*" a fact easily to be verified
from other sources, and in the notes (pp. 100-104) we
read that

> all the songs . . . are added by the translator . . .

This was about the only "metamorphosis" to warrant offering The Wild-Goose Chase to the public as a "comic
opera in four acts," as it was called in a favorable criticism under date of January 24th, 1800, in the February
issue of the Monthly Magazine and American Review.

Notwithstanding public approval of the modified version of Kotzebue's play, Dunlap must have altered The
Wild-Goose Chase immediately after the first performance,
for it was advertised in the "New York Daily Advertiser"

for performance on February 19th as "a comic opera, in three acts." But Dunlap was still unsatisfied, for when the next winter season opened, it was given on December 19th, 1800, as "the much admired Comic Opera of the Wild Goose Chase. Compressed in two Acts . . ."

In the meantime James Hewitt seems to have published the music (though I have been unable to find a copy), since Joseph Carr, when announcing in the "New York Daily Advertiser," February 3, 1800, his intention to publish "The Musical Journal," concluded the advertisement with the notice:

Next week, will be published, by J. Hewitt, the favorite songs in the Wild Goose Chase, as performed at the Theatre with great applause.

* *
*

In this survey of early American operas—*sit venia verbo*—I possibly have omitted a few, owing to the difficulty of access to the sources of information, to which I reckon in the very first place the scattered files of our early newspapers. Nothing substantially new, however, I believe, would be added even under more favorable conditions.

Early American opera was an offspring of English ballad opera and hardly contained any promises for a truly national art. The nineteenth century has by no means improved the outlook. During its first quarter the melodrama thrived simultaneously with the senile ballad operas. Then the definite importation of Italian opera inspired a few composers to bloodless imitations of Rossini, Donizetti, Verdi, etc. Meyerbeer, Gounod, and finally Wagner, stood godfathers to the more modern American attempts at opera, and to-day we are as far from American opera of artistic importance as we ever have been. Not that our composers lack the power to write dramatic music, but our operatic life has been trimmed into a hot-house product. The one Metropolitan Opera

House of New York supplies the whole country with opera, if we except the French company at New Orleans, the heroic struggle of Mr. Henry W. Savage for opera sung in English, and minor enterprises. Under these circumstances there is neither place nor time for the production of American operas, and our composers have almost stopped trying their hands at this sadly neglected branch of our art. The struggle against the apathy of the public, eternally in love with flimsy operettas, commonly called here comic operas (shades of Figaro!), and on the other hand against the commercial cowardice and avarice of the managers, seems hopeless. Whether or no a change for the better will take place, cannot be foretold. If not, then the task of the future historian of American opera will not be enviable, for he will have very little to say.

LISZT'S HULDIGUNGS-MARSCH AND WEIMARS VOLKSLIED

(Written 1914; published in The Musical Quarterly, 1918)

RECENTLY I had occasion to consult the following entry in the thematic catalogue of Franz Liszt's works:

Huldigungs-Marsch (componirt zur Huldigungsfeier (28. August 1853) S. K. H. des Grossherzogs Carl Alexander v. Sachsen-Weimar.) Berlin, Bote & Bock. Uebertragung: Fuer Pfte zu 2 Haenden vom Componisten. Berlin, Bote & Bock.

The natural inferences from this entry would be that the march was originally composed for orchestra and that it subsequently was arranged for pianoforte by the composer.

These inferences seem to be borne out by Lina Ramann in her Liszt biography (vol. II, p. 229):

. . . . (Komp. 1853) Huldigungs-Marsch[1] fuer grosses Orchester zur Huldigungsfeier (am 28. Aug. 1853) des Grossherzogs Carl Alexander v. Sachsen-Weimar . . . . . (Komp. 1857) Weimars Volkslied[2] (gedichtet von Peter Cornelius), dem feinsinnig ein Motiv aus dem Huldigungs-Marsch zu Grunde liegt, fuer vierstimmigen Maennerchor in Ausgaben mit Orchester, mit Klavierbegleitung, fuer gemischten Chor, fuer Kinderchor zu Schulzwecken, fuer Klavier, etc.

[1] Edirt Partitur 1858, Bote & Bock, Berlin.   Edirt Klavierausgabe vom Komponisten, 1863.
[2] Edirt in allen Ausgaben 1858, Bote, T. F. A. Kuehn, Weimar.

Why my sudden interest in the "Huldigungs-Marsch," one of Liszt's innumerable and forgotten minor compositions, little known even to the faithful of his own generation? I am free to confess that I had never heard of it, until I proceeded to consult the thematic catalogue, Ramann's biography and sundry other books for the purpose of identifying the manuscript of a "Marsch" scored for military band and bearing, on a fly-leaf preceding the first page of the score (23 p. fol.), this statement by A. W. Gottschalg, the distinguished organist and pupil of Liszt:

Festmarsch v. Dr. Franz Liszt (fuer Militaermusik von Raff). *N. B.* Dieser Marsch wurde spaeter als "Huldigungs-Marsch" benutzt; dem Grossherzog Carl Alexander gewidmet. Weimars Volkslied v. Liszt wurde zum Trio benutzt. Das vorliegende Autograph ist von Joachim Raff.

Of this unpublished band score [1] absolutely no mention is made in either the thematic catalogue of Liszt's works, or in Ramann's biography of Liszt, or in Schaefer's "Chronologisch-systematisches Verzeichnis der Werke Joachim Raffs."

Comparison between the band score of this "Marsch" and the orchestra score of the "Huldigungs-Marsch" published by Bote & Bock immediately established the fact that one march must have been derived from the other. True, the trios have nothing in common, but both marches begin (the thematic catalogue quotes merely the introductory fanfare):

After sixteen bars the marches part company structurally, the one for band being still more noisy and less plastic than the one for orchestra.

[1] Now in possession of the Library of Congress.

The question arises, to which of the two marches belongs the priority ?   Gottschalg claims that the manuscript band march was utilized later for the "Huldigungs-Marsch," whereas the thematic catalogue and Lina Ramann would have us believe that the "Huldigungs-Marsch" was composed in 1853.   Furthermore, Gottschalg claims that Liszt used his "Weimars Volkslied" as Trio for the "Huldigungs-Marsch," whereas Lina Ramann tells us that the trio of the march was used for "Weimars Volkslied." Finally, Gottschalg's statement would seem to imply that Liszt composed the "Festmarsch" for orchestra.   This, then, would mean that the orchestral score of the "Huldigungs-Marsch" is merely to a large extent a revised version of the "Festmarsch" with "Weimars Volkslied" as substitute for the original Trio.

In the following pages an attempt is made to reconcile these statements with the help of Liszt's correspondence, published by Breitkopf & Härtel.   Incidentally, it will be seen that Ramann's dates of publication, so far as they concern the "Huldigungs-Marsch," are incorrect.   Of course, Liszt's greatness as a composer is not affected by these inconsequential chronological notes, but biographical accuracy is better than biographical inaccuracy and, indeed, one never can tell just when or how chronological facts have a bearing on the history of a great composer's artistic evolution.

*   *

*

Grand Duke Carl Friedrich of Saxe-Weimar, who had drawn Franz Liszt to his court in 1842 and thus had shed new glory on Weimar, died on July 8, 1853, and Carl Alexander ascended the throne.   Immediately the preparations for the "Huldigungs" festivities on August 28 began and Liszt had occasion to write to Princess Wittgenstein on July 18, 1853, after a reception at court, as follows:

The company retired at 10 o'clock. Wishing me good-night, Monseigneur asked me to compose a march for his Installation-Huldigung on August 28th. I shall begin to-morrow; and, returning home in the carriage with the Prussian Lieutenant Colonel Hiller von Gaertringen, I believe I have found a fairly suitable motive which it is only necessary to develop further.

In his letter of July 22, 1853, to the Princess, Liszt again refers to the March in these words:

I finished yesterday my March for August 28th. It has more than 200 measures in 4 time and I seem to have succeeded fairly well. The leader of the military band will arrange it for his men and Raff will instrumentate it for the theatre orchestra. I have written it out merely for piano with but a few indications for the entry of the instruments. It is twice as long as Mendelssohn's march in the *Sommernachtstraum*—I believe that it will produce a fairly good effect.

Shortly afterwards Liszt took the waters at Teplitz, fully intending to be present at Weimar during the coronation festivities on August 28, for which he had also composed a "Domine salvum fac," but on August 25 he informed the Grand Duke that it would be impossible for him to return for the solemn occasion.

In the meantime, Liszt had written about the march to Joachim Raff, whose services from 1849 to 1857 as Liszt's amanuensis went far beyond suggestions as to "Hornverdopplungen und desgl." as Goellerich in his long-distance reminiscences of Liszt (1908) would have us believe in a gossipy report of a conversation with Liszt in 1884. We know from the correspondence between Raff and Liszt published by Raff's widow in "Die Musik" (1902) that Raff furnished the original instrumentation of Liszt's "Héroïde funèbre," reinstrumentated as the "Goethe Marsch," and not only assisted Liszt in the instrumentation of other works, but occasionally took a hand in the composition itself. That Liszt later, when his skill in orchestration had become equal to that of Raff, deviated from the jointly prepared scores, may be mentioned in passing, because that fact is not so well known.

It is in the correspondence alluded to that we find under date of August 5, 1853:

Do not forget to give Ludwig the score of the March so that the parts may be copied in time; and please do not send me a mere *brouillon* of the instrumentation of the "Domine." . . .

I send you herewith a few lines for Count Beust. Call on him either in the afternoon at Ettersburg or, more conveniently, in Weimar. It would be best to reach an agreement with him as to the performance of your Te Deum and of my March verbally and directly. There can not be the slightest difficulty, but should one be discovered on purpose, Count Beust has authority to remove it.

And again on August 24, 1853:

Several *rencontres* at Teplitz which might influence my future forbid my presence at Weimar on August 28th, contrary to my original plans. I regret that I shall not hear your Te Deum and I entrust entirely to your friendly care any performance of my March and Domine Salvum.

Pray recommend me to Montag and his two military band-corps, which will have to occupy themselves with my things —and please take care that they are not played in sloppy fashion.

Liszt was spared this danger, for the simple reason that the march was not performed. We know this from the correspondence between him and Grand Duke Carl Alexander, published by La Mara in 1909. Says the Grand Duke in his letter from Ettersburg, September 18, 1853, after some flattering remarks about "le produit incomparable de votre génie":

For fear of irritating my grieving mother by music in the castle I suppressed your march. I am obliged to you just the same and am still anxious to hear it. I hope and trust that I may soon have the opportunity.

Did such an occasion present itself? I find no allusion to a performance in Liszt's letters. Indeed, this march of 1853 does not appear to be mentioned again in his correspondence except in a letter to Hans von Bülow of April 26, 1857:

I welcome the opportunity for fulfilling my promise to Mr. Bock [of the firm of Bote & Bock, Berlin]; and I thank you for having pointed it out to me. Until now, I confess, I have not succeeded in discovering among my manuscripts anything suitable for him . . . ; but if Mr. Bock has a little patience I shall send him in July a March analogous [to the march "Vom Fels zum Meer"]. I would request him to publish it *brilliantly,* for it is a march which I composed for the *Huldigungs-Feier* of our Grand Duke. It will figure here on the program of the jubilee festivities for Charles August (September 3d). I should appreciate it if the arrangement for piano, about six or seven pages in print, appeared by then. I gladly make a present of the little opus to Bock.

What deductions are to be derived from these letters for our present purpose? In the first place, that Liszt, by command of the Grand Duke, composed and finished a march for the "Huldigungs-Feier" of August 28, 1853. Secondly, that he composed the march for piano with some orchestral indications. This, then, was the original version of the march, and it is quite clear that Liszt's loosely used words "arrangement for the piano" in his letter to Bülow are misleading. Not the piano version, but the version for military band, is to be looked upon as an arrangement. I say on purpose, the version for military band, because the second letter to Raff and the Grand Duke's letter to Liszt seem to compel the interpretation that a change in Liszt's plans had taken place. Apparently he dispensed with an arrangement for orchestra to be made by Raff, in favor of a band arrangement only. If Gottschalg was at all a judge of Raff's handwriting (and under the circumstances he must have been quite familiar with Raff's chirography), it would follow that Raff was entrusted with this band arrangement.

Furthermore, it is quite clear that this band arrangement was not performed on August 28, 1853, also that it has remained unpublished. It is equally clear that Liszt did not bestow a specific title on this march. He simply calls it "Marsch" and not once "Huldigungs-Marsch."

In other words, the entry under "Huldigungs-Marsch" in the thematic catalogue is misleading. As to the original version for piano, that, too, obviously was still unpublished in April, 1857, when Liszt thought of having it used by Bote & Bock. Curiously enough, though Liszt was willing to make a present of the original piano version to the publishers, nothing came of the affair. No such march was published in 1857. Indeed, this particular "Marsch" does not appear ever to have been published. More than this, though Liszt told Bülow that the "Marsch" would be performed at Weimar during the Grand Duke Carl August centenary festivities in September, 1857, it was not then performed. Or, to be more exact, the march was performed in the original version of 1853, which was still the only version in existence in April, 1857. With this assertion we have reached the second stage of the genesis of the troublesome "Huldigungs-Marsch." What had happened to induce Liszt to suddenly abandon his plan of April, 1857? Again his correspondence sheds light on the subject. The following letter from Grand Duke Carl Alexander to Liszt, written in Wilhelmthal, July 11, 1857, gives the key to the puzzle:

I wish to inform you of a desire, my very dear, [!] the realization of which I have much at heart, and which I entrust to your friendship and talent. Neither my country nor my house possesses a national hymn. On every occasion we find ourselves thrown back on the eternal *God save the Queen.* I beg of you to replace it by another hymn to emanate from your talent and to embody for present and future generations your own *cachet* of those elevated qualities with which God has endowed you. It is my desire that the festivities of September inaugurate this hymn. It must be something between a prayer and a *Volkslied,* serious rather than gay, neither too long nor too short—perfect. You alone can create it. Hence it is to you that I address myself.

The Grand Duke, in his somewhat Teutonic French, was ordering a national hymn for Weimar from his court-conductor, very much as he would have ordered a new

overcoat from his court-tailor. Liszt was too much of a diplomat to dive into his task without further consultation of the Grand Duke. Asked to whose poetry he would give preference, Carl Alexander replied on July 14, 1857, that he saw no reason for not asking "des accords à la lyre de M. Hoffmann" (von Fallersleben). At the same time he suggested unearthing from the theatre archives the text of the song often used on patriotic occasions during his father's reign and composed by the then court-conductor Johann Nepomuk Hummel. The comical side of this phase of the matter is that Liszt from the beginning had Hoffmann von Fallersleben in mind as the prospective poet of Weimar's prospective national hymn, and that in his subtle diplomatic way he was coaxing the Grand Duke into uttering a preference exactly for Hoffmann von Fallersleben, who, it will be remembered, was the author of "Deutschland, Deutschland über alles." (By the way, any one who takes the trouble to read the poem will see that, contrary to popular belief, "Deutschland, Deutschland über alles" is not an "offensive" but a "defensive" poem, substantially a plea for political German unity only.) Yet, when Liszt had accomplished his purpose, he did not compose Hoffmann von Fallersleben's poem after all, but one by Peter Cornelius. In a letter to his brother Carl from Weimar, August 3, 1857, Cornelius tells us how this change of front came about:

Liszt wanted a kind of *God save the King* for our reigning house and applied for it to Hoffmann von Fallersleben. But he delivered unto his hands an icy-cold, official nomenclature of Goethe, Schiller; Charles August and Liszt were not satisfied with that sort of thing. He thought that perhaps I could do better, and so I sent him yesterday the inclosed poem to Aix-la-Chapelle, where he is taking the *Kur.* I wrote the song as much from my heart as I could without hypocrisy or *Loyalitätschwindel*—to show Liszt that I complied with his wish with respect. Well, if he likes it and composes it, I shall have innumerable opponents, and the whole horde of know-betters (who have neither heart nor song in their make-up to turn out a poem of that type) will sail into me. Now please, my dear, worthy, erudite boy, roast my poem over the coals so that I may polish and improve it before venturing before the public, and can laugh at whatever the envious breed may say.

One begins to suspect that Gottschalg was correct in stating that "Weimars Volkslied," composed by Liszt *par ordre de Mufti,* was used by him for the trio of his "Huldigungs-Marsch." However, the following excerpts from Liszt's correspondence will prove that Gottschalg was mistaken. First we have Liszt's letter written from Aachen, July 23, 1857, to Princess Wittgenstein, and it will be noticed that Liszt then still had Hoffmann von Fallersleben in mind for the poetry of Weimar's national hymn:

This evening I shall begin to instrumentate the Goethe and Grand Duke marches which are to serve as *entr'actes* for Dingelstedt's Festspiel on September 4th. Magnolet perhaps can prevail on Hoffmann to send me a text for the hymn. Invite Hoffmann for lunch—the wine of Champagne will make his Germanic lyre foam.

One day later he writes to the Princess:

I am very busily at work on my marches, which I hope to finish in about a week.

And again one day later:

The whole afternoon was spent on retouching my marches, which have produced a *tintamarre* in my head. Alas, my good, my only and adored "Tintamarre" is far away! I advance more slowly than I anticipated with this business of my marches, though I am at it tenaciously. Perhaps they will succeed all the better for it.

On July 29 he informs the Princess:

My marches are almost finished. They take up more than twenty pages of my score-paper of thirty staves, each more than 200 measures in length. The Goethe march has 250 measures with the repeat. You will be satisfied, I hope.

And on July 31, with a sigh of relief:

> This march business is practically transacted and Sunday
> I shall begin to instrumentate the Fest prelude.

Without comment I pass on to his letter of August 5,
1857, to the Princess:

> Cornelius' verses [he means, of course, "Weimars Volkslied"]
> are to me what March is in Lent or rather the sun in summer.
> The choral melody of my march adapts itself to them miracu-
> lously well. Two birds with one stone . . . I am about to put
> my hymn on paper and I shall make a gift of the manuscript
> to Cornelius. In the meantime thank him for having re-
> sponded to my wishes so well. The stanza
>
> > Möge Segen dir entsprossen
> > Aus vereinten Sarkophagen,
> > Wo unsterbliche Genossen
> > Diadem und Lorbeer tragen!

is admirable.

From his next letter, that of August 8, 1857, we learn
nothing new, but its contents will help to flavor an otherwise dry narrative:

> All day yesterday Cornelius' verses laid siege to me. Impos-
> sible to rid myself of them either at dinner or at the theatre.
> Magnolet and Miss Anderson . . . would have died laughing,
> had they seen me light my cigar étui instead of the cigar and
> put claret into my coffee instead of sugar. But at last I have
> cleared my mind as to what to do, and I fancy that it will be
> something magnificent. To-day and to-morrow will be devoted
> to the task, for while preserving the popular character of the
> melody (to be sung *unisono* without alterations throughout the
> five stanzas), I shall vary noticeably the orchestral accompani-
> ment—which will call for 8 or 9 pages of orchestral score.
> However, the prospect of seeing you again in a few days stimu-
> lates me, and I hope to finish the hymn by to-morrow evening
> or the day after.

Finally, we have Liszt's letter of August 10, 1857, to
the Princess, still from Aix-la-Chapelle:

I required twelve pages of full orchestral score for the *Volkslied* of Cornelius—but I hope that the poet will be just as pleased with the composer as he is with the poet, and they will hug each other joyfully. I worked at it all day yesterday, from 7 o'clock in the morning until 9 o'clock in the evening, and again this morning. I shall now arrange it for performance either by a chorus or a male quartet with accompaniment of some brass instruments—work enough for four or five hours more.

At least one deduction from all these letters is self-evident; Liszt approached the task of giving to Weimar a national hymn through the medium of Peter Cornelius' verses with sincere enthusiasm. But also this further deduction is self-evident, that he did not compose new music for "Weimars Volkslied." He killed two birds with one stone by utilizing—as Lina Ramann correctly stated—the trio of the festival march composed in honor of the Grand Duke. This fact finds its corroboration in a letter written on August 12, 1857, to another friend. Says Liszt:

I believe I have succeeded well with the composition, and the *motif choral* of my march for the Grand Duke has done excellent service as support ("point d'appui") for this *Volkslied*.

With considerable satisfaction he reported to the same friend from Weimar on August 31, 1857, when writing of the rehearsals of the approaching festivities:

The *Volkslied* of Cornelius met with a complete success at court and in town.

It must have been quite a shock to Liszt that the final reception of "Weimars Volkslied," on which he had spent so much energy and enthusiasm, was followed by some severe criticism. The nature of this criticism appears from a curious letter written by Liszt to the Grand Duke on December 30, 1857:

You know that this *Volkslied* has been reproached for not being *volkstuemlich* enough. Without doubt I might reply that the appeal of both poetry and music is to a *cultured nation* and that the object of this *Volkslied* is precisely to glorify the *culture* of Weimar traditions; nevertheless, I shall not allow my unpopularity to seek shelter behind an act of respectful loyalty to your august house, unless . . . your Royal Highness finds that I was somewhat justified in raising the tone of my song and that it should be heard in public, though some persons might not see their habitual taste reflected in it.

In fairness to the critics of "Weimars Volkslied" I add that in after-years Liszt himself took a calmer and more critical view of the merits of this composition as a national hymn.

Do not let us modulate too much into minor, not even in *Weimar's Volkslied.* As for you, remain what you are, an exemplar of *noblesse,* very major.

he writes self-ironically from Budapest on January 25, 1881, in one of his touching, friendly, and fatherly letters to Bülow.

Every reader of the letters quoted above must gain the impression that Liszt, under considerable difficulties, had given birth to an absolutely new march for the Grand Duke! Without further knowledge of the real facts one could easily reach the conclusion that the "Huldigungs-Marsch" (incorrectly dated 1853 in the Thematic Catalogue) is totally different from the march alluded to in Liszt's letters of August, 1857. Liszt helped to pave the way for this possible confusion, by not once mentioning the title he was about to bestow on the march for the festivities in September, 1857. Yet, as was pointed out at the beginning of this article, the march for August 28, 1853, and the march for September 4, 1857, represent merely two different versions of the same piece. Liszt, with all his show of white fever-heat of creation, simply retouched and orchestrated his untitled and unpublished pianoforte march of 1853, suppressed the original trio and substituted a new trio with "motif choral." There was nothing either thematically or constructively really new about this march of 1857, later published and known as the "Huldigungs-Marsch," except its trio, and Liszt killed two birds with one stone by utilizing this trio for "Weimars Volkslied."

In the published version this trio is repeated for the final climax of the "Huldigungs-Marsch." Whether or no this was an afterthought, I cannot tell. Just how Liszt used the melody of the trio as "point d'appui" for "Weimars Volkslied" may be seen by comparing the beautifully harmonized melody as here quoted with the melody in the first edition of "Weimars Volkslied" in the version for a cappella male chorus:

1. Strophe
Frisch und kräftig

Tenöre.

Von der Wart-burg Zin - nen nie - der weht ein

Bässe.

Hauch und wird zu Klän - gen, hallt von Ilm und Saa - le

wie - der hell in fro - hen Fest - ge - sän - gen. Und vom

Land, wo sie er - schallten tönt's in al - le Welt hin-aus:

And these slight alterations not only weakened the melody but caused Liszt inadvertently to smoke leather instead of tobacco.

This is the genesis of the "Huldigungs-Marsch," so far as I was able to discover.   In passing, it may be mentioned that it attracted little or no attention in the musical press of the time.   Not even Franz Brendel thought it worth while to devote a few words to it in his report of the September, 1857, festivities at Weimar in the "Neue Zeitschrift für Musik," the only organ on which Liszt could count for a half-way decent and fair consideration of his importance as a composer.

Incredible as it may seem, in those days even Liszt's

publishers did not devote nearly as much space to advertisements of his works, as they did to a lot of worse than
mediocre rubbish.   Perhaps Liszt's hostility to the boost-
ing of his works by commercial means had something to
do with this attitude.   Liszt was so busy championing
the prospects of a host of other composers, that he neglected
his own.   His proud motto was, "Ich kann warten."
Perhaps he would still be waiting for recognition of his
greatness as a composer—in his best works he certainly did
attain greatness—had it not been for Bülow and the band
of the faithful who proclaimed and preached the art of
their idol, with a good deal of fanatic noise, it is true,
but also with that intuitive enthusiasm and willingness
of sacrifice against which the counter-currents of radical
opposition and even silent indifference became powerless
in the long run.

But back to the "Huldigungs-Marsch"!   If its history
as a composition is now tolerably clear, not so its bibliographic history.   Lina Ramann, it will be remembered,
claims that the "Partitur" was published by Bote & Bock
in 1858 and the "Klavierausgabe vom Komponisten" by
the same publishers in 1863.   Both dates are wrong,
Ramann committing a bibliographic salto mortale.   The
facts are that Bote & Bock announced the publication of
the "Huldigungs-Marsch" "pour piano" in their "Neue
Berliner Musik-Zeitung" on February 17, 1858—of course,
in its revised and final version of 1857, not in the original
version of 1853—and the publication of the "Orchester-
Partitur" not until April 18, 1860!   Thereby hangs a
ludricous episode, the humor of which the reader will
enjoy without unnecessary comment.

Hardly had the publication of the march been announced
by the publishers, when Hans v. Bülow, who was looking
after Liszt's interests, wrote to him from Berlin on February 28, 1858:

Are you very much displeased with the physiognomy of the

"Huldigungs-Marsch" as published by Bock? This is the second issue. The first was so disgraceful that I protested energetically. I am at dagger's point with him as with Schlesinger. Double profit, as you once remarked.

No further allusion of consequence to the "Huldigungs-Marsch" transpired in the correspondence between Bülow and Liszt until October 16, 1859, when Bülow, commenting on the publishers' "hesitation to publish anything except profitable compositions by Meyerbeer and Offenbach!" wrote,

Here is a copy of the letter which I saw myself obliged to send him in the matter of the Huldigungs-Marsch.

Fortunately for posterity this letter has been included in the fascinating collection of Bülow's letters published by his widow (Vol. III, p. 269–270) and though rather long I quote it here in full as an illustration of the spirit in which Bülow was fighting the battle of his revered father-in-law and master. The letter is addressed to Gustav Bock, and reads:

It is a very irksome task to have to write the following lines, since possibly their contents may discommode you and since, in view of your personal friendliness toward me, it would have been very desirable to spare me the regret at annoying you. About a year ago you applied to me for a manuscript of my dear father-in-law Dr. Franz Liszt. I sent you a manuscript, called "Huldigungs-Marsch," in orchestral score and in a version for piano, and you accepted it. An honorarium was not stipulated, but the condition was attached to the right of publication that simultaneously with the piano version (playable as a solo piece for piano) the orchestra score should be engraved and published.

The piano piece was issued, but circumstances of various kinds—taken into reasonable consideration both by me, Dr. Liszt's agent, and the composer himself—prevented you from carrying out your plan to fulfill the above condition.

Perhaps your admirably versatile activity caused the little matter to be forgotten; perhaps I have to censure myself for not having always pressed the demand of my father-in-law for publication of the score; perhaps, indeed, there is a misunderstanding—that I at the time failed to make said condition absolutely clear to you. I am led to this last explanation by the answer reported to me by Musikdirektor Truhn, who conveyed to you my query about the date of publication of said score. You rejected the friendly suggestion for pecuniary reasons and declared your refusal to publish at all the score of the Huldigungs-Marsch by Liszt.

Far be it from me to address to you, my very dear Sir and friend, any reproach; I assume the burden of the matter and complete responsibility to the extent of formulating for myself this obligation: to have said Huldigungs-Marsch by Franz Liszt engraved immediately in orchestral score *at my own expense.* Inasmuch as the piano score of said work was published by your house, I have now the honor to solicit your assistance in my effort to live up to *my* obligations and to spare me humiliation by my father-in-law. I adjoin the request that you inform me at your earliest convenience of the probable cost of publication—an advance inquiry to be pardoned on the grounds that I do not belong to the class of *rentiers.*

Characteristic as is this letter of Bülow's razor-like sarcasm concealed in a mouchoir of aristocratic politeness, Liszt's reply of October 19, 1859, is equally characteristic of this truly wonderful man, a gentleman born if there ever was one:

While regretting that I occasioned your disagreeable task of writing an explanatory letter to Mr. B., I could not help enjoying the reading of this little epistolary masterpiece, which would merit being printed at the head of the score of the Huldigungs-Marsch. However the little affair may end, please, I insist, avoid a falling out with B. on account of his editorial proceedings. Tell me simply his answer, and we shall take counsel for the best.

On the same day Bülow could report progress, which was to be foreseen either *pro* or *contra* after a letter such as his to Mr. Bock. Just what the latter replied, I am not in a position to know, but Bülow wrote to Liszt:

Here is Bock's reply to my recent letter. It was followed immediately by the engraver's visit, who wished to consult me about size, etc., of the plates. I have accepted the Leipzig edition of Glinka's works as the model. In three weeks the whole thing will be a matter of the past.

This prophecy was premature, for, as I said above, the orchestral score of the "Huldigungs-Marsch" did not appear on the market until April, 1860.

CIAMPI'S "BERTOLDO, BERTOLDINO E CACA-SENNO" AND FAVART'S "NINETTE À LA COUR"

A CONTRIBUTION TO THE HISTORY OF PASTICCIO

(Sammelbände der I. M. G., 1911)

THE late W. S. Rockstro contributed a two-column article on "pasticcio" to Grove's Dictionary which is a curious mixture of fact and fancy. Still, the article, though necessarily brief, is about the most comprehensive we possess on a musical *genre* which flourishes, as the editor of the New Grove happily adds, through the medium of the "ephemeral *musical comedies* of our own day," at least in England and America. It is surely not a survival of the fittest, but at any rate the survival of a practice once universal, indeed so universal that further histories of opera are in danger of being inadequate, unless some historian imposes on himself the task of first giving us an adequate history of *pasticcio*. This task will be difficult and laborious, but it will also be intensely interesting to him as a mere piece of research, and by the very oddity of the subject a refreshing incident to historical literature.

Rockstro defines "pasticcio, literally a pie" as "a species of Lyric Drama composed of airs, duets and other movements, selected from different operas and grouped together not in accordance with their original intention, but in such a manner as to provide a mixed audience with the greatest possible number of favorite airs in succession," and his definition is satisfactory for ordinary purposes, though any one who has occupied himself with pasticcios will miss the finer lines of distinction which so often compel us not to dispose of an apparently very simple

111

matter by such a sweepingly one-sided definition. However, it is easily seen that a pasticcio may be made up either from different works by one composer only, or from the works by two or more composers, and the more composers involved, the more pronounced the pasticcio character becomes. The first kind is not of much consequence in the history of pasticcio as a genre, and furthermore Rockstro's definition would not pass muster very long if every opera in which a composer deliberately used material from earlier operas, were called a pasticcio. For the history of opera the second kind of pasticcio offers hardly any historical nuts to crack, if the juxtaposition of two or more composers in one and the same opera was contemplated from the beginning as a mere matter of collaboration. Rockstro, citing the case of Mattei (first act), Bononcini (second act), and Haendel (third act), of Muzio Scevola 1721, as "perhaps the most notable pasticcio on record," bestows altogether too much attention on such collaborations, which one would almost be justified in not calling *pasticcios* at all. At any rate, such collaborations have never been very frequent, comparatively speaking, and in the history of *pasticcio* as a genre affecting the history of operatic life, they will be found to be more or less a negligible quantity. Really characteristic of the genre and puzzling are only those pasticcios which were an opportunistic afterthought, a mixture of heterogeneous ingredients, an operatic pie, made up of airs from different works by different composers, composed at different times for different cities; and most pasticcios are of this description. If one now considers that such concoctions, more frequently than not, retained the title of one of the operas which contributed to the mixture, that no reference was made to the other culinary ingredients, and that gradually the practice of thus mixing operas grew to extraordinary proportions, it is clear that a history of pasticcio is inevitable for an absolutely clear history of opera and operatic life in olden times.

This study is intended as a concrete illustration of the thesis, and an opera has been selected which in its day was second to none in popularity and which gave birth to a respectable number of imitations, such as Favart's "Ninette à la Cour," 1755, and Hiller's "Lottchen am Hofe," 1767—namely, Ciampi's "Bertoldo, Bertoldino e Cacasenno," or, as subsequently better known, "Bertoldo in (alla) corte." The lexicographers have been quite profuse in recording performances of this opera. Thus we find Venice 1747, Piacenza 1750, Paris 1753, Milan 1750, Venice 1749, Verona 1750, Piacenza 1747, Brunswick 1750, Bologna 1750, etc. It would be sheer waste of time to prove or disprove the correctness of these dates, some of which are simply impossible. They merely serve here to show what an area Ciampi's opera is reputed to have covered, and for a biographical notice of Vincenzo Legrenzio Ciampi (born at Piacenza in 1719) I simply refer to the short article in Grove, which is decidedly the best, whereas that in Eitner is about the worst imaginable. Ciampi is not of sufficient importance to the history of opera as an art-form that men with the tastes of Dent, Abert or Heuss should devote themselves to an investigation of his career or art (nor is he statistically interesting enough to arouse the bee-like industry of men like Piovano or Wotquenne) ; and perhaps for my purposes it is quite sufficient to quote Burney's several remarks on Ciampi in order to reach an adequate estimate of the merits of the man whom recent research (by William Barclay Squire) has almost with certainty established as the composer of at least one musical gem, "Tre giorni son che Nina," usually attributed to Pergolesi. Ciampi, in the course of his wanderings, came to London with a company of Italian singers and is said to have produced his operas there in person until at least 1762. So Burney, if anybody, had ample occasion to become familiar with Ciampi as a composer. He says in his History (IV, 477) under 1762;

The comic operas this spring were Bertoldo by Ciampi, with Le nozze di Dorina, and La famiglia by Cocchi. Bertoldo had been performed in 1751 or 1752, when Laschi, Pertici and Guadagni were here. The two first airs in the second collection that were now sung by Paganini, are gay and pleasing. Felton's ground was introduced, at this time, in the opera of Bertoldo, by Eberardi, but was become too common and vulgar for an opera audience, though sung by a favorite performer.

And on p. 459:

The productions of Ciampi strike me now as they did near forty years ago. They are not without merit; he had fire and abilities, but there seems something wanting, or redundant in all his compositions. I never saw one that quite satisfied me, and yet there are good passages in many of them.

And finally on p. 463:

The Didone of Ciampi [1754] is the most agreeable of all this composer's serious operas that were performed on our stage, here he is more frequently new, as well as graceful, than formerly.

As stated above, it is not worth while to attempt an elaborate analysis of such dates on the history of Ciampi's Bertoldo as are to be found in the many books of reference, more or less inbred. Only this much deserves to be stated here, that not one of them, except Towers in his opera dictionary, mentions the original title of Ciampi's libretto correctly, and Towers, when mentioning it, does not connect Ciampi's name with it. This original title was "Bertoldo, Bertoldino e Cacasenno" and not "Bertoldo" or "Bertoldo in corte" or "Bertoldo alla corte." The oversight is easily explained by a reference to Wiel's "I teatri musicali Veneziani," 1897, who enters under 1749:

Bertoldo, Bertoldino e Cacasenno. Drama comico per musica, in 3 atti. Poesia Carlo Goldoni. Musica (?)

or again by a reference to Spinelli's Bibliographia Goldoniana, 1884:

Bertoldo, Bertoldino e Cacasenno di Polisseno Fegejo [Arcadian name of Goldoni] da rappresentarsi nel Teatro Giustiniani di S. Moisè il carnovale dell'anno 1749. Venezia, Fenzo, 1749. p. 60.

or finally to Salvioli's Bibliografia universale del Teatro drammatico Italiano, 1903:

Bertoldo, Bertoldino e Cacasenno. Dramma giocoso per musica. Poesia di Polisseno Fegejo (Carlo Goldoni).—Musica di diversi autori.—Da rappresentarsi nel Teatro Giustiniani di S. Moisè il carnovale dell' anno 1749.—Venezia, Fenzo, 1749, in-8°.

Questa è probabilmente la prima rappresentazione del melodramma goldoniano. . . .

Lo stesso. Musica di Francesco Ciampi.—Rapp. nel Teatro Ducale di Milano l'anno 1750.

È noto che i Ciampi, maestri di musica, sono due: Francesco e Vincenzo Legrenzio, per di più contemporanei. Musicarono ambidue lo stesso dramma del Goldoni? Non avendo sott'occhio i libretti, non possiamo dirlo. Certo, nelle varie bibliografie e nei cataloghi troviamo riportati l'uno e l'altro nome. Musica di Francesco, dice il Ricci, la rappresentazione di Bologna (T. Formagliari) del 1750. Musica di Vincenzo, dice il Dic. Lyrique, una rappresentazione di Piacenza verso il 1750 (?), e nel catalogo N. 39 del Liepmannssohn è indicato un libretto con questo titolo e con musica di Vincenzo Ciampi stampato a Brunswich nel 1750 (testo italiano e tedesco). Non sappiamo poi comprendere da dove il Riemann (Opern Handbuch, 759) abbia tratto l'indicazione di una musica di Vincenzo Legrenzio Ciampi sul Bertoldo fatta a Venezia nel 1747! A Verona nel Nuovo Teatro dietro alla Rena fu data una rappresentazione del Bertoldo di Goldoni ma ignoriamo con quale musica.

This naïve accumulation of data is rather badly digested. Not that I deny that Francesco Ciampi, too, may have composed Goldoni's libretto, but there is absolutely no evidence for it and this particular setting of Goldoni's libretto which puzzled Salvioli is so certainly not by Francesco as anything can be certain in this world. "Musicarono ambidue lo stesso dramma del Goldoni?" Salvioli's own answer is of some importance for the present purpose: "Non avendo sott'occhio i libretti." Consequently his entry of Goldoni's libretto was not based on personal observation, but was derived from some unmentioned source or, as it looks to me, was compiled from several and more or less inaccurate sources. On the other hand, Wiel compiled his great work generally with the librettos before him; and the cast, which he mentions according to his industrious rule, corresponds with that in the Venice, 1749 libretto in the Albert Schatz collection at the Library of Congress, and since his entry in no detail conflicts with this libretto, it follows that he used a copy of the same edition. This agrees with Spinelli's entry except as to the words "di Polisseno Fegejo," which do not appear on our title-page; but Spinelli does not claim to have actually copied his title from a libretto which contains these words, and they may or may not be an editorial addition by himself or his source. This is more than probable, since his collation (Venezia, Fenzo, 1749, 60 p.) agrees with that of our libretto. Therefore, in the absence of further proof to the contrary, it is fairly safe to assume that the following represents the *original* edition of Goldoni's famous libretto, which the poet, to anticipate, does not mention at all in his memoirs:

Bertoldo, Bertoldino e Cacasenno, dramma comico per musica da rappresentarsi nel Teatro Giustiniano di S. Moisè il carnovale dell'anno 1749. (Venezia, Modesto Fenzo, 1749. 60 p. 14.5 cm.)

The libretto is in three acts, contains a preface and the cast, but neither Goldoni nor the composer is mentioned by name, hence, of course, Wiel's query "Musica?"

In the absence of any composer's name in the Venice, 1749 libretto—a practice of omission so exasperatingly frequent in old librettos—we would presumably be forced to concede that perhaps Ciampi did not compose the music for "Bertoldo, Bertoldino e Cacasenno," Venice, 1749, but shortly afterwards composed an opera really called from the beginning "Bertoldo in (*or* alla) corte." Fortunately, such methodical skepticism is out of place. The

Library of Congress happens to possess the following
librettos, all, regardless of minor differences (two of them
even down to the preface), identical with the "Bertoldo,
Bertoldino e Cacasenno" libretto of 1749 and *all mentioning Vincenzo Legrenzio Ciampi as the composer of the
music.* These are:

Bertoldo, Dramma comico per musica da rappresentarsi nel
Teatro Nuovo di Argentina (Argentina [Strassburg] Heitz,
1751). 46 p. 15 cm.

Then

Bertoldo in corte. Dramma giocoso per musica da rappresentarsi nel Teatro Bonacossi da S. Stefano il carnovale del-
l'anno 1755 . . . (Ferrara, Gius. Rinaldi, n. d. 48 p. 14.5 cm.).

And

Bertoldo, Bertoldino e Cacasenno. Dramma giocosa [!] per
musica da rappresentarsi nel Nuovo Teatro dell'Opera-Panto-
mima di Bronsevico (n. i., [1750?] 147 p. 18.5 cm.).

In the last the German title "Bertoldus, Bertoldinus
und Cacasennus" and text face the Italian and the libretto
is clearly identical with the one mentioned by Salvioli
as having been listed in Liepmannssohn's catalogue No. 39;
indeed, Mr. Schatz may have bought this very copy. At
any rate, it is a rather peculiar coincidence that one of
the librettos which caused Salvioli to be puzzled, should
turn out to be the very one which proves beyond doubt
that Vincenzo Legrenzio Ciampi was actually known about
1750 as the composer of Goldoni's "Bertoldo, Bertoldino
e Cacasenno." Hereafter, therefore, his opera should be
entered in histories and opera dictionaries under its original title with cross reference to its later and better known
title!

Whether or not Salvioli's "musica di diversi autori" is
correct—leaving it still open to what extent it is correct
—will depend entirely on the interpretation of the pertinent last paragraph in Goldoni's preface, which is now
quoted in full:

Amico Lettore.

Bertoldo, Bertoldino, e Cacasenno, sono tre personaggi, che hanno meritate le rime de' più celebri poeti italiani, gli quali in 20 bellissimi Canti hanno di questi tre successivi eroi formato si può dire, un poema. Ciò m'indusse a considerarli degni di comparir sulle scene, por far mostra, se non dei loro fati, almeno dei loro respettivi caratteri; cioè Bertoldo vecchio astuto, malizioso, e mordace: Bertoldino sciocco e goffo, ma fornito però di contadinesca malizia, facendolo io vedere, non ragazzo, come andò la prima volta alla corte, ma in età virile, ed ammogliato, dicendo di lui l'autore del Canto decimo nono alla trigesima settima ottava.

Da che moglie si prese è fatto accorte;

e Cacasenno in aria affatto di semplice, e bacellone. Per unir insieme questi tre soggetti, mi conviene fare una spezie di anacronismo, rispetto a Bertoldo, che non era vivo al tempo di Cacasenno per quello si leggi nel testo di Giulio Cesare Croce, ma spero mi sarà perdonato dal benigno lettore, come fu tollerato quello di Enea con Didone inventato con felicità da Virgilio, e seguitato con tanto applauso dal celebre Metastasio.

Io ho concepito il desiderio di porre in Teatro tutta la famiglia delli Bertoldi, onde ho con essi introdotta la Menghina, moglie di Bertoldino, avendo lasciata in pace la veneranda Marcolfa, perchè niuna delle signore donne avrebbe avuto piacere di avere un sì fatto nome, e di far la parte della nonna di Cacasenno.

Per salvar l'unità del luogo, fingesi che il re Alboino colla regina Ipsicratea sua consorte sia passato a villeggiare sul suo real palazzo di Bertagnana, territorio Veronese, e patria delli Bertoldi, come si legge nel Canto primo, ottava 19 dell'opera riferita.

L'unità del tempo è osservata, mentre nel giro di 24 ore può succedere quanto nella favola si rappresenta.

L'azione consiste nell'arrivo delli Bertoldi al Palazzo del Re, e nel retorno all'albergo loro.

L'amore del re per Menghina è l'episodio, che li fa andare alla corte; le gelosie della regina e di Aurelia sua cognata, è l'episodio, che li fa tornare alla campagna.

Le burle, i travestimenti, e le scioccherie di Cacasenno sono invenzioni per far ridere, che è l'unico oggetto di simili componimenti. Non mi sono però servito delle inezie, e puerilità descritte di Bertoldino, dal Croce, e di Cacasenno dal Scaligeri, sembrandomi quelle poco addattate alla proprietà del Teatro, ma ne ho ritrovate dell'altre, ricavate dal testo della mia testa,

le quali se non piaceranno non sarà colpa degli eroici protago-
nisti, ma del poeta.

A proposito del poeta, fa egli sua protesta, che le frasi, e le
parole poetiche non hanno a che fare col cuore Cristiano; e
che, se ha fatto un cattivo libro, in dieci giorni, non l'ha saputo
far meglio.

Circa le arie, alcune sono figlie legitime, e naturali del libro,
alcune addottate, altre spurie, ed altre adulterine per commodo,
e compiacimento de virtuosi, onde ec.

In this preface, Goldoni has not mentioned his whole
list of characters. It follows here with the original cast
as performed at Venice in 1749.

Ipsicratea Regina	La Sig. Livia Segantini
Alboino Re suo marito	La Sig. Anna Bastiglia
Aurelia Sorella del Re	La Sig. Redegonda Travaglia
Erminio suo Sposo	La Sig. Cattarina Baratti
Lisaura figlia del Re e della Regina	La Sig. Bassani d'anni 8
Menghina moglie di Bertol-dino	La Sig. Maria Angiola Paga-nini
Bertoldo	Il Sig. Carlo Paganini
Bertoldino	Il Sig. Francesco Carrattoli
Cacasenno	Il Sig. Giuseppe Cosmi

If at Brunswick the king Alboino has become "Il Conte
della Rocca, ricco gentil uomo," and the queen Ipsicratea
"la contessa Albina, sua moglie," these are, as will be
shown, comparatively insignificant modifications, but with
all the liberties taken in the replicas treated in this essay,
the Brunswick, Strassburg and Ferrara librettos are without any doubt based on Goldoni's libretto of 1749, and
though many changes were made in detail, the dramatic
motive remained absolutely and most of the plot practically
the same. Does the same remark apply to the replica
performed at Paris at the Académie royale de musique on
November 9, 1753, with partly the same singers (Anna
Tonelli, Pietro Manelli, Giuseppe Cosmi, Francesco Guer-
rieri)—one of them, indeed, having participated in the

original Venetian production, as at Strassburg in 1751?
Though the Paris libretto is not accessible to me, the question is easily answered, because Durey de Noinville in his
"Histoire du Théâtre de l'Académie royale de musique en
France" (2ᵐᵉ éd. 1757, v. 1, pp. 316–318) practically allows us to dispense with the libretto by saying:

Bertoldo in corte. Bertolde à la Cour. Intermède en deux
actes, représenté le vendredi 9 novembre 1753.

Acteurs.

Armire, veuve du roi Alboin, amante d'Emile	la demoiselle **Lepri**.
Emile, successeur d'Alboin...	le sieur Guerrieri.
Bertolde	le sieur Manelli.
Bertolin, fils de Bertolde	le sieur Cosimi.
Babet, femme de Bertolin....	la Dlle Anne Tonelli.
Sans-souci, fils de Bertolin & de Babet	la demoiselle **Catherine To-nelli**.

La musique est du sieur Vincent Ciampi, à laquelle on a
ajouté plusieurs ariettes de différens maîtres.

La scène est dans un village du territoire de Verona où étoit
un château du Roi Alboin.

Bertolde est un paysan qu'Emile fait venir à la cour avec
sa famille; ce prince aime Armire, & il en est tendrement aimé;
mais lorsqu'il a vû la charmante Babet il en devient éperdue-
ment amoureux; quelque attention qu'il ait de cacher son amour
à la princesse, elle s'en aperçoit & lui en fait de tendres re-
proches, il s'en défend le mieux qu'il peut, mais les yeux d'une
amante pénètrent aisément les sentimens du cœur de l'objet
qu'elle aime. Bertolin est aussi jaloux de sa femme, & il trouve
très-mauvais que le prince veuille lui en couter, il a beau lui
faire donner de même qu'à Bertolde de riches habits & de
l'argent, & leur procurer toutes sortes d'agréments, ils préfèrent
le séjour tranquille de leur hameau à toute la pompe & à la
magnificence de la cour d'Emile & ils le prient de les renvoyer
dans leur cabanner, ce prince faisant un effort sur lui-même,
renonce à son amour, renvoye Bertolde & sa famille dans leur
village, & épouse Armire.

Le poëme est assez bien écrit, mais on n'a pû en suivre le
style, scène per scène: l'action offre d'ailleurs beaucoup de jeu

de théâtre; presque toutes les ariettes sont d'une grande
beauté, & l'intermède en général a été très-bien exécuté, & bien
suivi jusqu'au 12 février 1754 que les musiciens Italiens ont
donné les Voyageurs dont nous allons rapporter l'extrait.

If we substitute "Bertoldino" for "Bertolin," "Menghina" for "Babet," "Cacasenno" for "Sans-Souci,"
"Ipsicratea" for "Armire," if we give Emile and Bertholde
their Italian equivalents, and if we bring Alboino back
to life, we have a synopsis of the original Goldoni libretto,
which fits it like a glove. But how strange a version
wherein the "Bouffons" killed off Alboino and made
Emilio, his erstwhile brother-in-law and rather shameless
purveyor of amorous pleasures, successor, not only to his
throne but to the love of his faithful wife. Verily,
habent fata sua libelli. However, the probabilities are,
that not one in a thousand knew what odd change of
worldly conditions and relationship had befallen the characters in Goldoni's libretto, and even had this been known,
it certainly would not have affected the fortunes of
Ciampi's opera at Paris, of which Clement and de Laporte
in their "Anecdotes Dramatiques," 1755, say, thus corrobo-
rating Durey de Noinville's estimate:

La musique de cet intermède est peut-être la plus brillante,
en ce genre, qu'on ait encore entendue à théâtre.
Bertholde à la Cour, dans sa nouveauté, attiroit à l'Opéra un
très-grand concours. Les Bouffons, dont le départ étoit arrêté,
donnoient cette pièce pour leurs adieux; comme elle plut presque
également aux amateurs des deux genres de musique, la ville
jugea à propos de les retenir encore jusqu'à Pâques . . .

It will have been noticed, that both, the king Alboino
and Erminia, are in Goldoni's original Bertoldo, Bertoldino e Cacasenno what the Germans call "Hosenrollen."
Such a proceeding was not at all original with Goldoni,
but perhaps the idea is not too far-fetched that he, whose
fund of fun was inexhaustible, wished to administer a
witty rebuke to the castrati nuisance of heroic opera.
Be this as it may, it certainly must have been ludicrous

to hear a petticoat king make violent love to a peasant woman, and a queen indulge in fits of jealousy towards a king whose voice alone was sufficient to betray the equality of his sex with her own. This grotesque effect was heightened by the fact that Erminio, too, the king's confidential aide de camp in his amorous escapades, was a woman, and still more whimsical was the idea of making this royal couple the parents of an eight year old child.

Goldoni had obviously introduced Lisaura for a funny scene between her and Cacasenno. Neither she nor "Aurelia" contribute anything substantial to the plot and it is therefore not surprising that other theatres simply dropped these characters. At any rate, this is true of the performances at Brunswick, Strassburg and Ferrara as represented by the librettos here discussed. The elimination of these characters helped to concentrate the interest on the main dramatic motive: The futile attempt of the amorous king to replace Bertoldino in the affections of Menghina. Of course, the whole idea is farcical and farcically treated, but then, Goldoni's farces are not intended as problem plays which respect the brutal logic of daily life. I do not believe anybody in the audience thought that Menghina, in real life, would have returned from such a court in her *status quo*. Everybody, I presume, went home perfectly satisfied as long as the poet did not carry his reckless flirtation with "the unpardonable sin" too far. He could, with impunity, build his first two acts dangerously near the slippery edge of gross suggestiveness, provided he frustrated the design of the "villain" and in the third act returned to the accepted standards of propriety. He could, with impunity, play havoc with the most sacred sentiments of his audience, provided he did so with genius, did not expect the audience to take his poetic escapades too seriously and, as it were, made them see themselves in the mirror held up to their own frailties and weaknesses, their faces beaming with innocent pleasure and laughter. This was true not only of Goldoni

and the Venetians of his time, it is true of playwrights
and audiences of our own time, though perhaps with this
difference, that nowadays the suggestiveness of low comedy
partakes too much of the *raffinement* of drapery and is
not naïvely frank enough to be harmless. A meagre plot
without much psychological development, like that of Goldoni's "Bertoldo, Bertoldino and Cacasenno," would to-day
be considered too primitively silly with its gay-hearted,
unveiled attempt to amuse the audience at any cost, in
fact unfit for the stage everywhere except perhaps in Italy
and especially in Venice, where the Goldonian spirit is
still tenaciously alive in the people.

If, as was stated above, other theatres dropped the characters of "Lisaura" and "Aurelia" for the obvious purpose
of dramatic concentration, they somewhat spoiled Goldoni's
libretto, because the slender plot really required much
embroidery in order at least to look substantial. The
annihilation of two members of the dramatic family probably was defended on the practical grounds of overpopu-
lation, but this argument cannot apply to the alterations
which a detailed comparison of the four librettos discloses.
These alterations, or differences, between the four
librettos, will catch the eye best in tabular form. The
first lines of each scene are given with the first line of
each aria in italics on a separate line, the words of scenes
which are identical with those in the 1749 libretto are
not repeated. Where only one line without italics appears, it means that the scene in question contains no aria.
Of course, where the line reserved for the opening of a
scene is occupied by a word in italics, it means that the
scene begins with an aria.

Venice 1749	Brunswick (1750?)	Strassburg 1751	Ferrara 1755
I, 1. (Camera nel palazzo del Rè) *Amor discenda lieto* (Chorus) *Germana, è questi il giorno* *Bastan gli affanni miei*	I, 1. (Piccolo boschetto) *Dolce amor, che del tuo fuoco* (Chorus) Amico, in questa alpestre	I, 1. (Camera nel palazzo del Rè) Regina è questi il giorno (no chorus)	I, 1. Amico, in questa alpestre
2. Ciò che si cela in cor *Qual'or di fiera ardore*	*Sono bresaglio e sdegno*	*Torbida notte intorno* 2. Preme andate in cerca	
3. Buon per noi, che lontani	2. Buon per noi, che lontani *Quel bel ciglio* = (1749, 4 1750, 10)	3. = 1749, 4	2. Buon per noi, che lontani *Vado che giusto siete* *Nel caro amabil volto*
4. Riverisco, o Signor, con umiltà *Quando s'in contrano*		4. Non mi spiace costui *Quando dilegua il fiero*	(4, 1749 = Ferrara, 8)
5. Non mi spiace costui	= (1749, 5 1750, 11)		(5, 1749 = Ferrara, 9)

6. Ah, sì pur trop-po è ver *Sento, che nel mio seno*	3. Ah si pur trop-po è ver *Il siren di quelle ciglia*	5. Ahi si pur trop-po è ver *Spero solo in quel bene*	3. = 1749, 7
7. (*Campagna vasta, e mon-tuosa . . .*) *Qua si fatica* (Chorus) *Ahi, ahi, non farò più*	4. (*Campagna vasta . . .*) *Qua si fatica* (Chorus) *Ahi, ahi, non farò più*	6. = 1749, 7	4. Povero Caca-senno *Ciascun mi dice* (= Brunswick)
8. Povero Caca-senno *Chi m'assomi-glia al fare-trato amore*	5. Povero Caca-senno *Ciascun mi dice*	7. Povero Caca-senno	5. Donna gentil, e bella *Bel volto credi-mi* *Io sò quel, che costumano*
9. Donna gentil, e bella *Io sò quel, che costumano*	6. Donna gentil e bella *Io sò quel, che costumano*	8. = 1749, 9	
10. Ora son im-brogliato *Sento ohimè, che il mio cervello*	7. Ora son im-brogliato *Quando io giun-to là sarò*	9. Ora son im-brogliato *Se mi sò far stimare*	

Venice 1749	Brunswick (1750?)	Strassburg 1751	Ferrara 1755
11. (Camera reale) Possibile che tanto *Teneri affetti miei*	8. (Camera) Possibile che tanto		6. (Camera reale) Possibile che tanto *Solo un ombra*
12. Nuovo spezie di pena	9. Signor, ecco seu viene	10. 1749, 12	7. = Brunswick, 9
13. Bondi a Vusignoria	10. Riverisco o Signor con umiltà (*see* 1749, I, 4) *Quando s'in- contrano*	11. 1749, 13	8. = Brunswick, 10
14. Oh che bel complimento	11. Non mi spiace costui (*see* 1749, I, 5)	12. 1749, 14	9. = Brunswick, 11
15. Oh, che bella figura *Ferma, ferma non conviena* (Duet)	12. = 1749, 12 13. = 1749, 13 in- cl. 14 14. = 1749, 15	13. Oh che bella figura *Ferma, ferma, no, non far*	10. = 1749, 12 11. = 1749, 13 12. = 1749, 15
II, 1. (Camera reale) Sire, qual im ponesti	II, 1. = 1749, 1	II, 1. (Camera reale) Vedo che bel- lezza	II, 1. (Camera reale) = 1749, 1
2. Largo, largo alla signora	2. = 1749, 2		2. = 1749, 2

3. Oh bella! oh disinvolta! *Maledetti quanti siete*	3. = 1749, 3		3. = 1749, 3
4. Quanto è pazzo costui! *Se di me gelosa siete*	4. = 1749, 4	2. = 1749, 3	4. = 1749, 4
5. Deh placate lo sdegno *Ah che nel dirle addio*	5. Deh placate lo sdegno *Ricordati ver mio*	3. Quanto è pazzo costui *La donna onorata* (= Brunswick, III, 5)	5. Deh placate lo sdegno *Contro il destin, che freme*
6. Ma voi, voi, che dovresse	6. Ma voi che dovreste *Deh tacete nel nesto pensiero*	4. Deh placate lo sdegno *Cara oh dio la vostra pace*	6. = 1749, 6
7. Erminio mi schernisce *Confusi i miei pensieri*		5. = 1749, 6	
8. Oh poveraccio me, cosa sarà? *Son ancora pi cinina*		6. Oh poveraccio me, cosa sarà *Se vi guardi ben*	7. = Brunswick, 7

Venice 1749	Brunswick (1750?)	Strassburg 1751	Ferrara 1755
9. Guardate, che pisciona! *Oh quanto con tento*			
10. Oh gran sem plicità *Non ho in petto un cor ingrato*	8. Oh gran sem plicità *Veglia sul caro oggetto*	7. Oh gran sem plicità *Ma che sorte mei cotesta?*	8. Oh gran sem plicità *Goderò ne' lab bri suoi*
11. (Notte. Sala con tavolino e lumi) Sta vita non m piace	9. = 1749, 11	8. = 1749, 11	9. = 1749, 11
12. Che fa mio padre collà lume spenta	10. = 1749, 12	9. = 1749, 12	10. = 1749, 12
13. E non vi ver gognate? *Zitto, e bel bello*	11. = 1749, 13	10. Voi mi diceste il vero *Tanta ver gogna*	11. = 1749, 13
14. Oh donne ma liziose *Mi par di ve derla*	12. Oh donne ma liziose *Donne belle donne care*		12. Oh donne ma liziose *Donne belle, donne care (see* Bruns wick, 12

15. Così è, ve l'ac certo *Superbo l'uomo irato*	13. *Oh caro amabil pegno Ti stringo a questo petti* (Duet)	11. *Volesse il ciel, che l'idol Giovani cori amanti*	13. Volesse il ciel, che l'idol *Sento mi aura*
16. Volesse il ciel, che l'idol *Cara sei tu i mio bene* (Duet)	14. Affè che l'ho trovata	12. Affè che l'ho trovata (but second half different, scene ending with the duet (1749, 16)	14. = 1749, 17 without the quartet which appears in the next scene
17. (Camera) Affè che l'ho trovata	15. Eccola con un altro cava liere	*Cara sei tu il mio bene*	15. = Brunswick, 15
Vuò conoscer quella Mar fifa (Quartet)	*Vuò conoscer quella Mar fifa* (Quartet)	III, 1. (Camera del rè) Sposo, e signor, questo piacer *Quel laccio d'amistà*	III, 1. (Camera del rè . . .) Sposo, e signor, questo piacer *Se al labbro suo non credi*
III, 1. (Camera de Rè con sedie) Sposo, e signor questo piacer *Sò, che fido ha il core*	III, 1. (Camera del con te, con sedie) Sposo, e signor questo piacer *T'amerà sarà contento*		

Venice 1749	Brunswick (1750?)	Strassburg 1751	Ferrara 1755
2. Qual merto a- vran costoro *Se non dorme il vostro core*	2. E ancor gelosa siete? *Tu nella ria Procella*	2. E ancor gelosa siete? *Al tremolar d fronda*	2. E ancor gelosa siete? *Aure che pla- cide*
3. Udiste? La ger mana *Non sì dà mag gior diletto*			
4. Vada, vada Menghina	3. Vada, vada, Menghina	3. = 1749, 4	3. Vada, Men ghina *Una donna come me*
5. Che commanda da me *Vogli darvi un aricordo*	4. Che comanda da me	4. = 1749, 5	
6. Venga Menghi- na. Questo *Se la moglie vi tormenta*	5. Venga Men- ghina. Ques- to *La donna ono- rata*	5. Venga Men- ghina *Sì caro sì*	
7. Anche questa ha voluto	6. Anche questa ha voluto *A riveder io torno*	6. Fermati, dove vai?	4. = 1749, 7 with aria of 8
8. Lo saprai, Ber- toldino *A riveder io torno*		7. Lo saprai Ber- toldino *Giammai l'oro non ricusa*	5. Che comanda da me *Più bella è la campagna* (Duet)

9. Or vanne, Er-minio, dalle nostre spose *Finchè bam-bino è amor*	7. Or vanne Er-minio dalla mia sposa	8. Or vanne Er-minio dall mia regina *Così fugge è spaventosa*	6. Or vanne, Er-minio, dalla sposa mia *Semplicetta tor-torella*
10. (Campagna vasta con col-lini . . .)	8. Si rende grazie al ciel (= part of 1749, 9)	9. (Campagna vasta con ca panna)	7. = 1749, 10
Belle le mie campagne *Che bel con-tento; che bel piacere* (Quartet)	9. (Campagna con colline) Belle mie cam pagne *Più bella è la campagna*	Belle le mie campagne *Qua si fatica* (= 1749, I 7)	
11. Mirate la fa-miglia *Dolce diletto* (Finale, quar-tet)	10. Mirate la fa-miglia *Dolce diletto* (a 3) *Che bel con-tento* (a 4)	Mirate la fa-miglia *Qua si fatica* *Belle campagne*	8. = 1749, 11

So many librettos, so many versions! The alterations evidently go far beyond condensations necessitated by the elimination of "Lisaura" and "Aurelia." Granted that the plot has practically remained the same in all four librettos, yet the changes by way of omission or substitution of arias are so numerous that the Strassburg, Brunswick and Ferrara librettos must be called adulterations of Goldoni's original "Bertoldo, Bertoldino e Cacasenno." And these are only three out of many that were published for performance of Ciampi's popular opera! I should have liked to add an analysis of the libretto as used at London, but unfortunately, it is not available at the Library of Congress. Still, the conjecture is perfectly sound that the liberties taken with Goldoni's original were very considerable. I base this conjecture on an analysis of

> The Favourite Songs in the Opera call'd
> *Bertoldo* by Sign. Ciampi.
> London. Printed for I. Walsh (n. d. l. p. l., 20 p. fol.).

The volume contains six arias (incl. duets) in skeleton score, all bearing Ciampi's name and the names of the singers, viz.: Nos. 2 and 6 sung by Guadagni, No. 3 by Ninetta de Roserman, Nos. 4 and 5 by Signora Mellini and No. 1 as duet by her and Guadagni. Each aria is headed "Aria nel Bertoldo," meaning of course, Bertoldo as performed at London, but only the first,

Ca-ra, sei tu il mio be-ne   Ca - ro fra dol - ci   pene
                                                           (Duet.)

appears in the original Bertoldo libretto in act II, sc. 16. As to the other five:

Fe - li - ce, fe - li - ce io so - no

Un vol- to a-ma- bi -le for- za à d'a - mar

Giu-ra il guer-rier tal   vol-ta, il guer-rier tal   vol - ta

Al por-to bra-ma - to del ven-to a se - con-da

Le va - ghe tu - e pu - pil - le, Deh

they do not even appear listed and certainly not under
Goldoni in Wotquenne's most useful though not exhaustive
"Zeno, Metastasio and Goldoni, Alphabetisches Verzeichnis
der Stücke in Versen aus ihren dramatischen Werken."
Nor are they to be found in the Strassburg, Brunswick
and Ferrara librettos.   Here then are five versions of the
same opera and all five distinctly and remarkably different!!

In the "Favourite Songs" the five arias which are neither
in the four librettos here analyzed nor listed in Wotquenne,
all bear Ciampi's name as composer, and we may therefore
take it for granted that they were really composed by him.
Immediately the question arises, were they interpolated
in the London "Bertoldo" from his other operas, or were
they composed for the occasion? I leave the question
open, as an exhaustive answer is neither possible for me
nor within the scope of this essay.   The probabilities are
that the correct answer will lie half-way between the two

possibilities.   On the other hand, it is possible, without
much effort, to trace with the help of Wotquenne's Verzeichnis, at least a few of the arias of the Strassburg,
Brunswick and Ferrara librettos which do not appear in
Goldoni's "Bertoldo, Bertoldino and Cacasenno" libretto
of 1749.   Thus

"La donna onorata" (Brunswick, Strassburg) is from Gol-
     doni's "Paese Cuccagna"
"Se vi guardo ben" (Strassburg) is from Goldoni's "I tre
     Gobbi"
"Contro il destin che freme" (Ferrara) is from Metastasio's
     "Antigono"
"Se al labbro suo non crede" (Ferrara) is from Goldoni's
     "Talismano"
"Una donna come me" (Ferrara) is from Goldoni's "Mondo
     della luna"
"Semplicetta Tortorella" (Ferrara) is from Metastasio's
     "Demetrio."

     Again the question arises, were these interpolations in
the Strassburg, Brunswick and Ferrara librettos selected from operas by Ciampi, or were they selected from
the works of other composers ? The bibliographical sources
for Ciampi's activity, at least so far as accessible to me,
are so hopelessly inadequate that I can only state that
Ciampi is known to have composed, of the librettos alluded
to, Goldoni's "I tre Gobbi" and Metastasio's "Antigono."
Therefore the conjecture is at least permissible that in
Strassburg "Se vi guardo ben" was selected from Ciampi's
"I tre Gobbi" and in Ferrara "Contro il destin che freme"
from his setting of Metastasio's "Antigono."
     Incidentally Wotquenne's Verzeichnis reveals the fact
that "Ah che nel dirli addio" in Goldoni's "Bertoldo,
Bertoldino e Cacasenno" libretto of 1749 is a parody of
"Ah che nel dirti addio" in Metastasio's "Issipile."   Im-
mediately now the final paragraph in Goldoni's preface is
remembered.

     Circa le arie, alcune sono figlie legitime, e naturali del libro, alcune addotate, altre spurie, ed altre adulterine per commodo, e compiacimento de' virtuosi, onde ec.

Clearly, Goldoni meant what he said, and though perhaps at this late date the exact percentage of the "alcune" may not be determined, there can be no doubt that Goldoni borrowed freely "dal testo della testa" of other poets, otherwise he would hardly have considered it advisable to take the reader into his confidence. Did Ciampi, one is now justified in asking, compose these borrowings anew, or did he utilize for them the original settings of other composers? The question, I fear, will have to remain open, since Ciampi's score of 1749 is not known to have been preserved. At any rate, not even the original "Bertoldo" libretto was wholly original, and it partook noticeably of the character of a "parody" as well as of a "pasticcio." Presumably the "parody" feature did not grow in the *replicas,* whereas it was shown above that the "pasticcio" feature of both text and music in their lyrical parts expanded considerably. For instance, of the twenty-five arias sung at Ferrara, only eight appear among the thirty-three sung at Venice in 1749! How utterly misleading therefore would the statement in the Ferrara libretto of 1755 "La musica è del Sig. Vincenzo Ciampi" be to him, who would attempt a study of Ciampi's opera from the Ferrara libretto alone (or score, if preserved)!

This concrete example surely illustrates the necessity of caution in basing historical estimates of old Italian operas on one libretto or on one score. Just as likely as not the historian will be criticizing *pro* or *contra* a composer who is not at all responsible for the aria examined. But, it might be said, Ciampi's "Bertoldo" is an exceptional example of the mania of interpolation; and though perhaps the practice was in force as regards lesser lights, the warning to be cautious does not apply to the men of genius who pushed the art-form of opera forward, and whose master-works surely were not subjected to mutilation. Against all arguments of this kind I simply refer to the preface of Fortunato Chelleri's "Temistocle" (Padova, 1721), libretto by Apostolo Zeno:

Il presente Temistocle è un' azzione scenica fatta in Vienna . . . l'anno 1701 [music by Ziani] . . . Questo adunque essendosi dovuto accommodarsi rappresentabile nel Teatro Obizzi di Padova, è stato soggetto alla dura necessità di aggiunte di nuove scene, cambiamenti di arie, ed acrescimenti di mutazioni. *Destino al quale ogni Drama vien sottoposto, dopo la sua prima comparso che egli fà sù i Teatri.* . . .

[This particular *Temistocle* is a scenic play written in Vienna in the year 1701 (music by Ziani). Consequently, this piece having to be adapted for successful representation at the Obizzi theatre in Padua, was constrained by stern necessity to submit to the addition of new scenes, changes in the arias, and new developments in the changes of scene. *A fate to which every drama is subjected after the first appearance it makes on the stage.*]

Though by no means the only one I found in my libretto studies, this is perhaps the most explicit admission of a pernicious practice which had grown into a deliberate system since the beginning of opera, for all students of the origin of opera will remember, how even in "La Dafne," in "Euridice" and in "Il Rapimento di Cefalo" traces of the "pasticcio" tendency are recorded. I do not mean the more or less legitimate practice of composers of borrowing, as for instance Händel so often did, from their own, older works material for new works, but the practice of tearing one composer's opera asunder and patching it together again with substitute arias from other operas, either by the same composer, or more often from operas of other composers, thereby causing an incongruity of style which throws a very peculiar side-light on the operatic life of olden times. I know very well that this is still done occasionally to-day, especially in ephemeral musical farces, and just as in former times as a matter of expediency; but that this expediency still has the force of a system, may fairly be doubted.

Granted that the system existed, what is its explana-

tion? If we except the quite excusable desire of managers
to replace weak or unsuccessful arias of the original score
by better or more successful substitutes, purely (as Goldoni so nicely puts it) the "commodo e compiacimento
de' virtuosi."

Of late years (see for instance Wiel) there have been
efforts to minimize the importance of this subserviency
to the singers, and the object of this historical flank-
movement has been to defeat by all possible means the
doctrine that Italian opera of the eighteenth century was
fast losing its right to be called *dramma* per musica. I
have never taken much stock in this doctrine, because contemporary evidence overwhelmingly proves that the poets
and the composers were in deadly earnest about the esthetic necessity that opera should be dramatic, notwithstanding the often indifferent attitude of (at least the
fashionable part of) the public. One need but refer to
Burney to notice that mere voice and vocal technique were
not considered sufficient in a singer to fill his part, unless
merely a lyric part, by those who frequented opera not
only as a social function. Emphasis is laid time and again
in contemporary sources on the singer's ability or nonabil-
ity to act his part in accordance with its dramatic contents
and to underscore them by "divisions" of his own invention. Whether or not the modern conception of how the
dramatic unity between words and music best be observed
and into what form the whole should be cast in order to
make of opera truly a musical drama, tallies with the
dramaturgic ideas of by-gone times, is a totally different
question. We have seen Meyerbeer vilified beyond the
bounds of propriety, yet I believe that even he was sincerely
striving after musical *drama,* and his contemporaries believed him to have accomplished his purpose. From the
beginning of opera the watch-word has been *dramma* per
musica, and I do not believe that Wagner was one particle
more in earnest about this knotty problem than his prede-
cessors who left their mark on the history of opera in the

seventeenth, eighteenth and nineteenth centuries. The difference of opinion has never resulted from the "what to do," but from the "how to do it." Then as now, many composers had no business writing operas, because they lacked the dramatic instinct; and then as now such composers were in the majority. Furthermore, then as now, many composers would compose into the hands of an applauding multitude and place the gratitude of singers for "thankful" parts above the esthetic demands of opera as an art-form. Then as now, many composers were simply not able to avoid the beaten path and to evade what had become inevitably stale by unimproved repetition; but, I believe, it is foolish to judge the constructive minority by the inert and, to a certain extent, destructive majority.

Having thus expressed my firm conviction that opera was never intended by real opera composers otherwise than as a sincere effort at the solution of the perplexing problem of musical drama, and that it is therefore *eo ipso* a psychological absurdity to think that Italian opera of the eighteenth century was not intended to be dramatic, I nevertheless take issue with what I called above a recent historical flank-movement. The history of opera and the history of operatic life are, if not absolutely, at any rate largely, two totally different things. A composer might set out with the best and clearest of intentions to write a perfect opera, and yet his efforts might come to grief through the conditions under which his work was to be performed. In Italy very much more than in any other country the system of *scrittura* exists and existed. Under this system the impresario wielded an influence, against the possible evil result of which the composer was powerless. He was simply a cog in the complicated wheel of conditions. Impresarios ever have been essentially men of business! It is their business to fill the house, by pleasing the public. If they can do so by upholding strictly the pure interests of art, they will surely do so, but if the preservation of artistic ideals means the depletion of their purse, they will surely let the artistic ideal go to the wall, unless they are fascinated by the prospect of bankruptcy. At the bottom of the history of operatic life is this purely commercial problem, and at every turn one will find that it has affected the history of opera as an art-form. No false esthetic sentimentality, no hypocritical contempt for the plain facts of daily life should blind even an historian against actual conditions, against the fact that opera is not merely a matter of art, but, as part of the history of operatic life, largely a matter of art-economics, and I venture to say that without this admission, perhaps mortifying for the lover of art, the history of opera will never be properly understood.

These remarks seem distant from the main theme. They are not so by any means. Under the system of *scrittura* the composer was engaged to compose a certain libretto for performance at a certain theatre. Maybe, as sometimes occurred, he had the choice between several librettos, yet, unless he declined to compose any of them, one he had to compose, whether he liked the libretto or not. Even if it suited his temperament and his individuality immensely, he was not at liberty to compose freely without further practical considerations. The public taste, the public demands at Venice differed from those at Naples, those at Naples from those at Turin, those at Turin from those at Rome, and so on. The composer was supposed to adjust himself to the taste of the city for which he received the *scrittura,* and as ample experience of many years had taught impresarios and composers just where the dividing lines of taste lay (generally a matter of traditional usage more than any real difference in ability to appreciate inspired music), this task was perhaps not difficult and not even irksome, since the librettos were modeled on the basis of these experiences. But this matter of local taste brought with it perplexing problems, when operas that had been successful, for instance, at Florence were imported to Naples. Immediately the impresario became, as it were, a tailor who, as best he could with the help of the accredited theatre poet and composer, endeavored to give to a garment of Florentine style a more Neapolitan cut. Frequently the impresario makes no mention in the libretto of this procedure; but frequently he does, either in those curious, longwinded, adulatory dedications to some potentate or person of rank, or in a notice to his "amico lettore." In every such case, of course, the people amongst whom the impresario has cast his lot are made to feel that they, and they only, possess the key to the secrets of beauty. I have come across more than one libretto in which some impudent flatterer of an impresario would justify his amputations of the original with the remark that the "barbarous" taste of Florence necessitated a thorough revision of the opera before he could bring himself to inflict it on the so highly cultivated and perfect taste of Neapolitans; and *vice versa.*

Perusing, as I have done lately, many hundreds of old librettos, one comes to the conclusion that the more insistent an impresario is on the demands of local taste, the more he has deviated from the original. The differences of local taste surely existed, and had their basis partly in a difference of climatic temperament, partly in traditions of local usage, like the indifference towards choruses or a fondness for incidental ballets or the craze for sensational scenic effects, and so on; but, just as certainly, the insistence on the demands of superior local taste was merely a cloak to hide the state of the impresario's purse. And exactly here enter the singers who, in the complicated structure of opera, stood just as much above the impresario as he stood above the composer and the librettist in moulding the destinies of opera. If a composer received the *scrittura,* he generally knew exactly what the cast, as engaged by the impresario, could accomplish. In a way this knowledge strengthened his hand, because he would skillfully remain within the vocal or emotional limitations of the singers for whom he composed the parts, and he would not risk flights of fancy on which the singers could not accompany him without inviting fiasco, due to an all too obvious contrast between intention and results. If it so happened that the composer had at his disposal a great cast, he would naturally be stirred to supreme efforts and, if it was in him, could attempt extraordinary things, thus carrying opera a little further in its development. On the other hand, the system weakened the composer's position, because it frequently prevented him from giving his absolutely best. Furthermore, tradition had rigidly fixed the relative importance of the several parts that were supposed to make up a well constructed libretto. It was, for instance, part of his business to observe strictly the rule that the part of the "seconda donna" should not be more effective than that of the "prima donna assoluta." To cope beforehand with the problem of rivalry and jealousy amongst the singers, was by no means the least difficult part of an opera composer's technique, a problem which a modern composer need fear not nearly as much. Marcello in his "Teatro alla moda" has so cleverly and convincingly shed the brilliant light of his satire on this whole rigid system with its many channels of corruption, silliness, laziness and stagnation, that I need not dwell on it here at all. The composer simply had to wind his tortuous way to success, handicapped at every turn by a code of conduct set up before him by those on whom, in the last analysis, the success of every opera depends—namely, the singers. In brief, he lived in an atmosphere of compromise, in which only the mere routiniers could breathe freely. And if this atmosphere of compromise hung like a cloud over a *scrittura,* how much more over a *replica,* over which the composer as a rule had no control whatever! The modern composer, as a rule, writes for a normal but imaginary cast, i. e., endows the characters of his opera with music that primarily fits the characters and is not beyond the capabilities of the forces of not a particular, but any theatre, that might accept the opera for performance. The composers of Ciampi's time very

often worked for a concrete cast, which might or might not
be normal.   Hence, they wrote music primarily to fit the
personal vocal or other characteristics of certain singers
who were to interpret certain parts.   If the composer succeeded in this to the singer's satisfaction, quite naturally
the singer would consider such parts as a kind of personal
artistic property, but quite as naturally singers who were
merely called upon to interpret such parts in a *replica,*
felt that the part was not really their own, that they wore,
as it were, second-hand clothes, and that they were placed
at a great disadvantage unless the music happened to fit
their own vocal and other characteristics.   Since the *scrittura* system, so to speak, conceded a part-ownership in an
opera to the singers, it was one of the logical consequences
of the system that in *replicas,* too, the music had to be ad-
justed to the cast.   An impresario, therefore, would not
and could not under this system, with its many ramifica-
tions into the whole "Opern-Betrieb," have any scruples
against modifying and altering a score and its libretto in
order either to cover up the defects of his company or to
display its strength to full advantage.   The easiest way
to do this was exactly to substitute for unsuitable numbers
such that either had already made a reputation for his
singers or, being newly composed for them, in the same
manner as a theatre-tailor would take their measure for costumes, were likely to fit them and thereby please not only
the singers but the public.   Inevitably, therefore, the
whole system led to *pasticcio,* and the more frankly a theatrical enterprise based its appeal to the public on the drawing power of "stars" rather than on the operas themselves,
the more openly the *pasticcio* feature would be developed
in all its phases.   Nor does it require much acuteness
to see that an impresario will have to lean heavily on the
sensational excellence of voices *per se* beyond the artistic
virtuosity of the happy possessors of these voices, where
the language of opera is not that of the audience.

In our own times, New York has been the paramount

example for this axiom; in Ciampi's time, and long after, it was London, and London in this respect still forms a twin-city with New York. It is therefore not at all surprising that in Ciampi's time the principle of *pasticcio* was in fullest bloom at London and there flourished with all the exuberance of an exotic plant. There its last consequences were reached by constructing whole operas around some particularly showy pieces in which the great operatic stars of the time took a personal interest. It was at London that Walsh flooded the market with "Le delizie delle opere." His, Bremner's and the "Favourite Songs" published by others run into the hundreds of volumes, and it is perfectly safe to say that they were not less the "favourite songs" of the singers than they were of the opera-going public. To say that every opera then given at London was a *pasticcio,* would be entirely too sweeping a statement, but how powerful a feature of operatic life at London the *pasticcio* had become Burney's history alone would prove abundantly. Very few Italian operas of the time—and London heard a great variety of the best of them and, of course, practically all in Italian—were given there, just as in Italy, Germany, Spain, or Portugal, without some more or less apparent modifications of the original score, or of the libretto; and, if we may trust the innumerable "Favourite Songs" publications, their majority partook remarkably of the *pasticcio* practice. The title and the dramatic body of the original would generally be retained, but, "per compiacimento de' virtuosi," the arias would be taken from anywhere and everywhere, and to such a degree as to make retrospective analysis impossible. Thus, in a standard libretto by Metastasio, he might have to share honors with Zeno, Goldoni, Stampiglia, Rossi and other librettists and Gluck, Ciampi, Galuppi, Cocchi, Jommelli, Latilla, Händel and several more might be pasted together for one and the same opera.

It is easy for us to condemn such a barbarous practice, but condemnation does not explain the cause, and it is the historian's business to find the cause before he condemns, lest he place the blame where it does not belong. A history of the *pasticcio* has yet to be written, and until it is written the history of eighteenth-century opera can never be made sufficiently clear in some of its most baffling aspects. The task will not be an easy one, but it will be a fascinating study in manners and customs, and once written, I believe, we shall find that Peri's bitter-sweet complaint in his "Euridice" preface,

Non dimeno Giulio Caccini (detto Romano) il cui sommo valore è noto al mondo, fece l'arie d'Euridice, & alcune del Pastor . . ., [etc.] E questo, perchè *dovevano esser cantate da persone dependenti da lui,* le quali Arie si leggono nella sua composta . . .

leads in a fairly straight direction and on a gradually broadening path to the foot-note of sweeping condemnation in Goldoni's Memoirs (I quote from the French ed. of 1787, v. 3, p. 363):

Les opéra-comiques de M. Goldoni ont parcouru plusieurs endroits de l'Italie. L'on y a fait partout des changements au gré des acteurs & des compositeurs de musique. Les imprimeurs les ont pris où ils ont pu les trouver, & il en a très peu qui ressemblent aux originaux.

*
*   *

If Ciampi's "Bertoldo, Bertoldino e Cacasenno" is conspicuous in the history of the Italian pasticcio, it also holds a prominent place in the history of that peculiarly French type of pasticcio, the *parodie,* and therewith becomes closely connected with the formative period of *opéra-comique*.

The history of serious—what an English-speaking public delights in labeling "grand"—French opera cannot exactly be called fascinating. The evolutional route is too straight and the subservience to the ballet too obvious.

Quite different the evolution of French *opéra-comique* (and comic opera), than which there is no more fascinating chapter in the history of music, fascinating because it developed so intermittently by way of curious obstacles, inoculations and odd evolutional phases. To go into details here cannot be my purpose. It will be sufficient to recall to the reader's mind just a few of the points of interest that make up the historical landscape. Thus he will remember how Molière at the "Comédie française" came pretty near finding his way from "Comédies-ballets" to "comédies-opéras"; how Lully, jealous of the privileges of the Académie royale de Musique, interfered, and how thus French opéra-comique received a first check. Then the Comédiens Italiens for the first time lost their opportunity, and instead of profiting by Molière's formative suggestions, they ran more and more to Harlequinades and burlesques with a strong leaning towards *real* "parodies en vaudevilles" (Font), filled with a curious mixture of vaudevilles, parodies, airs from "grand" operas by Lully and others, and airs made to order. They were suppressed in 1697 on account of the "saleté" of their productions. Enters, after a series of complications, "Le Théâtre de la Foire," with the ludicrous historical *écriteaux* episode. In his "Histoire du Théâtre de l'Opéra-Comique," Paris, 1769 (t. I., p. 5–7) Desboulmiers has so successfully and neatly described the share of the "Théâtre de la Foire" in the subsequent development, that it will be better to quote than to *parody* him. He says:

. . . je me contenterai de dire que le Théâtre de la Foire a commencé par des farces que les danseurs de corde mêlaient à leurs exercices, ainsi que le pratiquent encore Nicolet & les autres qui, avec plus de goût & d'intelligence, viendraient à bout de la ressusciter. On joua ensuite des fragments de vieilles pièces italiennes au grand mécontentement des Comédiens Français qui firent défendre aux Forains de donner aucune Comédie par dialogue ni par monologue: ceux-ci eurent recours aux écriteaux que chaque acteur présentait d'abord aux yeux des spectateurs; mais comme la grosseur qu'il fallait nécessairement donner aux caractères, les rendait embarrassans sur la scène, ont prit le parti de les faire descendre du ceintre. L'orquestre jouait l'air, & le spectateur chantait lui-même les couplets qui étaient présentés. Les acteurs imaginèrent avec raison qu'ils acquéreraient plus de grâce, chantés par eux-mêmes; ils traitèrent avec l'Opéra [l'Académie royale de musique] qui, en vertu de ses privilèges, leur accorda la permission de chanter. Le Sage, Fuzelier & d'Orneval composèrent aussitôt des pièces purement en vaudevilles, & le spectacle prit de ce moment le nom d'Opéra comique. On mêle peu-à pres de la prose ou des vers avec les couplets pour mieux les lier ensemble ou pour se dispenser d'en faire de trop commens; car alors il n'en était pas ainsi qu'à présent, on pensait qu'il était nécessaire de mettre dans chaque de l'esprit ou du sentiment. Telles furent toujours les pièces de l'Opéra comique, jusqu'à ce qu'il ait succombé sous l'effort de ses ennemis, après en avoir toujour été persécuté.

The last sentence refers to Monnet's reformatory but ill-fated management, 1743–1745. He was too successful for the Comédie Française, ever watchful of her own prerogatives and interests. The Comédie obtained an injunction against the Théâtre de la Foire to the effect that the spoken work in whatever form was there forbidden. This forced the management and its playwright collaborators, principally Favart, to fall back in 1744 and 1745 on the older form of "comédie toute en vaudevilles" and finally, though the manager of the Académie de musique used his influence to save the undertaking with Favart as accredited playwright and *régisseur,* it was suppressed in 1745.

Parfaict took his preface almost verbatim from the preface of Le Sage & d'Orneval's famous libretto collection "Le Théâtre de la Foire, ou l'Opéra-Comique," 1737, and a foot-note to the first *écriteaux* libretto tells us how the amusing subterfuge was accomplished:

Les écriteaux étoient une espèce de cartouche de toile roulée sur un bâton, & dans lequel était écrit en gros caractère le couplet, avec le nom du personnage qui aurait dû le chanter.

L'écriteau descendoit du ceintre, & étoit porté par deux enfans habillez en amours, qui le tenoient en support. Les enfans suspendus en l'air par le moyen des contrepoids, dérouloient l'écriteau; l'orchestre joüoit aussitôt l'air du couplet, & donnoit le ton aux spectateurs, qui chantoient eux-mêmes ce qu'ils voyoient écrit, pendant que les acteurs y accommodoient leurs gestes.

Le Sage and d'Orneval's collection is arranged chronologically, so that it is easy to study the structural and other developments of the librettos. They themselves have divided this development into three stages, by first giving, as they put it, "trois par écriteaux," then "celles qui sont en purs vaudevilles chantez par les acteurs & enfin les pièces qui sont mêlées de prose." For chronological reasons two men did not receive in the "Théâtre de la Foire" collection of 1737 the credit which is due to them historically as the heirs and successors of Le Sage, Fuzelier and d'Orneval. The one was Pannard, who brought a little more morality into the plays—and that had become quite necessary; the other, young Favart, whose refined esprit became necessary to keep the whole genre from degeneration. What went without saying in Le Sage and d'Orneval's time, at least requires an explanatory hint in our own and that is, that many of the works performed at the Théâtres Forains were bona fide parodies not merely of the plays given at the Comédie Française, but of the operas and ballets at the Académie royale de musique. Thus, for instance, Favart's "Harmonide" 1739 (one act in vaudevilles varied with prose dialogue) is a parodie of Royer's heroic ballet Zaide; and Favart, Laujon and Parvi's "Thésée" (1745, one act entirely "en vaudevilles") a parody of Lully's opera Thésée, which had just been revived. As to the music, for a long time Gilliers was the accredited composer and arranger of the company, whose duty it was to arrange and instrumentate the vaudevilles, to compose not only the ballet airs, but generally also the last vaudeville, a function in which no less a master than

Rameau at times participated, who indeed at one time was the conductor!

In the meantime (since 1716) the Comédiens Italiens had again appeared on the field. We possess an excellent collection of their repertory in the "Nouveau Théâtre Italien," 1753 (a pendant to Gherardi's collection of the old Comédiens Italiens), and the preface to the first volume contains a fairly satisfactory historical survey of the new company's accomplishments. Then, we are told, they at first performed only Italian pieces in Italian, but, as might have been expected, the public gradually ceased to encourage the undertaking exactly for this reason. To regain their patronage the Comédiens adopted the plan of distributing the argument of the plots together with the cast. This plan they followed up with "le canevas italien & français" scene by scene, so that "il n'y manquoit que la forme du dialogue," and then by the complete comedies of which the French translations were printed facing the original Italian, a practice, by the way, necessarily in vogue wherever Italian operas were or are sung in languages other than that of the audience. At last, having learned the French language, the Comédiens Italiens began to add performances in French, either translations of Italian works or French works written for them. Not being able to subsist on pure comedy, and not being allowed to compete with the Comédie française, much less with the Académie royale de musique, quite automatically the Comédiens Italiens were forced to intersperse their comedies with ballet divertissements and the inevitable vaudevilles, but towards 1750 the musical features become quite noticeably less prominent. Even with these musical admixtures, their comedies would not have kept the Comédiens Italiens above water, and they were even prudent enough to lay special stress on parodies with or without music. Says the "Calendrier des Théâtres," 1751:

L'usage où l'on était autrefois de faire les parodies de toutes les tragédies ou des opéras nouveaux était encore pour eux d'une grande ressource: le public qui avait versé des larmes à *Ines de Castro* venait en foule les essuyer chez *Agnès de Chaillot,* et l'on venait rire au *Mauvais ménage* de ce qu'on avait pleuré chez *Hérode et Mariannine.*

After all, the parodies were only more or less clever arrangements and travesties without much opportunity for composers of operatic talent to do original work, and therefore sterile, so far as the art-form of opera is concerned; and the comédies en vaudevilles, either entirely so or in prose mixed with such, were but a species of *ballad opera.* Consequently, though perhaps they were cleverer and more developed than the English ballad operas, their possibilities would very soon have been exhausted after so many years of inbreeding. However, it is futile to discuss what might have happened. The fact is that the somewhat barren field was irrigated from a different source, and it is therefore impossible to separate this influx of fresh suggestions from the problem. On October 4, 1746, the Comédie italienne produced Pergolesi's "La Serva Padrona," of course in Italian; the reception, though warm, was not such as to encourage the Comédiens to familiarize Paris with a genre of which the city was just as ignorant as of serious Italian opera. The novelty wore off without causing much comment and it was not until Grimm's "Lettre sur Omphale" on the revival of Destouches' Omphale in 1752 at the Académie that the clouds of esthetic discussion began to gather on the musical horizon of Paris. The storm broke when the Académie engaged Bambini's *opera buffa* troupe for performance of comic Italian operas as intermèdes or after-pieces. Strange to say, now the very same "Serva Padrona" with which Bambini opened his season on August 1, 1752, and which in 1746 had caused no excitement whatever, led to the famous *Guerre des Bouffons* with its avalanche of pamphlets written either for Italian against French music or for French music against Italian, and the fury of excitement had not quite spent itself when the Bouffons found it advisable to quit Paris in March, 1754.

Font has neatly summed up (p. 263 of his book on Favart) the results of this storm in a teapot by saying:

> Elle avait jeté une semence qui allait germer dans un sol bien préparé à la recevoir; le fruit devait être une renaissance qui transfigure le genre de la comédie musicale et créa l'opéra comique. Cette rénovation se fit par degrés, d'abord on traduisit en français les intermèdes italiens, puis on imita leur musique, enfin, on rivalisa avec l'étranger par des qualités originales et françaises.

And speaking of Favart's share in this development, Font states that he started out on March 6, 1753, with a translation of Doletti's "Giocatore"; then, on August 14, 1754, he tried Bauran's translation of "La Serva Padrona" on a public which by this time was in the midst of the ludicrous esthetic battle. "On avait," says he, "une nouvelle preuve que la langue française pouvait se marier aux chants italiens." Be this as it may, Favart finally got away from mere translations and, continues Font (p. 265):

> D'abord il employa la musique de tel d'entre eux à des paroles nouvelles et pour une comédie originale: telle est *"Ninette à la cour ou Le Caprice amoureux"* . . . puis il cessa de leurs emprunter des airs, chargea des musiciens d'en composer dans le goût italien, et mêla aux ariettes à l'italienne les meilleurs de vaudevilles: dans ce genre est écrite la petite pièce d'*"Annette et Lubin,"* mêlée d'ariettes et de vaudevilles (5 février 1762).

From this last quotation it becomes quite clear that Favart was not an innovator or even capable of grasping the point at issue without compromises between the inevitably new and the inevitably antiquated. Favart, at his best, was an opportunist, and Dauvergne and Vadé, whom Monnet in 1753 engaged to compose and write "Les trocqueurs" in French (though still with due respect for

their Italian models), were far in advance of him as
fathers of the French opéra-comique. This Font neither
affirms nor denies, but at least he is impartial enough to
attribute Favart's "Ninette à la cour" to "ces curieuses
pièces de transition."

On the other hand, Petit de Julleville in the appendix
"La comédie-vaudeville ou opéra-comique" to the vast
"Histoire de la langue et de la littérature française" (v.
6) exaggerates considerably when he calls Favart

> le premier, qui mêle aux vaudevilles des ariettes parodiées,
> c'est-à-dire des airs nouveaux empruntés aux pièces italiennes.

but we may gladly accept his authoritative estimate that

> Le modèle du genre est *le Caprice amoureux* ou *Ninette à la
> cour :* le ton s'y élève, l'esprit abonde avec la satire piquante de
> la cour, et une aimable fantaisie, et les couplets légers et
> frétillants.

With this estimate and with Font's "tel d'entre eux"
we are brought back again to Ciampi, who perhaps was
not gifted enough to compose a masterpiece himself, but
who at least was destined to stimulate the writing of a
literary masterpiece. However, before it is shown just
how he stood sponsor to Favart, it is necessary to gain the
proper distance from that double-headed term *parodie*
so often used in these pages.

Though a fine line of distinction divides the two, we,
of this age, ordinarily treat *parody* and *travesty* as equivalents, and for all ordinary purposes we are justified in
so doing. At any rate, we should not hesitate to accept
the definition of "La Grande Encyclopédie":

> *Parodie.* Imitation burlesque d'une œuvre sérieuse.

Not so simple and not so emphatic about the burlesque
characteristics is the definition in Diderot's Encyclopédie
(1774):

> On peut réduire toutes les espèces de parodies à deux espèces

générales, l'une qu'on peut appeller *parodie simple & narrative;* l'autre *parodie dramatique.* . . Quant à la manière de *parodier,* il faut que l'imitation soit fidèle, la plaisanterie bonne, vive & courte, & l'on y doit éviter l'esprit d'aigreur, la bassesse d'expression & l'obscénité.

Of musical parodies not a word in Diderot, and yet the operatic woods were full of them in his time, before his time, and ever after. Still, the musical parodies which most readily come to one's mind, generally were or are parodies in the sense of burlesque imitations of both the text and the music of an opera, and such reminiscences would lead us widely astray should we apply them to the musical parodies of Favart's time. Undoubtedly most of the parodies given at the Théâtre de la Foire and at the Comédie italienne were burlesque imitations of serious works, but they generally were *real* parodies only with reference to their texts. In other words, it was not so customary, as the term *parodie* would lead us to suspect, also to make a travesty of the music. Very much more often than not, the original music was transplanted more or less *notatim* into the parody of the text without an attempt to imitate, for instance, Lully's musical characteristics and mannerisms in a burlesque manner. It is for this reason that I have called the term *parodie* a double-headed term. To-day it is generally used, if applied to music, in the strict sense of burlesque imitation, but in Favart's time it was generally used in a totally different sense, indeed, *without* burlesque tendencies, in a merely derived sense, as defined in the "Nouveau Larousse,"

Parodier un air. Composer sur cet air des paroles autres que les paroles connues.

and in this sense the term is still used in France side by side with the other, original sense, thus occasionally causing confusion in a foreigner's mind.

Pointed as is the definition in the Nouveau Larousse, it lacks all the esthetic and historical suggestiveness and surprising inclusiveness of older definitions. For instance, of that in Framery, Ginguené and de Momigny's "Encyclopédie méthodique," Paris, 1818:

Parodier. C'est faire des paroles sur un air donné, ou sur un morceau de musique quel qu'il soit. La parodie demande un poëte qui sente bien la musique, ou qui soit guidé par un musicien.

Il faut de la flexibilité dans le talent du poëte qui parodie, ce qui tient à une abondance d'idées et de mots dont il peut disposer à son gré.

On devroit avoir un certain nombre de poëtes distingués pour cet emploi, qui, comme l'a très-bien dit le célèbre Grétry, seroient d'une très grande utilité pour embellir de l'expression de la poésie les meilleurs compositions instrumentales qui peuvent se prêter à ce perfectionnement. La parodie serviroit à les faire comprendre à ceux auxquels il faut une traduction, dans leur langue, pour connoître la vraie expression d'un morceau de musique. (De Momigny.)

Equally interesting is Castil-Blaze's attitude towards the practice of parody. He says in his "De l'opéra en France" (1820), in the chapter "Des traductions, parodies et centons" (the latter the equivalent of pasticcios):

Parodier, c'est ajuster au chant de nouvelles paroles dont le sens n'a souvent pas le moindre rapport avec celles qu'il avait d'abord; il suffit que le parodiste se conforme au caractère des morceaux de musique, & s'applique surtout à calquer son dessin sur celui du musicien, pour qu'il y ait une parfaite concordance dans les images.

Castil-Blaze adds some really keen esthetic remarks on the practice and then plunges against the parodies into a propaganda for translations. Of course, being responsible for translations (?) of operas by Mozart, Rossini and others, he is arguing for himself and, needless to say, carries his point to his own satisfaction, but it is quite significant that a Frenchman should find it necessary to champion the cause of translations—significant, because to this day France prefers to limit herself more or less to the French operatic repertory rather than to build up,

after the German fashion, a wide cosmopolitan repertory
by way of translations.

Both de Momigny and Castil-Blaze expressed their views
of *parodies* at a time when this genre had become less and
less of an esthetic actuality.   Quite different at the time
of the "Guerre des Bouffons."   Then the genre, already
indispensable to theatrical life, seemed to open itself to
future possibilities full of esthetic vitality and educational
values, such as de Momigny alludes to in the definition
just quoted.   But exactly because the genre was then or
had become a problematic actuality, it is not surprising
that about 1750 the partisans of parody were carried away
by its assumed possibilities as a characteristically French
contribution to the esthetics, not only of opera, but of
music in general.   Of course, Rousseau with his bull-
headed contention in the "Lettre sur la musique françoise,"
1753, that

> Les François n'ont point de musique et n'en peuvent avoir;
> ou que si jamais ils en ont une, ce sera tant pis pour eux.

far from showing the optimism of the parodists, attacks
them savagely in the foot-note that closes his "Lettre":

> Je n'appelle pas avoir une musique que d'emprunter celle
> d'une autre langue pour tâcher de l'appliquer à la sienne, &
> j'aimerois mieux que nous gardassions notre maussade & ridi-
> cule chant, que d'associer encore plus ridiculement la mélodie
> italienne à la langue françoise.   Ce dégoutant assemblage, qui
> peut-être fera désormais l'étude de nos musiciens, est trop
> monstrueux pour être admis & le caractère de notre langue ne
> s'y prêtera jamais.

Undoubtedly Rousseau's position would have been un-
assailable if the problem merely turned on the issue
whether or not the parody with its mixture of heterogeneous
elements could be esthetically as satisfactory as Italian
music set to Italian texts; but that was not the problem,
and others saw more clearly where Rousseau, blinded by
his preconceived theories against French music, was fight-

ing windmills. As I see it, what really interested those who gave differentiating thought to the matter was the same question that interested Castil-Blaze, namely: is it more satisfactory to produce an opera written in a foreign tongue in a more or less literal translation which only rarely will preserve the racial or national flavor and the poetic charm of the original, or is it more satisfactory to use a parody, i. e., a text which, while expressing the sentiments of the music faithfully, is written anew around the music in a language whose spirit and characteristics will immediately appeal to the audience?

Seen in this light, the problem of parody is by no means disposed of by ill-tempered or hasty epithets like monstrosity, hybrid form, etc., and these epithets gain force only from the fact that the parodists, not having their problem quite in hand or being unduly and irresistibly under the influences of the tendencies of their time, undermined the esthetic possibilities of pure *parodie* by an adulteration with the esthetic impossibilities of *pasticcio*, as will presently be seen in the case of "Ninette à la cour." For us it is easy to see the source of their error, but it should be kept in mind that they had grown up with the *comédies en vaudevilles*, a genre which, in the last analysis, just like that of the ballad opera, is a species of pasticcio, and it is but logical that they could not of a sudden outgrow the genre.

How differently some of Rousseau's contemporaries felt from him on the subject of parody cannot be better illustrated than by the article on "Ninette à la cour" in Parfaict's "Dictionnaire des théâtres de Paris," 1756 (t. 7, p. 425-42):

C'est une nouveauté véritablement digne de ce titre qu'on prodigue tous les jours à des ouvrages dont la forme même n'est pas nouvelle. Si l'auteur du grossier *Bertolde de l'Opéra* [Goldoni!] avoit eu plus de délicatesse, il auroit imaginé quelque chose d'approchant de *Ninette à la cour;* si Pergolesi vivoit encore, il feroit exprès de la musique sur des paroles Françoises plus dignes de l'exercer que les paroles italiennes de *la Serva padrona,* & ne soffriroit pas qu'elles fussent déhonorées par de la musique bien inférieure à la sienne & qui ennuyeroit souvent, si elle n'étoit dans la bouche de Madame Favart & du Sieur Rochard . . .

A l'égard de la manière dont *le Caprice Amoureux* est représenté, ce Molière, ce juge sévère & attentif, à qui le défaut de vérité déplaisoit autant dans les acteurs que dans les auteurs de son temps—ne trouveroit pas *Ninette* indigne de ses éloges.

De tous ceux qu'a obtenus dans cette occasion-ci M. Favart, le plus flatteur pour lui-même & pour notre nation, c'est celui qu'on n'a pû lui refuser d'avoir prouvé que la musique italienne peut s'allier à des paroles Françoises, puis qu'il a réussi à allier des paroles françoises, aussi ingénieusement que naturellement écrites, avec de la musique italienne. Il résulte de là que les sons n'ayent point de patrie, & l'idiome faisant la seule distinction réelle entre les deux musiques, celle de musique françoise & de musique italienne tombe absoluement, & que quand même on voudroit supposer plus de talens aux compositeurs italiens qu'aux nôtres, supposition de la vérité de laquelle nous sommes bien éloignés de convenir, rien n'empêcheroit que l'émulation de nos musiciens ne nous mit en état dans peu d'années, d'enlever la palme aux Italiens en ce genre, comme en presque tous les autres.

Favart's "Le Caprice amoureux ou Ninette à la cour" was not the first parody which Ciampi's "Bertoldo in corte" brought to life at Paris. His opera with the interpolation of *ariettes* by other masters, as was said at the beginning of this study, was first performed at the Académie royale de musique in 1753. Parfaict, stating that it was given as after-piece to Rousseau's "Le Devin du village," dates the performance November 22, 1753, but Durey de Noinville, it will be remembered, has November 9, and our modern historians still disagree on the exact date, Chouquet siding with Parfaict and Castil-Blaze with Durey de Noinville. However, all sources agree that the opera scored an emphatic success and that it was largely instrumental in keeping the *Bouffons* at Paris until Easter, 1754.

Just previous to their departure appeared at the Opéra-Comique (the Théâtre de la Foire) :

Bertholde à la ville. Opera-comique, en un acte. Représenté pour la première fois sur le Théâtre de la Foire S. Germain le 9 mars 1754.

These data are taken from the anonymous libretto (55 p.) as published by the widow Duchesne in 1766 with the "Airs de Bertholde" on p. 31-55 of the libretto. The score, as published by De la Chevardière without date (1 p. l., 39 p.), adds no further clew. Indeed, it omits the date of performance, and on this as on the authorship of the libretto the authorities disagree. Parfaict, for instance, says "par Messieurs * * * * * Vadé, Anseaume & Hautemer, représenté le samedi 9 mars 1754" and adds "Paris Duchesne." (Since the 7th vol. of his "Dictionnaire" was published in 1756, clearly the libretto mentioned by him is much earlier than that at the Library of Congress.) Clément et de Laporte in their "Anecdotes dramatiques," 1775 agree with Parfaict as to the year of performance but do not specify the date and mention "l'abbé de Lattaignan & Anseaume, & le M. de S. pour les ariettes," as the literary and musical authors. De Léris in his "Dictionnaire portatif des Théâtres" also names de Lattaignan and Anseaume as authors and the marquis Lasalle d'Offemont (the "M. de S." of Cl. & de Lap.), but he dates the first performance as March 8, 1754. If we turn to modern books of reference, we find *inter alia* that Clément & Larousse's opera dictionary attributes the text to Anseaume alone, whereas Wotquenne in the Brussels catalogue (I, 382) follows de Léris, or Clément and de Laporte, but both authorities fix the date of first performance as March 9, 1754. It is therefore presumably safe to accept this date, and unsafe to attribute the text definitely either to Anseaume alone or to the teams de Lattaignan and Anseaume, or Vadé, Anseaume and Hautemer. By a more satisfactory consensus of opinion the marquis Lasalle d'Offemont is credited with the arrangement of the music for this, it seems, only slightly

successful first French parody of Ciampi's once so popular
opera, and those interested in the career of this titled
amateur will find half a column under Lasalle d'Offemont
(1734-1818) in Fétis.

Of "Bertoldo, Bertoldino e Cacasenno" nothing was
left in this parody except the essence of the plot, and the
whole is carried on by only four characters:

> Bertholde, paysan des environs de Paris.
> M. Dorimon, traitant,
> Mlle. Catin,
> Lisette, jeune paysanne.

Of course, Dorimon has designs on Lisette, who inno-
cently accepts his invitation to reside at his hôtel on condition that Bertholde, her sweetheart, be made secretary
to Dorimon.   Inasmuch as Dorimon is made to believe
that Bertholde is her brother, he accedes to this ludicrous
stipulation, but the trio overlooked Mlle. Catin.   The
result of it all is, that Lisette turns in disgust from Dorimon, and Mlle. Catin, wounded in her pride as mistress,
casts Dorimon out of her sphere of interest, quite satisfied
that at least half a dozen noblemen will be only too glad
to take Dorimon's place.

This harmless yet not too insipid story is constructed
on the lines of the older *comédie toute en vaudevilles,*
that is, the dialogue is not spoken, but carried on by means
of the music of vaudevilles, and it is easily seen how this
procedure, by the incongruity of airs and words and the
resulting associations in the mind of the audience, could
be made quite witty.   For instance, Mlle. Catin in her
rage sings to the air "L'amour n'est pas un jeu" some
lines which end

> Vous le savez, pour une actrice,
> Changement n'est qu'un jeu.

It goes without saying that the vaudevilles were not
used merely for the argumentative part of the libretto,

but also for the lyrical, and, in addition, this contained
six Ariettes.[1]   Lasalle d'Offemont's share in the parody
was therefore twofold; first, he had to select a sufficient
number of familiar *vaudevilles* called *airs* and to arrange
their accompaniment, and secondly to select and arrange
the music of suitable arias (*ariettes*) from popular operas.

Just how he did this and how, in fact, a *comédie toute
en vaudevilles* looked, will best be understood from a first-
line or thematic analysis of his operatic trifle.   The words
in italics represent the titles of the vaudevilles.   To the
musical themes has been added the source of selection,
which is not given in the libretto or in the score, but was
traced for the Brussels Catalogue by Mr. Wotquenne.   His
statement, however, that the parody contains "sept morceaux" is slightly misleading.   At any rate, the libretto
contains only six ariettes and Wotquenne's fifth "Les
grandeurs, les honneurs–Adapté sur le menuet d'Exaudet"
while appearing in the printed score as

Les grandeurs, les honneurs,   la   for - tu - ne

figures in the libretto not as an ariette, but as the vaudeville "Nous sommes précepteurs d'amour."

BERTHOLDE À LA VILLE
Air.

Scene 1.   *Rossignol, ton chant est beau:* Morbleu que voilà
que c'est beau.

Du haut en bas: Qu'on est heureux.

Hélas! la pauvre fille: Ah, ma pauvre Lisette.

Pelsambleu Monsieur le curé: Eh oui-dà Monsieur
le Galant.

2.   *Mon père aussi ma mère:* Mais j'apperçois Lisette.

Non, non, Colette n'est point trompeuse: Non, non,
Lisette n'est pas légère.

De la coupe enchantée: Quand tu me fis de si ten-
dres promesses.

[1] It may be mentioned that Rousseau in his "Lettre" waxes quite sarcastic over the custom of dubbing *vaudevilles* "Airs," and real "Airs"
(Arias) *ariettes.*

Ariette première.

Quand le ha-sard en-sem-ble, les ras-sem-ble
(= "Quando s'incontrano, Ciampi's B., B. e C.)

Si des galans de la ville: Des beaux messieurs de la ville.

Ton petit minois sans défaut: Ma chère enfant, la clef des cœurs.

Des sabotiers italiens: Ne suis-je donc pas fille d'honneur?

Ariette seconde.

Tel qu'un pe - tit oi - seau
(= Amore è fatto come un uccellatore, from Cocchi's La Mascherata.)

Des fraises: Jure donc que l'on rompra.

3. *N'y a pas de mal à çà:* Ah le téméraire.

Laire là, laire lanlaire: Quoi! c'est ton frère, mon enfant?

Des billets doux: Pour Secrétaire je le prends.

Dans le fond d'une écurie: Plutôt, si c'est votre envie.

Ma raison s'en va beau train: Soit, par ce moyen.

Pour la baronne: Avec mon frère j'y peux rester avec plaisir.

Paris est au Roi: Mon cher, en ce cas.

4. *Ah qu'il y va gaîment:* Pour son rival il est galant.

C'est une excuse: De le tromper, j'ai du regret.

5. *Ton humeur est Catherine:* Parlez donc, Mademoiselle.

Du cap de Bonne-Espérance: Ma fureur est sans égale.

Sans le savoir: Faites-vous donc au moins connoître.

Menuet de Grandval: Voyez-vous la sainte mitouche.
(This was used as early as 1716 in the so-called opéra-comique of "Arlequin traitant.")

Mariez, mariez-moi: Je n'ai point l'esprit jaloux.

On n'aime point dans nos forêts: Moi me marier! Ah vraiment.

Vous m'entendez bien: Comment, les filles parmi vous.

Est-ce que ça ce demande: D'un engagement sérieux nous évitons la gêne.

Nous jouissons dans nos hameaux: Pour sortir de l'obscurité.

Ariette troisième.

Vo - tre   cœur en vain mur - mu - re
(not found by Wotquenne.)

Allez, Lison, ne craignez rien: Je reconnois votre candeur.

6. *De l'amour tout subit les loix:* Que de gens on voit à Paris.

   Nous autres bons villageois: Je puis donc en liberté.

   Ah mon Dieu! que de jolies filles: Mais quelle est cette jolie femme.

   Madame, en vérité: Votre habit est du dernier beau.

   Comm' 'là qu'est fait: Monsieur sans paroître incivile.

   Tout roule aujourd'hui dans le monde: C'est que j'ai vu certaine Belle.

7. *Jupin de grand matin:* Mon frère, dès ce jour.

   Entre l'amour et la raison: Il se déclare mon amant.

   Petits moutons, gardez la plaine: Est-ce pas interêt qu'on aime.

   Je me ris de qui fait le brave: Si l'on m'aimoit, comme on vous aime.

   Non, je ne serai pas: Lison, vous me fuyez.

8. *Babet, que t'es gentille:* Oui, je t'offre ma main.

   Ah, Phaéton: Ah Dorimon, est-il possible.

Ariette quatrième.

A tant de   charmes, Ren- dez les   ar - mes
(not found by Wotquenne.)

La fontaine de jouvence: Les beaux sentiments qu'elle étale.

Je n'saurois: Oui, c'est vous seule que j'aime.

Les filles de Montpellier: Et toi, mon cher écuyer.

Nous sommes précepteurs d'amour: Les grandeurs,
Les honneurs, La fortune. (See above.)
Vous qui vous mocquez par vos ris: Osez à mes
yeux la prier.
De la bisogne: Allons donc mon bel écuyer.
Laire là, laire lanlaire: Je ferois volontiers cela.
J'entends, le souper qui m'attend: Comment?
Demandez à Lisette.
Ma raison s'en va beau train: Ton amant! ah, qu'as-
tu dit?

Ariette cinquième.

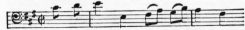

Dieux! quel paix de ma ten-dres - se

(=Maledetti quanti siete, from Ciampi's B., B. e C.)

L'amour n'est pas un jeu: Hé bien, donc, Monsieur
Dorimon.
Bouchez, Najades: L'un d'un côté, l'autre de l'autre.

Ariette sixième.

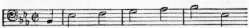

Le ciel va rendre à mes vœux

(= A riveder ritorno, from Ciampi's B., B. e C.)

Decidedly more developed, more pretentious and in
every respect more important was Favart's parody, commonly known since early times as "Ninette à la cour."
But this is really a sub-title, an alternative title, as appears
conclusively from Clément et de Laporte, Parfaict, and
other contemporary sources. The real title appears on
the title-page of the libretto with cast by Duchesne of
Paris in 1759 (86 p.; in the Library of Congress):

Le caprice amoureux ou Ninette à la cour, comédie en deux
actes, mêlée d'ariettes, parodiées de Bertolde à la cour par
Monsieur Favart. Représentée pour la première fois par les
Comédiens italiens ordinaires du Roi, le mercredi 12 mars

1756 et ci-devant en trois actes le 12 février 1755.   Nouvelle
édition corrigée & conforme à la représentation.

Besides containing the correct title, the libretto gives
practically all the chronological, etc., data that one cares
to have.   A copy of the original three-act version has not
come to my notice, but at least I can refer those interested
to Parfaict's statement in 1756 that a libretto of the
three-act version had been published at Paris by Delormel
& Prault fils, and Parfaict's enthusiastic review of "Ninette
à la cour" quoted above serves the purpose sufficiently
of showing with what delight Favart's exceedingly clever
parody had been acclaimed upon its appearance at the
Comédie italienne.   Yet Favart reduced the piece from
three to two acts, and the current theory (not shared by
me) is, that he felt the comedy to be too long.

As will be seen, Ciampi's music was allowed to grace
Favart's Ninette only to an almost negligible degree.
Quite different Goldoni's text.   Favart parodied it as
closely as one possibly could without furnishing a translation.   The term which one so often meets on German
librettos, "frei bearbeitet," would here be fully applicable,
so much so indeed, that a synopsis of Favart's plot becomes
unnecessary.   This will appear without further proof by
quoting the list of characters with the cast of 1756:

Astolphe, roi de Lombardie................ M. Rochard.
Fabrice, confident d'Astolphe.............. M. Desbrosses.
Émilie, comtesse, amante d'Astolphe........ Mlle. Catinon.
Ninette, villageoise....................... Mme. Favart.
Colas, villageois.......................... M. Chanville.
Dorine, Suivante.......................... Mlle. Astrandi.
Clarice,   "   .... Mlle. Desglands.

Obviously, all the essential characters in Goldoni's
libretto, at least so far as they deal with Menghina's and
Bertoldino's career at court, are here represented.   Not
only this, but Favart parodied closely the construction of

the plot and did not forget to utilize that farcical scene in Goldoni where the ever-serviceable trick of extinguishing the candles serves to introduce a number of (easily imagined) ludicrous *quid pro quos*. However, in my opinion, Favart turned here the harmless though frank drollery of Goldoni into a scene which would to-day hurt the sensibilities of many. Ninette extinguishes the candles and pushes the neglected countess Émilie towards her faithless lover Astolphe, who, believing her to be his intended prey, Ninette, makes violent love to her, a proceeding which Ninette encourages by guiding him on over the shoulders of Émilie. Nothing new in opera, of course, and perhaps very funny, but somewhat disgusting, because Émilie is made a tool and an object of charity in a manner mortifying to every refined and faithful woman. Ninette relights the candles, she and Colas fairly burst with laughter, Astolphe changes from disappointed rage to an unconvincingly sudden repentance, and the hapless Émilie, as faithful women so often do in mediocre French comedies and comedies in the French taste, by order of the playwright meekly subdues her pride and practically accepts Astolphe out of the hands of Ninette, as if a lover had a perfect right to maltreat his bride in whatsoever manner he pleases. Font, in his book on Favart, calls this a "situation plaisante," and brushes aside all objection with the glib remark, "Astolphe, en homme d'esprit, obtient son pardon d'Émilie."

Still, I suppose, such things should be interpreted historically or racially; and there can be no doubt that "Ninette à la cour," aside from such matters of racial or changed taste, is a very clever piece of play-writing and fully deserves its literary reputation. Certainly, Favart's parody is so typically French that it simply could not fail to please the public and presumably very much more so than if, as would have happened in the case of a translation, even a free translation, the peculiarly Italian flavor of Goldoni's original had been preserved. Menghina above

all, this naïve and somewhat primitive but shrewd and
quick-witted Italian peasant woman, has become in Favart's hands a typically Parisian *villageoise,* equally quick-
witted but no longer naïve or primitive. Far from it,
she has been turned into a very dexterous type of stage
coquette, and if all ends well, I wonder if there did not
pass through Favart's mind, nevertheless, those slightly
similar interviews between Mme. Favart and the Maréchal
de Saxe which form such a sad chapter in the life of the
Favarts and which, so Font claims, did not end so happily
for the then "Ninette." However, if Gounod's Marguerite
is a strikingly French edition of Goethe's Gretchen, not
less so is Favart's Ninette of Goldoni's Menghina, and
for exactly the same reasons.

Just how the three-act version of "Ninette à la cour"
differed from the two-act version (title quoted above) only
the comparison of the respective librettos could disclose.
Unfortunately, the Library of Congress does not possess
the libretto of the three-act version, which appears to be
exceedingly rare, and whose title perhaps reads as entered
in Parfaict:

Caprice (le) Amoureux, ou, Ninette à la cour, comédie françoise au théâtre Italien, parodiée de l'intermède Italien intitulé
Bertholde à la cour, trois actes en vers libres, mêlés d'ariettes,
aussi parodiées de celles de cet intermède, & autres représentés
au théâtre de l'Opéra. Le *Caprice amoureux* est de M. Favart
& a été donné pour la première fois le mercredi 12 février
1755. Paris, Delormel & Prault fils.

The same comparison might be made from the score,
but the three-act version is not known to exist in score.
Mr. Wotquenne, under No. 2025 of the Brussels catalogue,
is inclined to suspect that such a score was printed. He
says:

n'ayant pu rencontrer un exemplaire de la partition de la
parodie en *trois* actes, nous ne pouvons affirmer qu'elle ait été
publiée, mais il y a grande apparence que cette question doit

être tranchée affirmativement, car l'éditeur Desœur, de Liège, toujours à l'affût des nouveautés du jour, a fait paraître vers 1755 un recueil des airs détachés de Bertholde à la ville [*sic*] en *trois* actes.

Wotquenne then proceeds to analyze the publication. I fear that the eminent Belgian bibliographer will not succeed in proving the existence of the three-act *score* in this direction, because the Library of Congress acquired from the Weckerlin collection a publication with Parisian imprint so identical in all other respects with Desœur's that his gives the impression of a pirated edition, or, to put it more mildly, of a mere reprint. The three volumes (44, 42, 44 p.) are bound in with a copy of the "L'année musicale," 1755-1756, and the title-page reads:

Ariettes de Ninette à la cour. Parodie de Bertholde, acte premier [—acte 3ème] A Paris, Aux spectacles et aux adresses ordinaires. Gravé par Melle Vendome.

If one compares this publication, or that of Desœur, with the libretto of the two-act version and with the score of the two-act version, one is led to believe that the contraction into two acts did not change the body of the dialogue substantially, but was brought about more or less by a mere rearrangement of the scenes into two instead of three acts and the suppression and also the *addition* of several ariettes. Of this score the Library of Congress possesses two copies, both alike as to contents, but slightly different bibliographically, inasmuch as the second lacks the words "Imprimé par Tournelle" on the title-page and on its verso contains a very much more extensive catalogue of De la Chevardière's publications, thus proving its later date. The title-page of the score reads:

Ninette à la cour. Parodie de Bertholde à la ville, comédie en deux actes, mêlés d'ariettes par Mr Favart. Représenté sur le théâtre de la Comédie italienne (Paris, De la Chevardière [n. d.], 1 p. l., 73, 76 p. fol.)

The title-page describes adequately the *genre* of the score. It is indeed a mere comedy with incidental arias (the embryo of *opéra-comique*) and structurally calls for no further comment than that all the arias begin without recitatives. The orchestration, just like that of Lasalle d'Offemont's parody, is not clearly indicated. Nor was this customary in such skeleton or compressed scores; but from occasional hints, at least flutes, horns and oboes must have been employed in "Ninette à la cour" besides the strings. Still, these hints are not sufficient to throw full light on the question of how the Italian originals fared at the hands of the parodists—an interesting question, but not within the scope of this essay.

At the end of the libretto of the two-act version, 1756, Duchesne printed a *"Table* des ariettes de Ninette à la cour, gravées en quatre [!] parties." Duchesne did not print the music, but refers to the engraved score (De la Chevardière's publication?) by a foot-note:

Les ariettes marquées dans la table par une S, ne se chantent point à la représentation, mais se trouvent gravées dans la musique.

The table is here reprinted, substituting * for the S:

Première partie.

		page
1.	Travaillons de bon courage..............	2
2.	Fillettes, n'allez jamais seulettes...........	3
3.	Que le nom de Ninon......................	4
4.	Oui, je l'aime pour jamais.................	5
5.	Agité par la fierté.......................	8
6.	Un doux penchant.......................	11
7.	Tout va vous rendre aimable..............	13
8.	Tu nous perdras, Colas...................	18
*9.	En tourbillon, un papillon................	23
10.	Ahi, ahi, il m'a fait grand mal............	30
11.	Je renonce au village....................	33
12.	Auroit-on cru cela d'elle.................	39

Seconde partie.

13. Ah! quelle gesne................................. 2
14. Ah! comme me voilà......................... 4
15. Donnez-moi deux cœurs..................... 6
16. Viens, espoir enchanteur.................... 9
17. Dans nos prairies............................ 12
*18. Au sein des allarmes........................ 15
19. Le nocher loin du village................... 20
20. Maudite race 24
*21. Qu'il a de gentillesse........................ 28
22. Une dame vous enflame..................... 33

Troisième partie.

*23. Je veux tirer vengeance..................... 2
*24. Assise sur le bord d'une onde................ 5
*25. Non, non, je n'ai peur....................... 9
26. Où Ninette est-elle?....................... 13
*27. Quatuor 14
28. Je sens, par la morguenne.................. 33
29. La cour n'est qu'un esclavage.............. 38
30. Ariette oubliée du premier acte............. 42
     (He means: "Je vois du plus beau jour," which
     should have been printed as the sixth ariette.)

Quatrième partie.

31. Comme la cloche du village................. 1
32. Contente je chante......................... 8
33. Quelle aisance! 10
34. Ariette de l'écho ["Ce cœur qu'il possède"]... 14
35. Quatuor: Toute mon âme................... 17

How does this table agree with the "Ariettes de Ninette
à la Cour. Parodie de Bertholde. Acte premier
[— 3ème]," as printed at Paris and reprinted by Desœur
of Liège?

Act 1.   page

1. Tra-vaillons, tra-vail-lons de bon cou-ra - ge   2

2. Fil-let - tes fol-let - tes n'al-lés ja-mais seu-let - tes   3

3. Que le nom   de Ni - non   ê - cla - te   4

4. Oui, . . je l'ai - me pour ja - mais   5

5. A - gi-té . . . . par la fier-té   8

6. Un doux   pen - chant m'en - traî - ne   11

7. Tout va vous ren-dre hom-ma - ge   13

8. Tu   nous per-dras, Co - las, ne souf - fle pas   18

*9. En   tour - bil - lon   un   pa - pil-lon   23

10. Ahi!   Ahi!   il m'a fait grand mal   30

11.   Co - las, je   re - non-ce au vil - la - ge   33

12.   Au - roit - on   cru   ce - la   d'el - le   39

Act II.

13.   Ah quel - le   ges - ne   2

14.   Ah com - me   me voi - là   4

15.   Don - nez- moi deux   cœurs   6

16.   Viens, es - poir en - chan - teur   9

17.   Dans nos prai - ri - es tou-jours fleu - ri - es   12

(Not mentioned by Wotquenne as in Desœur, presumably overlooked.)

*18.   Au sein des al - lar - mes   15

19.   Le   no - cher loin du   ri - va - ge   20

20. Mau - di - te ra - ce, lais - sés de grâ - ce   24

*21. Qu'il a de gen - til - les - se   28

22. U - ne da - me vous in - flam-me   33

Act III.

*23. Je veux ti - rer ven - geance   2

(According to Wotquenne this melody is the same as "Quelle est cette tristesse" in Sody's parody of Rinaldo da Capua's "La donna superba," Paris, 1752.)

*24. As - si - se sur les bords d'u-ne on - de pu - re   5

*25. Non, non, je n'ai point peur   9

26. Où Ninette est - el - le? en vain je l'ap-pel-le   13

(Quartet)

27. Suis - je en - core un-e trai-tres - se?   14

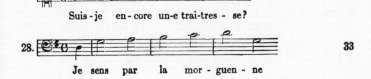

28. Je sens par la mor - guen - ne   33

29.   38

La   cour   n'est qu'un es - cla - va - ge

30.   42

Je   vois du   plus beau jour

(Printed in v. 3, p. 42–44 as omitted by mistake in its proper
place as sixth ariette of the first act.)

To facilitate comparison, asterisks (needless to say, no
such marks appear in the three-act "Ariettes") have been
prefixed in this thematic list to those themes which in the
two-act libretto were designated as suppressed in the performance. This comparison proves that Duchesne's table
and the contents of the three volumes of detached ariettes,
even down to the pagination and the omission of what
should have been the sixth ariette from its proper place,
tally throughout, Duchesne's *quatrième partie* excepted.
This does not appear at all in our (clearly complete and
perfect) copy of the "Ariettes," nor evidently in Desœur's
publication of these ariettes as analyzed by Wotquenne.

The pagination given by Duchesne makes it unmistak-
ably clear that he refers to the Paris edition of the "Ariettes" and not to a published *score,* and thereby a bibliographical fact, perhaps hitherto unnoticed, comes to light,
namely, that a fourth part was issued as a supplement
and this supplement must have been issued *after* the reduction of "Ninette à la cour" by Favart into two acts, because the ariettes of the *quatrième partie* are to be found in
this two-act version only. Nos. 31, 32 there appear as
belonging to act I, sc. 1; No. 33 to act II, 8, No. 34 to act
II, 18, and No. 35 to act II, 19. Just why No. 32 ("Contente je chante") should have been printed as a separate
ariette is puzzling, since it is identical with the second ari-

ette, "Fillettes, n'allez," and indeed the words "Contente je chante" form the second couplet of the so-called No. 32. By referring to the score of the two-act version we are enabled to supply the themes of the other supplementary ariettes:

31. Com'la clo - che du   vil - la - ge

33. Quelle ai - san - ce,   quel - le   grâ - ce

34. Ce cœur qu'il po - sè - de   cè - de,   cè - de,

35. Tou - te   mon   a - me pour toi s'en - fla - me

Further comparison proves that musically the indications in the two-act libretto agree absolutely with the two-act score, even down to the fact that No. 19 of the thematic list of the three-act version "Le nocher loin du rivage" appears, both in the libretto and in the score, *not* in the middle of the second act as in the "Ariettes" but as the *last* ariette in this act. *Consequently, Nos. 20 to 29 helped originally to form the third act.* Furthermore, since Nos. 31 to 35 do not seem to have belonged to the third-act version, but were *added,* and, as, therefore, the reduction to two acts resulted in a net reduction of two ariettes only, the current theory that Favart reduced his parody because it was too long, is weakened considerably. It now appears more likely that the alteration was made simply because Favart believed two acts, arranged as indicated, to be more effective than three.

The impression will have been gained that the libretto and the score coincide. This impression is generally correct, yet differences between the texts are noticeable that deserve to be pointed out to those who might have occasion to study "Ninette à la cour" for one reason or another. Disregarding such slight verbal differences as in act I, 4 (Astolphe), "Je n'ose l'aborder" (libretto) as against "Elle se parle" (score), the omission from the score in the same scene (Astolphe) of "Hélas! quelqu'un qui vous adore," the words of Colas ending the seventh scene of the score "Je suis petrifié" are the opening words of the ninth scene of the libretto, and in the latter the ariette No. 11 forms the eighth scene, whereas in the score it belongs to the seventh, a different numbering of the scenes thereby resulting. In the second act, the dialogue of scene 3 is, towards the end, very much shorter in the score than in the libretto; the fourth scene opens slightly differently, and the ariette No. 16 of the libretto forms scene 6, whereas in the score it forms part of scene 5, with corresponding differences in the continuation of the act. It should also be noticed that the score does not contain the music of the "Divertissement" which in the libretto is announced to follow the final quartet "Toute mon âme"; but to omit such ballet music from the scores was then more or less customary. It contained, as appears from the indications in the libretto, the ariette numbered 29 in the thematic list.

In the Brussels catalogue M. Wotquenne set himself the task of tracing the musical sources of several parodies which resulted from the Guerre des Bouffons. That he was not able completely to excavate their musical foundations is not at all surprising, and it certainly required extraordinary patience and true bibliographical instinct to accomplish what he did. As to "Ninette à la cour" he traced the following:

Act I.

Comme la cloche du village = Quando senti la campagna, from Latilla's "La finta cameriera."

Oui, je l'aime pour jamais = Zerbinetti d' oggidi, from Selletti's "Cinese rimpatriatro," Paris, June 19, 1753.

Je vois du plus beau jour = Amore è fatto come un uccelletto, from Cocchi's "La mascherata."

Un doux penchant m'entraîne = Per pietà, bell'idol mio, from Vinci's "L'Artaserse."

Tout va vous rendre hommage = Io sono una donzella, from Selletti's "Cinese rimpatriato."

Tu nous perdras, Colas = Quando s'incontrano, from Ciampi's "Bertoldo alla corte."

Ahi! ahi! il m'a fait grand mal = Ahi! Ahi! no'l farò più, from Ciampi's "Bertoldo alla corte."

Aurait-on cru cela d'elle = "Maledetti quanto siete," from Ciampi's "Bertoldo alla corte."

Act II.

Ah! quelle gêne! = Mi stà d'incanto, from Selletti's "Cinese rimpatriato."

Viens, espoir enchanteur = Spera forse anch'un dì, from Doletti's "Giocatore," Paris, 1752.

Quelle aisance, quelle grâce! = Con occhiate e con inchini, from Jommelli's "Il Paratajo."

Une dame vous enflamme = Sei compito e sei bellino, from Selletti's "Cinese rimpatriato."

Le nocher loin du rivage = Vò solcando un mar crudele, from Vinci's "L'Artaserse."

Ce cœur qu'il possède, cède = Se giammai de speco l'eco, from Pergolesi's "Maestro di musica."

Toute mon âme = O dell' Egitto, final chorus in Rinaldo da Capua's "La Zingara"; the same as and probably borrowed from "Dea delle selve"; Act I, No. 3, Hasse's "Leucippo."

Since those ariettes which Wotquenne could not trace were also parodied from Italian operas, "Ninette à la cour" presented itself as a neat little anthology from the repertory of the Bouffons, and if there ever was a pasticcio, Favart's "Ninette à la cour" certainly is a shining example of the genre as practised in France. Ciampi, however, did not fare very well in this anthology, and if it should develop that neither the three ariettes traced to "Bertoldo alla corte," *given at Paris as a pasticcio,* nor any of the ariettes not yet traced, were by Ciampi, we should have the curious spectacle that a parodie-pasticcio could sail under a composer's colors without being at all recruited from his opera! Wotquenne does not inform us of his method of tracing the ariettes, and, to be frank, it is a mystery to me how he traced the three ariettes to Ciampi's "Bertoldo alla corte," since the score of this opera does not exist, and since the three ariettes do not appear among the six arias bearing Ciampi's name in Walsh's "Favourite songs in . . . Bertoldo." However, Wotquenne is not in the habit of making claims without substance, and we are therefore justified in accepting his statements. What then is the net result? Five of the arias in Walsh were interpolations for London and, as was shown, did not belong to the original version of Goldoni's "Bertoldo, Bertoldino e Cacasenno." Only the first, the duet "Cara sei tu," can be traced with certainty to the original libretto. In addition, we have the three ariettes "Quando s'incontrano," "Ahi! Ahi! no'l farò più," and "Maledetti quanto siete," parodied according to Wotquenne from Ciampi's opera and therefore, probably, though not necessarily, by Ciampi himself. To these must be added the *ariette sixième* in Lasalle d'Offemont's operatic skit, parodied from "A riveder ritorno" in the original Bertoldo libretto. At best, then, five arias out of the original thirty-three have so far been traced to Ciampi. Surely a very meagre crop for any attempt to reconstruct the score of an opera once so popular as Ciampi's "Bertoldo, Bertoldino e Cacasenno"!

It remains to fix, if possible, the responsibility for the musical arrangement of "Ninette à la cour." Favart possessed a keen ear for music. He is even known to have composed some airs. That he and his equally musical wife supervised the selection of ariettes for "Ninette" and made suggestions, goes without comment, but Favart hardly possessed the necessary technical training to put these selections into orchestral shape, etc., for performance. One naturally turns to Font's book on Favart for explicit information on this point, and finds:

(p. 270.) Le napolitain Duni, l'ami de Pergolèse, retoucha cette partition de Ciampi; il écrivait pendant longtemps des airs à l'italienne pour les paroles françaises des livrets de Favart et d'Anseaume. Par la simplicité, par la naïveté de ses mélodies, il travailla à l'éducation du public. Il habitua les oreilles à goûter et à exiger la sincérité de l'inspiration. Ses airs, si peu français, préparèrent les voies aux partitions si françaises de Grétry.

In the "Chronologie des pièces de Favart" Font adds to this or rather modifies it by saying (p. 346):

Mme. Favart a choisi les airs de l'original, Duni a retouché et arrangé la musique.

Font does not mention his authority for these claims, which are not corroborated by any of the contemporary sources mentioned in these pages! As far as Duni is concerned, it looks to me as if Font in turn merely retouched the current statements of lexicographers. Says, for instance, Fétis in the Biographie universelle under Duni:

Après avoir visité Gênes, il fut chargé [no date given] d'enseigner la musique à la fille de l'infant de Parme. La cour de ce prince étant presque toute française, Duni se hasarda à écrire quelques petits opéras dans cette langue. Son coup d'essai fut la Ninette à la cour de Favart; le succès fut si grand, qu'on lui envoya *la Chercheuse d'esprit* et *le Peintre amoureux de son modèle.* En 1757 il revint à Paris . . .

Of course, Fétis' article on Duni was used, copied and *parodied* by all subsequent lexicographers, and thus we find Duni as *composer* of "Ninette à la cour" in Riemann, Mendel-Reissmann, Towers, Eitner, Grove, Clément et Larousse, etc. Such a claim is absurd on the face of it and should be expurgated from all future reference books.

Font was more careful, and merely insists that Duni *retouched* and *arranged* the score of this parodie-pasticcio, but even this claim calls for close scrutiny.

Unfortunately, Duni's biography is not at all clear, and even Fétis' short article is subject to revision. The point at issue simply depends on the year of Duni's arrival at Parma. Fétis does not mention the date. Mendel-Reissmann give the impossible 1746, and Grove 1755, but no variance of opinion appears on the year 1757 as that of Duni's arrival at Paris, when his "Le Peintre amoureux" was performed, presumably translated from his "Pittore inamorato." If Grove is correct, then Duni's collaboration with Favart is hardly credible, since "Ninette à la cour" was performed as early as February 12, 1755, and Duni is not known to have been in Paris late in 1754. Riemann says that "Ninette à la cour" was performed at Parma *and* Paris in 1755. If this is correct, then the Parma performance of necessity was merely a replica of the one at Paris, and in that case, of course, Duni may have retouched the score *for Parma;* but our last court of appeal is Paolo Emilio Ferrari's "Spettacoli Drammatico-musicali e coreografici in Parma," 1884, and in this voluminous work Duni is first mentioned as in Parma for the winter of 1754–55 with his "Olimpiade" and for 1756–57 with a "La buona figliuola." Of other operas by Duni in 1755 and particularly of "Ninette à la cour" not a word, and moreover the supposedly predominant French taste at Parma about 1755 is a myth, since only two or three French works appear to have been performed then under Du Tillet's management.

The conclusion, it seems to me, is practically safe that Duni had nothing whatsoever to do with Favart's "Ninette à la cour" of 1755, and a collaboration of his with Favart is possible only for the two-act version of the parody, if, as Font claims in one place, the revival took place in 1758, a supposition which is promptly confuted by the solid fact that the two-act version was first performed in 1756.   If therefore Duni drops out, it still remains an open question, who assisted Favart and his wife in keeping Ciampi's name, though only fragments of his opera, before the public.

THE FIRST EDITION OF "HAIL, COLUMBIA!"

(The "Pennsylvania Magazine of History and Biography,"
1916.)

In the April, 1910, number of the "Pennsylvania Magazine of History and Biography," Mr. Charles Henry Hart had an article called "Hail Columbia and its First Publication. A critical inquiry." It was followed in the January, 1912, number by a supplemental note, headed "The First Edition of Hail Columbia."

Mr. Hart's critical inquiry was prompted by the statement in my essay on the history of "Hail Columbia" that "no copy of this original edition of 'Hail Columbia' has come to light," i. e., of the edition advertised in "Porcupine's Gazette," Philadelphia, Friday, April 27, 1798, as to be published on the following Monday, April 30, at B. Carr's Musical Repository, "ornamented with a very elegant Portrait of the President."

John Adams was then President and quite naturally I inferred that Carr was to publish the "New Federal Song," as Joseph Hopkinson's text of "Hail Columbia" adapted to Philip Phile's President's March originally was called, with the portrait of John Adams. Mr. Hart, however, adduced strong evidence that it was Carr who, though without his imprint, published "The Favorite New Federal Song Adapted to the President's March" not with the portrait of John Adams but with an oval, profile to left, bust portrait by an unknown etcher after Joseph Wright, with inscription on ribbon beneath bust, "G. Washington." The portrait is not engraved on the plate, but is a separate print mounted in the blank centre-space of the title and above the curved and engraved quotation of the first line of fourth stanza in Joseph Hopkinson's poem, "Behold the Chief who now Commands." Mr. Hart also drew attention to the fact that the same portrait (of course, without the quotation) had been used in December, 1797, for "The Battle of Trenton, A Sonata," and was used again in 1798 for the song "New Yankee Doodle," both pieces issued with the joint imprint of J. Hewitt, New York, and B. Carr, Philadelphia. Mr. Hart held that the edition of the "New Federal Song" with the Washington portrait and the quotation was the first and earlier than one with engraved American eagle in place of mounted portrait and quotation, which edition Mr. Louis C. Elson, the owner of a supposedly unique copy, in turn had claimed to be the first edition of "Hail Columbia."

To Mr. Hart's findings I wish to add some remarks which occurred to me after the Library of Congress, too, had acquired a copy of the American eagle issue.

Mr. Hart identified the oval portrait used as number 157 in his Catalogue of the Engraved Portraits of Washington. Inasmuch as this number 157 shows "overhead, to left, a female Victory. . . . On extreme left, a whole-length figure of Goddess of Liberty. . . . At base, drum with Eagle . . ." the oval portrait must have been secured by utilizing the whole print number 157 only in part. That this was the procedure appears from the same portrait as mounted on our copy of "New Yankee Doodle": it plainly shows traces of the paraphernalia enumerated above.

Comparison of our American eagle issue with the practically exact-size facsimile of the portrait issue of "The Favorite New Federal Song" in Mr. Hart's article discloses further facts.

1. *The music plates used in both issues are identical* in every respect, inclusive of distance-measurements of the lettering in the title, but exclusive of course of the American eagle. With this exception, the copies of the song

extant represent *impressions from the same plates.*

2. When mounting the oval portrait in the blank space left between the words "New/Song" and "Adapted/President's" and above the words "Behold the Chief," etc., in the title it became necessary to let the portrait protrude as much as one centimeter on the music sheet beyond the impression of the upper margin of the music plate. (This is the simple explanation of a puzzle which will mystify all who fail—as I did for some time—to notice that the impression of the upper plate margin is visible even in Mr. Hart's facsimile. Unless one notices this marginal impression one may easily be led to argue that the distance-measurements in the title in both issues of the song are different, that two different plates were used and that therefore the two issues represent two different editions.)

3. Examination of our copy of the issue of "The Favorite New Federal Song," with the engraved American eagle with clouds broken by sunrays in the background, by Prof. Rich. A. Rice of the Prints Division of the Library of Congress, convinced him that the American eagle, etc., was engraved after the surrounding words had been engraved, principally for the reason that a few of the cloud lines clearly run through the line of flourish of the word "Adapted" in the title. This in itself, of course, does not argue that the American eagle was added to the plate later for a second issue of the song, but it does argue this: if the American eagle had been engraved on the plate at the time the song was first published—thereby establishing the issue with the American eagle as the first and earlier than the one with the Washington portrait—then its later erasure from the plate to make place in a later issue for a substituted mounted portrait of George Washington would have left visible traces even in a facsimile. Since no such traces appear, Prof. Rice agrees with me that the American eagle did not originally form part of the plate, that the space was left vacant, and that the American eagle was added noticeably later, carefully

utilizing the available space for the design, but with the *lapsus stili* noted above.

Against all this might be adduced the fact that Carr advertised the piece in "Porcupine's Gazette" for Friday, April 27, 1798, as "On Monday afternoon will be published," and in "Claypoole's American Daily Advertiser" for Wednesday, May 2, 1798, as "just published" ". . . ornamented with a very elegant portrait of the President." The President was then John Adams. This fact would call for *his* portrait, not that of George Washington. No copy of "The Favorite New Federal Song" with the portrait of John Adams has come to light, whereas Mr. Hart has shown that the song exists with the portrait of George Washington mounted above the engraved words "Behold the chief who now commands." This is a quotation from the fourth and last stanza of Joseph Hopkinson's poem, and the stanza runs:

> Behold the Chief who now commands
> Once more to serve his country stands
>   The rock on which the storm will beat
>   The rock on which the storm will beat
> But arm'd in virtue firm and true
> His hopes are fix'd on Heav'n and you
>   When hope was sinking in dismay
>   And clouds obscur'd Columbia's day
> His steady mind from changes free
> Resolved on Death or Liberty
>   Firm, United, let us be, etc.

Lines second to end would have no meaning unless they refer to George Washington. They would seem to imply that also the first line refers to George Washington. Now, in April and May, 1798, President John Adams was *ex officio* the Commander-in-Chief of the American forces, not George Washington. The latter was not nominated Commander-in-Chief by John Adams until July 2, 1798. (The nomination was confirmed by the Senate on July 3.) Consequently, so the argument would probably continue,

July 2 or 3, 1798, would be the earliest possible date of issue of "The Favorite New Federal Song" with the words "Behold the Chief who now commands" joined to a portrait of George Washington.

And this is about as far as an attempted argument in favor of the priority of the American eagle issue as the first issue of "Hail Columbia" would get in this direction. It is blocked by the fact that Joseph Hopkinson wrote the line "Behold the Chief," etc., in April, 1798, when it could have applied only to John Adams; and by the counter-argument that, for the reasons stated above, the issue without the American eagle is prior to one with the eagle. Therefore, the argument would prove only that the issue with the portrait of George Washington was not published before July 3, 1798, that the issue with the American eagle instead of the portrait was published still later, and that—inasmuch as the song was published by May 2, 1798, with "a very elegant portrait of the President"—*both these issues were preceded by one with the portrait of John Adams,* of which issue no copy has come to light!

Into this curious dilemma those are driven who, like Mr. Hart, interpret the line "Behold the Chief who now commands" as addressed by Joseph Hopkinson to George Washington. By this anachronistic interpretation Mr. Hart and others are ungracious enough to credit Judge Hopkinson with a rather poor knowledge of the Constitutional prerogatives of the Presidents of the United States. However, Mr. Hart is mistaken if he seems to think that the first two lines of the fourth stanza are applicable to George Washington only. His quotation

> Behold the Chief, *who now Commands*
> *Once more to serve his country stands*

without the third ("The rock on which the storm will beat") is faulty and forced; it leaves the third line dropped off in mid-air. Furthermore, we know from contemporary evidence—"Aurora," April 27, 1798—that the Anti-Federalists looked on the song (which Joseph Hopknison had intended as a non-partisan song) as "the vilest adulation to the anglo-monarchical party and the two Presidents," i. e., the only two our country had so far had, George Washington and John Adams. Now Hopkinson's first two stanzas ("Hail Columbia—happy land" and "Immortal patriots, rise once more") are wholly impersonal. The third ("Sound, sound the trump of Fame / Let Washington's great name") deals with the first President. That leaves only the fourth stanza for John Adams, if the impression of vilest adulation of *two* Presidents could be created. It is but necessary to read this extract from an editorial report in "Porcupine's Gazette," April 28, 1798, on the political enthusiasm created by Mr. Fox's singing of "Hail Columbia" on April 27, at the New Theatre as it had been on occasion of the *première* of the song on April 25, and to combine with it the editorial political remarks about the President's recent letter to Congress, to know that indeed at least the first line of the fourth stanza was considered a direct reference to John Adams: "but no sooner were the words

Behold the Chief who now commands

pronounced, than the house shook to its very centre; the song and the whole were drowned in the enthusiastic peals of applause, and were obliged to stop and begin again and again, in order to gain a hearing."

That Joseph Hopkinson referred with that line to the only "Chief" of whom he could possibly say in April, 1798, "who *now* commands," namely John Adams, must be clear from all this internal and external evidence. But Gilbert Fox, to whose lot it fell to "create" (as the French would say) "Hail Columbia" on April 25, 1798, must also have been the first interpreter to query the *address* of all the other lines in the last stanza. Did they, too, refer to John Adams, or do they, with the second line,

"Once more to serve his Country stands," suddenly turn back to George Washington, just as if the author in his flights of fancy had tried in vain to emerge for more than a few seconds from under the shadow of the first President?

Hopkinson's commas in his autograph text at the Pennsylvania Historical Society afford us little help:

> *Behold the Chief,* who now commands,
> Once more to serve his coùntry stands,
> The rock on which the Storm will beat.

"Porcupine's Gazette," the first newspaper to print the poem (in the issue for April 28, 1798) improved on this feeble interpunctuation, though not settling the case of Adams *versus* Washington:

> Behold the Chief who now commands,
> Once more to serve his country, stands
> The Rock on which the Storm will beat.

I realize that the normal interpretation of lines second and third, especially with Porcupine's interpunctuation, would be "George Washington, who stands ready once more to serve his country as the rock," etc. Yet I believe that it is not the interpretation desired by Joseph Hopkinson. I suspect that it is merely the case of a very minor poet endeavoring to cram too much historical and patriotic symbolism into a few lines without the power of unequivocal, contrasting statement.

It is inconceivable that a man like Joseph Hopkinson can have referred to any but the actual President as "the Chief who now commands." It is equally inconceivable that, after having devoted one whole stanza, the third, to George Washington, he should have turned by way of poetic contrast to John Adams only to the extent of one line and have succumbed to "Washington's great name" again for the rest of the poem. Hence, we may feel morally certain that the *plan* of his *whole* last stanza was

a reference to President John Adams.   This conclusion
in nowise interferes with the fact that the plan miscarried
by way of misleading phraseology, mixed metaphors, etc.,
with the result that without further analysis and without remembering the constitutional prerogatives of a
President, in matters military, almost any reader would
see in the fourth stanza a direct reference to George Washington.   Perhaps Hopkinson's idea was (with a modicum of that poetic license which disregards chronology)
to symbolize in the abstract and impersonally the President of the United States as ready to serve his country
again as the rock, etc.   Perhaps unconsciously he voiced
an anticipation that John Adams would step aside in
favor of George Washington as the Commander-in-Chief
of our military forces.   Perhaps the association of "The
President's March" with its memories of George Washington exercised too much pressure on his mind.   Whatever the cause, the threads of our poet's imagination became twisted, and by using the words *once more* to serve
his country" he inevitably switched the attention of the
reader from the *de facto* "Chief" John Adams to George
Washington.

And Benjamin Carr, the first publisher of "The Favorite New Federal Song" that within a few days became
known as "Hail Columbia"?   Who can tell why a music
publisher (of the eighteenth century, of course) did this
or that?   When he advertised the song with a portrait
of the President, he knew full well that John Adams was
the President and not George Washington.   But perhaps
no suitable engraved portrait of John Adams was available for his purposes; perhaps he really held the erroneous
belief (pardonable enough in a music publisher comparatively "lately from London") that George Washington
was still the Commander-in-Chief of the American forces
and ready to serve his country against France as he had
against England; perhaps it was a better business propo-
sition after all to twist the facts a little and to sell the

song with a picture of George Washington rather than that
of John Adams; perhaps—but enough of conjectures.
The unalterable fact is, whatever its explanation, that B.
Carr published "The Favorite New Federal Song" with
a portrait of George Washington and the quotation, "Behold the Chief who now commands."

To sum up, the history of the first edition of "Hail
Columbia" would appear to be this: Joseph Hopkinson
wrote it in April, 1798, as a non-partisan song for the
benefit of Gilbert Fox, who sang it at the New Theatre,
Philadelphia, for the first time on April 25, 1798.   It
was advertised as to be published on April 30, 1798,
and on May 2, 1798, was advertised as published in Philadelphia, at the Musical Repository of B. Carr.   It was
published, though without Carr's imprint, as "The favorite
new Federal Song Adapted to the President's March,"
composed by Philip Phile.   The engraver of the music
plates so spaced the title as to leave space in the centre
for the insertion of "a very elegant portrait of the President" as advertised by Carr.   Instead of John Adams'
portrait, however, a profile to left, bust portrait of George
Washington engraved after Joseph Wright appears to
have been used.   It was mounted above the engraved
quotation from Hopkinson's text, "Behold the Chief who
now commands."   Either because his supply of prints was
not equal to the demand for the "favorite" song or because
he wished to rectify his mistake in calling Washington
the "Chief" or because of some other reason B. Carr appears to have substituted some time later (probably in
1798) on the same plate, for the mounted portrait of
George Washington and the quotation from Hopkinson's
text, the design of an American eagle with American
shield in beak and clouds in the background broken by
sunrays neatly engraved in the available space in the centre of the title.   This, then, would be the second issue
of the first edition; whereas the issue with the Washington portrait would be the first issue of the first edition,

unless, after all, a genuine copy of "The favorite new Federal Song" should be discovered not with George Washington's portrait but with that of John Adams, as Carr's advertisements would imply. In that case the issue with Adams' portrait would be the first and its date would be April 30 or May 1, 1798. The issue with George Washington's portrait would then be the second and the line "Behold the Chief who now commands" would point to July 3, 1798, the date of Washington's appointment as Commander-in-Chief in the threatened war with France, as the earliest date of publication and the issue with the substituted American eagle would be the third, though probably still of the year 1798.

GUILLAUME LEKEU
(1870–1894)

(Written 1916; published in the "Musical Quarterly," 1919)

Enfin, ce pauvre Guillaume Lekeu, tempérament quasi génial, mais mort à vingt-quatre ans avant d'avoir pu se manifester d'une manière complète. (Vincent d'Indy in his chapter on the "artistic family" of *"père* Franck.")

To die at the age of twenty-four and to leave a permanent mark in the Book of Art, of itself bespeaks genius. That is precisely the sad but proud record of Guillaume Lekeu. His case is more tragic than that of Schubert or Pergolesi. They, too, died young, but not before Nature permitted them to shower on us the fruit of ripened genius. Fate treated Lekeu more cruelly: his life-thread was cut before he could possibly refine all the crudities of youth in the crucible of a mature mind. It would be futile to deny this, and no friend of Lekeu's art has yet failed to acknowledge that occasional "écriture inégale" in his music on which Henri Maubel in his "Préfaces pour des musiciens" dwells feelingly and understandingly. Yet no friend of Lekeu's art—and my own efforts in his behalf first took concrete form about as long ago as 1905— need apologize for his public espousal of an artist admittedly immature, for Lekeu's immaturity is more acceptable by far than the maturity of those unfortunate artists who long outlive their over-ripe productions. If Guillaume Lekeu did not live long enough to earn the full title of genius and master, his are at least the credentials of one almost a genius and almost a master. They have

been honored as such by more critics than any other artist
of so premature a death, I believe, has ever inspired to
encomia, not to mention exponents of his art among conductors and performers. If men like d'Indy, Closson,
Maubel, Pujo, Séré, de Stoecklin, Destranges, Tissier,
Gauthier-Villars, Dukas, Vallas, Lyr, Debussy, Hale did
not disdain to lay wreaths of laurel on the tomb of Guillaume Lekeu, the humble music-lover, if thrilled by Lekeu's
music as those men were, need not take seriously professional myopes whom Lekeu's youth misleads into dis-
respectful remarks about his music.

*   *
*

Claude Debussy, who had introduced Lekeu's "Unfinished Quartet for piano and strings" to a Parisian public
on February 1, 1896, under the auspices of the *Société
nationale* (since 1871 so valiant a herald of new talent),
in his contribution to Landormy's enquête on the present
state of music in France ("Revue bleue," 1904) wrote:

"César Franck is not French, he is a Belgian. Yes, there is
a Belgian school. Next to Franck, Lekeu is one of its most
remarkable representatives, this Lekeu, the only musician to my
knowledge whom Beethoven really inspired."

The same year that Debussy made this startling statement—to be more specific, on Nov. 16, 1904—the Hoffmann Quartet with Miss Alice Cummings introduced the
"Unfinished Quartet" to Boston. It elicited from the
critic of the "Boston Journal" the terse comment:

Everywhere it breathes genius and causes regret for the un-
timely death of its creator at 24.

This was as close a replica of the usual French comment on Lekeu's art as one could desire. Philip Hale, so
brilliant and able a champion of modern French music
in those and earlier years and ever since, shared, of course,

his colleague's opinion. He remarked in the "Boston Herald":

Lekeu's voice was his own. His music is not like that of other men; he thought in his own way and his emotional eloquence in this quartet is genuine and convincing. . . . Such music does not suffer when played after a noble work by Beethoven, but it makes a work like that of Dvorák's which followed unendurable.

In fact, if I am not very much mistaken, it was Philip Hale whose voice was first raised in America in behalf of Lekeu with that authority and power which compels lazy ears to listen attentively. At any rate, as early as the year 1900, when Lekeu was still practically unknown in America, Philip Hale in his and L. C. Elson's remarkably up-to-date new series of "Famous Composers and Their Works," included this striking critical estimate of Lekeu based on Ernest Closson's biographical sketch in "Le Guide Musical," 1895:

Lekeu was distinctively of the young French school, and his music shows all the good qualities and all the faults of that school: independence of form, predominance of the idea, a gift of perhaps too refined tone color, fastidiousness in style, excessive boldness in harmony. But it should not be forgotten that the young composer was intoxicated with his freedom from pedagogism and fixed and fired with a ferocious hate of all applauded commonplaces and vulgarity. Chiefly remarkable in his writing are inexhaustible richness of invention, the very melodic character of his inspiration, and the fiery spontaneity and the peculiar intensity of individual feeling. His musical sentiment is characterized by tenderness, compassion and a premonition of death.

Still more critically concentrated, I think, is the opinion of Marcel Orban, who edited a few of Lekeu's letters for the "Courrier Musical" in 1910:

If sometimes the tumultuous current of his ideas interferes with the neatness of the total ensemble, an extremely rare, a unique quality—the power to move—makes us forget imperfections which result from a magnificent superabundance of ideas, and silences criticism.

Curiously enough, while Mr. Hale in 1904 so emphatically favored Lekeu's unfinished Quartet, the Boston correspondent of the German musical magazine "Die Musik," himself a German, was utterly nonplussed. So were most of the German critics when Stavenhagen and Berber played Lekeu's Violin Sonata about that time at Munich, Berlin, Leipzig. "Unclear," "vague," "amateurish," "sterile," these were some of the unfriendly epithets hurled at the sonata in addition to "immature." In good faith, of course, and without any *intentional* chauvinism. However, it would lead entirely too far, though it would be easy, to account for this strange exhibition of a misapplied nationalism which appraises the intrinsic value of a foreign work of art according to the presence or absence of the influence of one's own national art thereon and is responsible for the frequent undervaluation of César Franck in Germany just as much as for that of Johannes Brahms in France.

Other quotations might have been adduced as testimonials to Lekeu's talent or genius, whatever term one prefers; the above owe their selection in part to special reasons. They embody both a misconception and a contradiction which, unchallenged, might confuse the student of Lekeu and obscure the appreciation of his racial individuality. The contradiction lies in this—that Philip Hale (and others) unreservedly group him with "the young French school," whereas Debussy (seconded by Jean Huré and other French nationalists) emphatically considers him a Belgian, not a Frenchman, and sees in him one of the most remarkable representatives of the Belgian school, next to César Franck. Debussy's sharp distinction will startle those whom wisdom or convenience has led to affix the same national label to Franck, Lekeu, d'Indy, Chausson, Debussy, Ravel, *e tutti quanti*. It will not startle those whose ears never quite could accept the doctrine that Franck's music sounds wholly Latin, much less wholly French. Now Debussy, whom no one will accuse of underestimating Franck's greatness as composer as he did that of Wagner, though he really owes very much more to Wagner than to Franck, cannot very well be accused of establishing a difference between tweedledum and tweedledee, inasmuch as the Belgians themselves will have none of the customary critical melting-pot and take a similar separatist view. The very fact that Lekeu, after the disappointing study of certain cantatas by Paul Gilson and Edgar Tinel, could exclaim in one of his letters: "Is a Belgian school of composers merely an illusion and a snare?" proves that the Belgians take the existence of a distinctively Belgian school for granted. Now Lekeu confesses his inability quite to follow Tinel because the text of his cantata is in Flemish, of which language he understands not a word! Wherewith the genealogists of music face the discomforting fact that the Belgian nation is a combination but not an amalgamation of two racial groups, different in language, temperament and consequently in art. Paradoxical as it may appear, if there is *one* Belgian school of music, there must of racial necessity be *two*. The whole matter has been summed up very neatly for those who are at all capable of reforming their opinions, by Mr. René Lyr in his chapter on Belgian music in Lavignac's remarkable "Encyclopédie de la musique du Conservatoire" (1914). *Without the contributions of our musicians, surely French music would not be what it is,* he avers (quite correctly) and on this claim in behalf of Belgian music in general he superimposes the clear-cut distinction between a Flemish-Belgian school (Germanic) and a Walloon-Belgian school (Gallic-Latin), the one differing essentially from the modern French, the other from the modern German. Thus he presents Blockx and Benoit as Belgian composers of Flemish characteristics, César Franck and Lekeu as Belgian composers of Walloon characteristics. (In Franck's case, moreover, he records a German substratum, by reason of descent. Hence, a recent American program annotator was wiser than his smiling readers suspected when he compounded César Franck into "a French composer, Belgian by birth, but of German stock"). Only if one takes into due account this belief and pride of Belgians in a dual Belgian school, can one fully comprehend the significance of the comment of Lekeu's biographer Tissier on the impression created by his premature death: "The blow was crushingly cruel to all, for in Lekeu the qualities of heart and character reached up to his genius as an artist." The personality of their young friend endeared him to men like Ysaye, Crickboom, Voncken, Kéfer, but their jubilation over every new sign of progress in his art, their love and admiration for him and their public espousal of his works, struck a deeper source than his sympathetic qualities of heart and character; they had seen in Guillaume Lekeu a young compatriot so richly endowed with promise that their fervent hope for an eventual successor to César Franck had come to be centered in him.

*   *

*

Premonition of death was at one time supposed to have inspired Brahms' "Vier ernste Gesänge" as well as Tschaikowsky's "Symphonie pathétique." It did in neither case, and it did not in the case of Lekeu's "Unfinished Quartet for piano and strings." Mr. Hale simply voices a current tradition which Alexandre Tissier in his authoritative pamphlet on Guillaume Lekeu (Verviers, 1906) took pains to shatter by declaring that "contrary to what often has been said, Lekeu never ceased to be of a gay, jolly, exuberant, enthusiastic disposition and never at any time had a premonition of his premature death." Indeed, such a premonition of death would have been a rather protracted affair, of several years' standing, since the same element of sombreness, if not of piercing lament, pervades all of

Lekeu's works and not only his "Unfinished Quartet." [1]
Apparently Lekeu's frequent and characteristic "wail"
was a matter of temperament with him. For that reason
he might have developed into a kind of Leopardi of musical
art without in the slightest letting this very same "wail"
disturb or perturb his daily life as a mere human being.
And if Tissier's statement is not accepted as binding,
then we possess in its support a long series of letters
written by Lekeu to his parents and Louis Kéfer during
the years 1889–1893 and published with a prefatory note
by Paul de Stoecklin in the "Courrier Musical" of 1906.

There is in these letters not the slightest trace of an
abnormally gloomy disposition or view of life, much less
of a premonition of death. They are the letters of a
"serious young gentleman" of extraordinary mental equipment, who enjoyed life, held his chosen art sacred and
sought to live up to his motto, "Everybody works, and that
is decidedly the only way to arrive at happiness."   I
quite agree with Marcel Orban, who ridicules the *presenti-
ment of death* idea which people love to ascribe to great
men, and says that Lekeu was thinking of life only, with
the gayety and exuberance of his age, with enthusiasm,
with an ardent desire for instruction and the creation of
beautiful things. His mental evolution was simply more
rapid than in ordinary mortals, and that accounts for a
seriousness of mind not often met with in artists so young.
It accounts also, I think, for that remarkable self-critical
attitude assumed by Lekeu toward his works as soon as the
first flush of satisfaction with a piece of work well done
had passed. Pride in his own accomplishment is noticeable, of course, but it seldom partook of that youthful
naïve, overweening self-esteem on which most of us have
reason to look back with amusement and which most of us
coupled with (in retrospect) amusing annihilation of
composers against whom we conceived for this or that

[1] Lekeu's art reminds me of Dante's lines in the "Purgatory": A place
there is below not sad with torments, But darkness only, where the lamen-
tations Have not the sound of wailing, but of sighs.

reason an esthetic grudge. Lekeu had his antipathies, too—for example, he took an impulsive dislike to Magnard, sneered at the "nullities" of Ambroise Thomas, expressed disgust with Bruneau after he had succumbed to the pernicious influence of Zola, waxed sarcastic over the preferment of Massenet and his "Esclarmonde" to César Franck, felt his heart "frozen and bleeding" over a situation such as retarded the publication of Franck's scores, and elicited from the great master at sixty this pathetic excuse for his publishers: "If I perchance should become celebrated";—but his remarks on younger contemporary composers reveal a decided aptitude for benevolent critical neutrality and a judgment as well-balanced and clairvoyant as if it had been written to-day, not more than twenty years ago.   But more important for the present purpose than Lekeu's characterization of certain works by d'Indy, Fauré, Charpentier, Chausson, Bordes and others is his artistic *credo* on the one hand and his conception of the essence of music on the other, since they open for us the road to a readier appreciation and easier grasp of Lekeu's art and aims.   The pertinent observations to be culled from his letters to Louis Kéfer will speak for themselves, I think, without further comment on my part:

To Louis Kéfer, December 16, 1889.
[César Franck's Rédemption.]   This is absolutely a colossal masterwork. . . . It is for me (Wagner's works always aside, it goes without saying) the work of purest genius in sacred music since the D minor mass of the *God* Beethoven. . . .
[When reading a trio by Kéfer] I have observed there again a psychological phenomenon which I often felt: revery proceeding from mild and serene joy leads to melancholy and thence irresistibly to the idea of God.

To Louis Kéfer, January 18, 1890.
. . . Later I may be able to answer your recent question: *What does Franck think of program music?*   I have not yet discussed this matter with him; yet, on the basis of his habitual attitude, I consider myself safe in telling you that his opinion

of this problem (at bottom easier than it looks) coincides with
that of Beethoven. . . . *Mehr Ausdruck der Empfindung als
Tonmalerei.*

To Louis Kéfer, February 1, 1890.

I have asked Franck at last for his opinion on program music
and here is his answer:

Whether music be descriptive, that is, busies itself with
awakening the idea of something material, or whether music
confines itself simply to a translation of a purely internal and
exclusively psychological state of mind, matters not! It is
merely necessary that a work be *musical* and above everything
else *emotional.*

I do not know what you think of this opinion, which I consider reasonable enough; but to be perfectly candid, I do not
believe that master Franck has weighed this problem often or
carefully, a problem which to my way of thinking led Berlioz
astray, though its solution presents no forbidding difficulties.

However, I should always prefer the last page of the *Quintet,*
the first *Trio,* the *Symphony,* the *Quatuor* of Franck to his
Djinns, notwithstanding the fact that the expressiveness of that
piece, within its limits, is wonderfully musical.

To his mother, March 1, 1890.

[On hearing "le 15ᵉ quatuor du Dieu" Beethoven (Op. 132)
on which he subsequently wrote a brief expository essay, reprinted in the "Courrier Musical," 1906.] I am still trembling
with the fever produced in me by that work; my impression
certainly was the same as that of a blind man cured of cataract
by a skillful operation.

To his musical deities Beethoven, Wagner, Franck, here
revealed, we must not fail to add Bach, an hour with
whose "Well-tempered Clavichord," for instance, he did
not hesitate at Bayreuth to prefer to a reception at "Wahn-
fried"!

*   *
*

Guillaume Lekeu was born at Heusy near Verviers on
January 20, 1870. His parents moved to Poitiers (France)
in 1879. There he entered the Lycée. Always one of
the first in his class, he developed an aptitude for scientific

knowledge so pronounced and an interest in literature ancient and modern and the plastic arts so keen that he could not fail to impress his friends with his remarkable intellectual endowment. He graduated in 1888, entered the university at Paris and in due course took his bachelor's degree in philosophy before switching entirely to music as a profession.

We have Tissier's testimony that Lekeu's musical talent hardly revealed itself before his fourteenth year. He played violin a little and amused himself with the banalities of the day—when some pieces of Beethoven accompanied by a friend gave the first real impetus to his musical evolution. This was in 1885. On the strength of a few pianoforte and solfeggio lessons he then spent four years in assiduous study of Beethoven, Bach, Wagner, particularly of Beethoven, whose quartets he is said to have carried with him constantly. At Paris he had the good fortune to be thrown together with the many intellectual notables who gathered at Stephane Mallarmé's receptions. Equally stimulating was his friendship with Gabriel Séailles and Théodore de Wyzewa. It was the latter who dissuaded Lekeu from entering the Paris Conservatoire and induced him to begin his professional musical studies under Gaston Vallin, a former *prix de Rome*.

When Lekeu finished his harmony course under Vallin in less than three months, his friends bethought themselves of César Franck as the only master capable of controlling effectively Lekeu's incredibly rapid development. They effected an introduction through the good offices of M. Read, a mutual friend. At first Franck is said to have demurred, but from the moment that he accepted Lekeu as pupil he appears to have taken a fatherly interest in his musical welfare. Tissier and with him de Stoecklin claim that Lekeu had only about twenty lessons from Franck at the rate of two lessons a week. I doubt that even a César Franck could have imparted to so talented a pupil the mysteries of the most complicated types of

counterpoint in twenty lessons.   Lekeu's letters prove that
to be a legend, for he began his studies under Franck
some time in 1889 (probably in early fall) and continued
them until a very few days before Franck's death on
Nov. 8, 1890.   His progress, as under Vallin, was exceedingly rapid, and Franck apparently did not believe
in applying the professional speed-limit.   Lekeu, in his
letters to Louis Kéfer, the director of the conservatory at
Verviers, has given us a vivid description of Franck's
method.   He taught him counterpoint orally, without the
aid of a text-book, for the simple reason that he considered all text-books deplorable.   Basing the counterpoint
studies principally on themes of sacred music such as the
Stabat Mater, or the *Dies irae,* he demanded that the
contrapuntal embroidery

1.   sound well (*i.e.,* be musical),
2.   above all else be expressive.

He believed that only in this way could the studies be in-
fused with *life,* and that otherwise they would be mere
documents of extreme dryness.   His principal aim (as
throughout his career as teacher) was to stimulate the
productive imagination of the pupil, first by guiding him
into every nook of the workshop of a Bach or Beethoven
and secondly by urging him on to unconventional musical
utterance of his own.   "That marches as on wheels,"
he would exclaim, and would encourage Lekeu to write
from lesson to lesson as much as he possibly could, with
the result that three or four days later the fascinated
pupil would submit ten or twelve pages of music for examination by a master than whom there was no greater
teacher in all Europe!   Franck wished to reach the study
of fugue as rapidly as possible, so that it might run parallel
to a study of counterpoint in its more complicated aspects.
And Lekeu perceived the *rationale* of his procedure as
early as Nov. 19, 1889, when he wrote to Kéfer:

I have finished my studies in three-part counterpoint . . .
This kind of thing is not exactly amusing, but I feel that it
gives to my musical pen an incredible fluency, and I attend to
it seriously.

And as Lekeu descended deeper and deeper into the in-
tricacies of counterpoint the more affectionate the rela-
tions between the two grew, the master spending with open
hand in valuable advice from the treasure-house of his
experience as a composer, the pupil seeking it with open
heart and reverential respect for his teacher's genius.
Then César Franck died in November, 1890. We know
from Lekeu's letter to Kéfer on April 15, 1891, how completely Franck's death stunned him:

In December [*sic!*] the death of my "cher Maître." When,
at the beginning of the new year, I saw myself freed from my
extravagant occupation [he had substituted in the fall of 1890
as a teacher of Greek], when I could set myself to work again,
I succeeded only in writing horrors without name, which I have
grouped under the title of a *Trio* for piano, violin and violoncello.

I was completely bewildered; I passed four or five days a
week smoking and watching the implacable rain pour down
and telling myself how wise it would be to jump out of the
window. But, since verily there are other things to do than
to watch the downpour, I forced myself, as best I could, to do
regular work. I plunged back into counterpoint, double chorus
and fugue, and that sort of thing now marches *cahincaha*. . . .

Also, Vincent d'Indy, whose acquaintance I was fortunate
enough to make, urges me in the friendliest spirit to work a
lot. At every meeting he asks me if I have something new to
show him. Thus I do not despair of being seized again by that
fever for work which held me captive all last year.

It was indeed fortunate for Lekeu (and for us) that
Vincent d'Indy, artistically *père* Franck's greatest son,
stepped into the breach to act, as it were, as step-father to
the orphan and as the pilot without whom, perhaps, after
all, Lekeu would have drifted on the rocks. Needless to
say, Lekeu fully appreciated at their true value the emi-

nent qualities of Vincent d'Indy as a teacher of composition.   And when the time had come to put his talents and
his technique to an actual concrete test, he followed Vincent
d'Indy's advice to compete, nothwithstanding his extreme
youth, for the Belgian Rome prize in 1891, though it prevented him, very much to his regret, from journeying
to Bayreuth.   Victor in the preliminary test for admission
(counterpoint and fugue) his cantata received but the
second-second prize.   Utterly disgusted with the verdict
of the jury, Lekeu forthwith renounced all ambition for
further trial of strength in similar competitions, without,
however, decrying the benefit of self-assurance to be derived from such contests.   The next two years and a half
were devoted to work incessant and fruitful, with no biographical incidents worth recording here, except perhaps
his trip to Aix-la-Chapelle in October, 1892, to hear Schumann's *Paradies und Peri*.   "A sublime work of incomparable poetry" as he calls it in a letter of October 28,
1892, from Heusy to his mother, which contains this observation:

But what an astonishing thing the German public is!
While fully appreciating and loving this or that interpreter, it
does not tender them a personal ovation; all applause is delayed
until after the last note of the work and then is intended for
everybody, for choristers, orchestra, conductor, soloists, but above
all for the memory of Robert Schumann. From the start it is
not a question of the singer, but of the work and its beauty.
Just the reverse of the French and Belgian practice. It explains
in good measure the depth of thought in German musical works;
the composer knows that he will always have a "listening"
audience. What perpetual encouragement! To know that one
will be judged on the merit of one's case!

In the fall of 1893, just when he began to enjoy full
control of his powers and shortly after the first performance
of his *Fantaisie symphonique* on two folk-songs of Anjou
at Verviers under his own direction, he showed the initial
signs of his lingering illness, contracted, it was diagnosed,
from contaminated sherbet.   Surrounded by his family

Guillaume Lekeu died of typhoid fever on January 21,
1894, at Angers. On April 29 his friends organized a
concert in honor of his memory so that the public might
share their conviction of the great loss sustained by the
world of music. The concert took place at Paris, at
the Salle d'Harcourt, under the direction of Vincent
d'Indy and with the coöperation of Mme. Deschamps-
Jehin, Eugène Ysaye and A. Pierret. The program consisted of Lekeu's song "Sur une tombe," a scene from his
ill-starred cantata "Andromède," his Violin sonata and
his *Fantaisie symphonique* just mentioned.

*   *

*

Lekeu's best-known works found their way into the
concert-hall rapidly, but only gradually to the printing-
press after Vincent d'Indy had sifted the manuscripts
and prepared them for publication. Presumably that explains the surprise expressed by some critics at the light
bagage left by the young composer. This impression was
faulty. A glance over the list of his works printed by his
principal publisher, E. Baudoux & Cie (now Rouart,
Lerolle & Cie) of Paris on the cover of Lekeu's Violin
Sonata, or into the bibliography appended by Octave Séré
to his chapter on Lekeu in his valuable book on "Musiciens
français d'aujourd'hui" (1911), leads to a totally different
conclusion. Here it is, with a few added or corrected
dates:

Pianoforte: Tempo di Mazurka (comp. about 1887, Poitiers,
Alb. Alliaume).
    Trois pièces: 1. Chansonnette sans paroles. 2. Valse oublie.
3. Danse joyeuse (comp. 1891; Liége, Veuve L. Muraille, 189–).
    Sonata (comp. April, 1891; Baudoux, 1900).

Songs: La fenêtre de la maison paternelle (A. de Lamartine;
comp. 1887. Unpublished).
    Chanson de Mai (comp. 1891; Jean Lekeu; Baudoux, 1900).
    Trois poèmes (Guillaume Lekeu): 1. Sur une tombe. 2.

Rondo. 3. Nocturne (comp. 1892; Baudoux, 1894. The "Nocturne" exists also with string orchestra accompaniment by Lekeu himself).

Mélodie—L'ombre plus dense (G. Lekeu; comp. 1893. Liége, Veuve L. Muraille).

Les Pavots (A. de Lamartine; Rouart-Lerolle, 1909).

Chamber music: Adagio pour deux violons et piano (1888; unpublished).

Sonate pour piano et violon (comp. 1892; Baudoux, 1894 or 1895; [1] a transcription for piano and violoncello by Ronchini published by Rouart, Lerolle et Cie, 1912).

Trio pour piano, violon et violoncelle (1891; Rouart-Lerolle, 1908).

Sonate pour piano et violoncelle (unfinished; prepared by V. d'Indy for publication by Rouart-Lerolle, 1910, but apparently not yet published).

Quatuor pour piano, violon, alto et violoncelle (comp. 1893, unfinished; prepared by V. d'Indy for publication by Baudoux, 1896).

Orchestra: Première étude symphonique: *Chant de triomphale délivrance (1889)*, Rouart-Lerolle, 190–; score *en location.*

Deuxième étude symphonique: 1. *Sur Hamlet* (unpublished). 2. *Sur le second Faust* (Goethe; comp. 1890; Rouart-Lerolle, 190–; score *en location*).

Adagio pour quatuor d'orchestre, Op. 3 (comp. 1891?; Rouart-Lerolle, 1908).

Poème pour violon et orchestre (unfinished and unpublished).

Épithalame pour quintette à cordes, trois trombones et orgue (about 1891; unpublished).

Introduction et Adagio pour orchestre d'harmonie avec tuba solo obligé (1891; unpublished). Probably identical with:

Concerto for tuba and orchestra. Manuscript said to be lost; unpublished.

Fantaisie symphonique sur deux airs populaires anjevins (comp. 1891–1892, Rouart-Lerolle, 1909; also 4 hd. arr. publ.).

Operas and choral works: Barberine (A. de Musset; 1889; sketches; unpublished).

Les Burgraves (V. Hugo; fragments; unpublished).

Chant lyrique pour chœur et orchestre (1891; unpublished).

[1] Séré gives 1899, but that is impossible, since E. Closson in the Guide Musical, April 12, 1895, mentions among the works so far published by Baudoux Lekeu's Violin Sonata, with allegorical title-page figure by Carlos Schwabe, "à la mémoire de notre Guillaume."

Andromède, poème lyrique et symphonique pour soli, chœurs et orchestre (Jules Sauvenière; comp. 1891; vocal score, Liége, Veuve L. Muraille).

Baudoux's list is even more extensive than this as regards unpublished songs, pianoforte and chamber-music; it reaches the formidable total of about sixty compositions finished or unfinished or existing merely in the form of sketches. And all this in less than seven years; and his weighty works in barely four and a half! What renders this record of industry still more amazing is the fact that sickness and other circumstances would force upon Lekeu a cessation or retardation of work for weeks and even months at a time, or when, during the last three months of 1890, he substituted for a friend as teacher of Greek, Latin, etc. Furthermore, it appears from his letters that he was not or at least did not consider himself a rapid worker. An amusing illustration of this fact he has recorded for us in a letter to Kéfer, June 15, 1891. Commenting on his diffidence to enter the *prix de Rome* contest because of the short time (three days) allotted to the candidates for the fugue in four parts and chorus with orchestra in the preliminary test, he writes:

I have never been able to write a fugue in less than six days. As for the chorus with orchestra, I have tried to compose one in as short a time as possible, with the result that it took me eight days.

*   *

*

Brief as was Guillaume Lekeu's career and restricted the number of his works available for performance, his position in the history of modern music—music of *yesterday* if confronted with Schönberg or Scriabin, but modern nevertheless—is prominent enough to warrant as comprehensive a presentation of biographical data as is possible or as space will permit. For that purpose Lekeu's letters published by Mr. de Stoecklin in the "Courrier Musical" (1906) and repeatedly quoted in the preceding pages, are biographical documents of prime importance. So far as I know, these letters have not been accessible heretofore in English, and to students and admirers of Lekeu the translated extracts forming the major part of this essay will therefore, I hope, be welcome, grouped somewhat differently from the original publication in order to accord with chronology as nearly as possible. They not only afford a clear view of Lekeu's character and of biographical episodes, but they disclose the genesis of some of his best and most ambitious works, whether actually completed or not. Mr. de Stoecklin published the letters with numerous elisions. This perhaps accounts for the absence of reference or for the meagreness of reference to certain works, as for instance the Violoncello sonata, the Pianoforte sonata, the *Fantaisie symphonique* on two folk-songs of Anjou. It is more than probable that these gaps would be filled by a publication of Lekeu's other correspondence not yet accessible in print. One would wish to know more about the genesis of these works, as also of the *Chant lyrique for chorus and orchestra* (the score has been permitted to rest unpublished in the archives of the Société royale d'Émulation of Verviers after the first— and last—performance of the work at a concert of this society on December 3, 1891, had met with an "enormous success" according to Marcel Orban) or of the *Concerto for tuba and orchestra*. This odd concerto, according to the same authority, has remained absolutely unknown to the public, though it contains "wonderful things." To make matters worse, a certain Mr. Faniel, for whom it was composed, claims to have lost the precious manuscript.

That the letters do not mention Lekeu's pianoforte pieces need not be regretted: few critics would hesitate to throw them out of court. Division of opinion about Lekeu's songs is more probable, yet again few critics would care to go as far as Destranges and Closson in their praise. My own estimate is this: Lekeu, like Beethoven, does not appear always to have been quite at ease when writing for the voice. I doubt that he would have become a great master of the *Lied*. For instance, his "Chanson de Mai" (June 23, 1891) to words by his brother Jean is not very valuable; a certain youthful swing and tenderness cannot be denied to this spring-song, but it is not original and its profile is marred by the excessive employment of pot-boiler chords of the ninth. The simple, notturnesque "Mélodie" to Lekeu's own words stands higher. If the poet perhaps was inspired in his apostrophe to "this night of December" by memories of Poe's "Ulalume," the musician vividly, at least in the middle section, recalls Beethoven. On the title-page this song is called "Œuvre posthume, 1893," whereas Lekeu's most important songs, the cycle of his own "Poèmes: Sur une tombe—Rondo— Nocturne," are dated 1892. (They were actually finished in December of that year. Without these dates every one would claim for these songs a wide step forward!) Famous as these songs are said to have become in France and Belgium, they do not impress me as deeply as does Lekeu's chamber music, mainly because they are not essentially vocal in style. The voice-part is not treated badly, on the contrary, but it is not independent enough of the piano-part. Indeed, the songs almost gain if arranged as pieces for the piano with Lekeu's own poems as mottos instead of the lines by Lamartine, Verlaine, Hugo, that are prefixed as such. When the voice does not travel *unisono* with the piano, the separation follows declamatory more than stylistic reasons.

Apart from such more or less technical objections, the *Poèmes* in all fairness demand serious interest and respect. They strive toward that freedom of musical speech which is so characteristic of latter-day songs and which will conjure the censure of incoherence the moment the voice-part is severed and studied away from its twin, the piano-part. Though the "Rondo" is full of esprit, almost catchy, "Sur une tombe" and the "Nocturne" lent themselves best to Lekeu's introspective, brooding manner, a conclusion verified by the fact that the young composer took pains to provide his favorite, the "Nocturne," also with an accompaniment transcribed for orchestra, which is said to be impressively beautiful. The three songs are very difficult of interpretation, and this difficulty will always stand between them, the singer and the public. But thoughtfully interpreted they must conquer every sensitive connoisseur of song. Yet he would find that the impression created does not result wholly from the music: Lekeu, the poet, deserves his share of approval, since his exquisitely impressionistic free verse leads the composer without effort to interesting rhythmical experiments and to melodic curves of extraordinary breadth. As a specimen of Lekeu's poetic gifts, his "Nocturne" (a landscape seen with the eyes of the soul, as it has been called) may follow here:

Des prés lontains d'azur sombre où fleurissent les étoiles, descend, lente et précieuse, la caresse d'un long voile d'argent pâli dans le velours de l'ombre.

From distant meadows of sombre blue, where the stars flower, descends slowly and exquisitely the caress of a long silvery veil, pale in velvet shadows.

Aux branches des bouleaux, des sorbiers et des pins, la tenture suspend ses long plis de mystère où dort le sommeil des chemins et l'oublieuse paix de rêve et de la terre.

From the branches of birches, sorbs, and pines the drapery suspends its long mysterious folds, where rest in slumber the paths and the forgetful peace of dreams and of the earth.

L'air frais et pur, dans les feuilles,
Laisse mourir un lent soupir
Si doux qu'il semble le désire
Des défuntes vierges aimées
Cherchant l'invisible joyau
Que va berçant près du ruisseau
La chanson murmurante et douce
De l'onde rieuse en la mousse

The fresh and pure air lets die in the leaves a slow sigh so sweet that it resembles the desires of maidens once loved, now dead, but still in search of the invisible jewel that lulls asleep in the moss near the rivulet the murmuring, lovely song of its smiling ripples.

La lune resplendit comme une agraffe d'or! et parfumant la plaine heureuse, la bruyère s'endort dans l'ombre lumineuse.

The moon is resplendent like a golden locket; and wafting delicious odors through the happy plains, the heath is lulled asleep in the illumined shadows.

In July and August, 1889, Lekeu, in company with his friends de Wyzewa and Guéry, made a musical pilgrimage to Germany, visiting Munich, Frankfort, Nuremberg and especially Bayreuth. Even to-day his letters home make good Wagnerian reading and will revive memories of similar Wagnerian impressions in those of us who in those days, too, had their first full taste of the magician of Bayreuth. For instance, on August 1 he wrote from Munich:

The day before yesterday I saw at the Munich opera an immense masterpiece: *The Flying Dutchman* of Wagner. Simply prodigious! And the performance! Yes, Germany is a country in every way more than extraordinary. . . . It is a powerful and admirable work proceeding without intermission from *Fidelio*. What will it be at Bayreuth?

And on August 12 from Bayreuth, after having heard *Tristan,* the *Meistersinger* and *Parsifal:*

. . . Wagner can absolutely not be understood from the piano; to hear or rather to see one of his dramas is to enter an entirely new world of which until now I had no conception. One cries almost all the time: *Parsifal* has made me passionately religious and I feel a smothering longing to go to Mass (for that is the only thing resembling Wagner's superhuman revery). And to think that I am to hear again *Tristan* and after that the *Meistersinger.*

From these quotations one might infer that Lekeu did not begin to sketch his opera "Barberine" until after he had come under the spell of Bayreuth. Yet his letter to Kéfer of November 19, 1889, undermines this inference:

My humble felicitations [on the success of Kéfer's symphony] may appeal to you like mustard after supper, and yet, my dear Sir, I beg of you to accept them and to believe in their sincerity.

My uncle recently informed me of the kind interest with which you spoke of me. I hardly know how to thank you for this new sign of affection and I cannot find suitable words to thank you for your request of a musical work through my uncle. I should very much like to be at your service, but I really cannot as yet. Please listen instead, my dear Sir, to this recital of events.

. . . Since May I am working on a scenic study in three characters (I omit three others, as they are of no importance for the sense of the work): a study after Alfred de Musset's charming comedy, *Barberine.* My score will have two acts; I hope to finish in one or two months (let us say by January 1) the first act. Though not completely. I sketch the music on three, four, five or even eight and ten staves, multiplying the instrumental indications, but the orchestral score has not even been started, very much less the arrangement for piano, the very thought of which makes my hair stand on end. So you see that I have at least a year of work ahead of me, and serious work at that, before I shall reach the end of my little drama.

So far I need not complain about myself. Indeed, I confess quite frankly that I have realized my intentions fairly well. Without false illusions, however, about the value of this first work for the stage, since I feel only too well how the master of Bayreuth rests with all his formidable weight on my thoughts; after all, I merely sought to follow him, to be straightforward and accurate in the declamation, expressive and musical in the instrumentation, and furthermore scenic. Now to-day a friend of mine, an actor at the Odéon, asures me that Mme. Lardin, sister of de Musset, would never permit the performance of the work (if by some lucky chance that opportunity should arise) nor the performance of excerpts at a concert. It would seem that she rejects absolutely all the numerous requests for permission to adapt musically her brother's dramas and comedies. . . . At any rate, if an orchestra is willing, I can always at my expense and unhindered by Mme. Lardin have the purely symphonic parts of my work played. But I find only two excerpts fit for concert performance and the first will lose much, I fear, away from the stage: a fragment of the second scene of the first act and the prelude for the second.

My first act will have no prelude; I thought this best, since the principal character does not appear until the second act.

The prelude, then, is reserved for this entry in the second act; it will depict the loveliness of Barberine, her goodness of heart, her love and her devotion to her husband. This is a fine program, to be sure, but . . . I have not yet written a note of it. Without doubt (since four fifths of the first act are finished) I may avail myself of several of the motives as a foundation for this symphonic piece.

Still, I shall require two or three other motives. Because useless for the first act, I have reserved them exclusively for the second; the business, then, remains of putting all these themes in order for a concise piece of orchestral music.

I propose to put my hand to this prelude the moment the end of the second act is in sight. As soon as it is finished I shall show it to my master Franck and it will give me a real pleasure to send you the score. . . I have also an introduction to *La Coupe et les lèvres* in my head, but that is practically only in the state of a mere project.

To Kéfer, Paris, Dec. 16, 1889.

. . . Recently I wrote to you about my "future" scenic essay, *Barberine*. I have abandoned it. For this very *intime* drama I composed a Prelude. I showed it to Franck; it pleased him very much and he did not withhold his compliments (far from it!). Yet he advised me against writing for orchestra too soon. I shall follow his advice. Nevertheless, the orchestration of this Prelude is entirely sketched; nothing remains to be done except to transcribe it in score. The same applies to a symphonic study in form of a *Chant de triomphale délivrance* which I finished about a month ago on four or five staves surcharged with instrumental indications. These two pieces and my fugue, there you have a list of my works since October.

The above reference to his "first symphonic study" called *Chant de triomphale délivrance* disposes of the assertion by Tissier, de Stoecklin (who edited the letters!) and others that the work was first performed under Kéfer in 1889, before Lekeu "had received a single lesson in composition." That is at best a doubtful compliment. We must not forget that in November Lekeu had already developed the habit of taking his oracle in counterpoint, César Franck, into his compositional confidence, and certainly not without profit. As a matter of fact, the *Chant de triomphale délivrance* was not performed by Kéfer, to whom it is dedicated, at a concert of the Verviers conservatory until April 13, 1890. The history of this performance is sufficiently outlined for biographical purposes in the following three letters:

To Kéfer, Paris, January 18, 1890.

. . . You will receive with this mail a manuscript which without doubt will impress you as being unreasonably long. Excuse me, its length and my boldness in dedicating to you my first work for orchestra. But I believed that this dedication was yours of right because of all the kindness you have shown me and because, of all the things that I have concocted so far, it is the only one that satisfies me. I have worked on it since November. The last five or six pages of the score I attacked six or seven times. I finally saved only the version which appeared to me to be the most concise and precise. . .

Tell me frankly what you think of it, for I am very young, and at twenty one hardly ever has the good fortune to meet so devoted a friend as you: in other words, it would not pain me in the slightest, not even after the happy news from you, if I had to wait some time, even some years, before appearing in public. Above all I must ripen.

March, 1890, to his mother.

I heard yesterday the first rehearsal of my *Étude symphonique.* On the whole, I was satisfied. It sounds well; it is an orchestra à la Beethoven and Kéfer has again told me, warmly pressing my hands, that the fugue is "prodigieusement charpentiée." However, I shall make a few little changes, not melodic or harmonic, but orchestral. Yesterday's rehearsal took place under particularly disadvantageous conditions. For an hour and three quarters Kéfer had kept the musicians busy rehearsing his symphony; tired, they were about to leave the hall, when Kéfer called them back and requested them to try over a work by one of their compatriots. They went about it sawing and blowing as best they knew how, but the horns and trombones, not knowing the work at all, missed many entries. When they had finished they began to applaud and I had to rise (I was seated hidden in a corner of the hall) and bow my acknowledgments right and left; after which I had to shake hands for five or six minutes. All that will make you laugh, and yesterday I felt like doing likewise. The main point, however, is, it is good music and feasible.

At the next concert a piece (Again!) by *Voss' éfant* will be performed. This little piece (which you will certainly hear) is a *bonne blague* invented by me and Massau [violoncellist, professor at the Conservatory of Verviers].

First a violin and violoncello take their place at their desks, all others remaining vacant. They wait a little while for the others, who do not appear, and then play a motive of "Crampignon" (first the violin; then the violoncello takes it up, accompanied by the violin in imitative counterpoint).

While they are playing, an alto arrives, sits down and takes up the motive. And during all the succeeding entries (in a goose-march, as it were) of the string instruments, a little fugue is rolled off without interruption.

Then comes an oboe: he wants to take up the theme, but bizarre chords impose silence on him after two futile attempts. In the meantime a clarinet has entered and chants a melody, calm and interpretative of the pleasure one feels when making music with friends. This melody is treated in an adagio of five or six lines. Then the horn and bassoons take part in the sport; the volume of sound increases; finally the violins intone victoriously the chant of the clarinet and at the same time the basses, doubled by the bassoon, take up the theme of *crampignon* which served as subject for the fugue. (Just as in the *Master-singers*.)

You see, my dear Mother, one can write *blagues* [hoaxes] in music as well as in literature. But I have tried to make this caprice amusing and yet very musical. I believe it will sound marvelously well. Almost all the successive entries are amusing and unexpected; especially a fortissimo entry of the double-bass solo.

I have not been able to identify this reversed shadow of Haydn's "Abschieds-Symphonie" in Baudoux's list of Lekeu's works. Perhaps the score has disappeared. That would be regrettable, for an opportunity to hear Lekeu's whimsical piece ought to prove most entertaining on a suitable occasion. Indeed, just for the fun of it—and we need a little more fun in music—one might wish to see Lekeu's *blague* and Haydn's *blague* put in juxtaposition on a program.

Again it is a letter to Kéfer which acquaints us with the conception and genesis of one of Lekeu's "serious" and ambitious works, nothing less than a triptych, however incongruous. He writes from Paris, on May 22, 1890:

> . . . I have undertaken *une grosse machine* in three parts for orchestra (and male chorus in the third). I shall tell you below of the subject and the plan. Here, first of all, my reasons for hoping to hear this work at an early date. M. Voncken [violinist, professor at the Verviers conservatory] has requested of me for the annual concert de l'Émulation a work for orchestra and chorus. Furthermore, recently I was introduced to M. Louis de Romain, who with Jules Bordier is in charge of the artistic enterprise of the concerts at Angers. This gentleman treated me charmingly and asked me to let him have in August, when he next visits Paris, the score of a symphonic piece. I have set myself the task of finishing for his purpose and by that date the first part of my *Poème.*
>
> Here is the point of this heavy job: I should like to make a Musical Study after Shakespeare's *Hamlet.* The first part has for a motto *"To die—to sleep;—To sleep! perchance to dream. . . "* You see that this is precisely Hamlet's character.
>
> But this character, I feel neither old nor strong enough to adequately depict: that task requires a Beethoven! But at least I can attempt to illustrate musically some principal traits of the character: the thirst of death, the march of his mind toward this idea: seeing first in Death a deliverance and then fear of finding beyond the grave painful surprises; his hatred, thereupon, of all the rank evil which surrounds him (his counselors, his mother, his step-father). Thus I am also led to reveal the honesty of this extraordinary soul, his profound love of the good, his eternal attachment to his father.—You see that this is not a small affair. Many things will still have to be considered and translated, for the complexity of this character (so astonishingly *one,* after all) is truly crushing.
>
> Well! I have resolutely set my hand to the task! Even before leaving for Verviers I was spending much thought on it.
>
> I have finished the first part. Now I must prepare the entrance of the themes of hate and combine them symphonically with the motives of the Invocation of Death.
>
> The second part will have as epigraph: *"Das Ewig-weibliche zieht uns hinan"* (the last words of the second Faust): the consolation that Death will not perhaps procure and which the troubled soul asks for Love. But there again, complete deception; and the themes of grief return still more certain of their victory.

The third part will have as epigraph: *"O proud Death!
What feast is toward in thine eternal cell, That thou so many
princes, at a shot, So bloodily hast struck?"* This is the definitive
triumph of Grief.—There is one thing against which I must
guard myself: to want to narrate in music concrete facts (program music), for instance, the apparition of the ghost and other
bêtises. Under no circumstances do I wish to attempt rewriting
in music Shakespeare's drama. My desire is merely to essay
a translation into music of some of my impressions gained from
the frequent reading of *Hamlet.* For example, the third part
will not be a funeral march (Berlioz has made one on this subject), but a piece of music (in very moderate tempo) into which
I shall try to put utmost sorrow, deriving it nominally from
the Invocation of Death and the heinous imprecations of the
first part.

Was "Hamlet" performed at Angers in 1890? Probably letters of Lekeu not yet published would answer that
question. Those edited by Stoecklin (with elisions) do
not. Yet one feels inclined to deduce an affirmative answer
from the tenor of Lekeu's letter to Kéfer on April 15,
1891, the one informing his friend of the depressed state
of mind in which the death of his "cher maître" Franck
had left him:

"At Angers [the letter was written in Paris, apparently after
a return from Angers] I heard a good rehearsal of a little
orchestral piece which I composed last summer (the second part
of an *Étude symphonique* in three parts) [obviously the "Faust"
movement], and as it did not sound disagreeable, I took a little
courage. . . I shall revise completely, I might say re-compose,
the first part of this my second symphonic study, for when I
set about writing the third part, the first impressed me as being
more *nulle* than the collected works of Ambroise Thomas.

That he did not carry out this plan, is a further deduction from his letter to Kéfer. At any rate, it would offer
a plausible explanation of the fact that the "Hamlet"
(and also the third) movement remained unpublished,
whereas the score of the second, the *Faust* movement,
seems to have been printed, though, in keeping with that

regrettable practice of French and Italian publishers, *en location* only.

"Horrors without name, which I have grouped under the title of a Trio for piano, violin and violoncello." With these not very flattering remarks Lekeu in his letter to Kéfer of April 15, 1891, would seem to refer to the least known (and least coherent) of his chamber music works, finished early in 1891 after he had recovered from the blow dealt him by Franck's death, but commenced early in 1890, and apparently, after the completion of the first movement, laid aside in favor of his *grosse machine* in three parts. I say on purpose "would seem to refer," because the letters quoted below in which other references to the *Trio* occur contain a contradiction. In one of them he mentions a trio for piano, violin and *alto* (underscoring the word *alto*), which leads us almost to suspect that Lekeu at that time was actually working on two different trios, one for the customary combination of piano, violin and violoncello, the other for the rather unusual combination just mentioned! The earliest allusion to a trio I find in Lekeu's letter to Kéfer from Paris, February 1, 1890:

> I just left my admired master, Franck, who for half an hour bombarded me with compliments on the first four pages (all I have written in a month) of a Trio for piano, violin and violoncello.—But enough of this.

On April 26, 1890, Lekeu then informs Kéfer that César Franck is

> quite satisfied with what I have shown him of the Trio on which I am busy. He warmly encouraged me to persevere in this heavy and irksome task. Hence, I have thrown myself into it with refreshed strength.

It is in his letter to Kéfer of May 22, 1890, that the *alto* is mentioned instead of the violoncello. In these words:

I work much. I do not mean counterpoint; one has to submit to these annoying but indispensable scholasticisms! I have finished the first movement of a Trio for piano, violin and *alto*. The adagio will have been written (at least I hope so) in one or two months. I showed the work to father Franck, who is very much satisfied with it. In fact, I expect to dedicate it to him (which is but natural).

Between these letters falls one written from Heusy on March 1, 1890, to his mother, which affords a further valuable clew to Lekeu's type of mind as a composer. (After all, he *was* a "programmatic" composer and not a formalist.) The letter runs:

The last piece of my Trio is definitely attacked: two pages are written. The rest simmers feverishly in my head. Here is what I should like to express in this first movement. I have all the themes:

1⁰. *Introduction:* Grief, a ray of hope, fugitive, too short, brusquely driven off by the sombre reverie which, alone, expands and prevails.

2⁰. Allegro molto: The sorrow of melancholy; always to be in battle with matter and with the memories of victory over matter! temporary and torturing. Grief reappears; cries of hate resound and the malediction has plain sailing. The violin issues an appeal of despair: who will deliver me from this torture? The hellish ritornelle answers; the violoncelle [sic!] unites with the violin to proclaim anew the supplication; once more the ritornelle replies. A contest ensues, desperate, between the two ideas. (Here is where I have stopped.) The plan of the rest is as follows:

The contest seems to come to an end. Is it to be the end of the suffering?

The melody of Hope of the Introduction reappears. But brusquely Grief, as if irritated by this consoling calm, takes possession of her empire. The cries of hate become more numerous, the fugue in its winding course sweeps them away. Melancholy, too, in an attempt to rend the clouds, is driven off; expelled also all hope; and in impotent lassitude the first section ends as if proclaiming in darkest silence the triumph of Evil.

But, dear Mother, rest assured that the other sections correct the first, and the finale will be the luminous development of *Goodness,* if I am at all able to cope with that task worthily.

I am satisfied with what I have done so far. With patient

travail I hope to reach the end of this work, which I feel to be so beautiful, above all so expressive, and I compel myself to put my whole being into it. Let us hope that you may hear it within a year.

On April 15, 1891, Lekeu had occasion to thank Kéfer for his willingness to lend the string section of his orchestra for the performance of a little piece composed for the approaching marriage of his friend, A. Guignard. It was his unpublished *Épithalame:* "This ensemble of strings, trombone and organ ought not, I think, to sound full of holes." April, 1891, is also the date affixed to the printed score of his "Sonate pour piano," yet I can find no mention of this work in the letters published by de Stoecklin. Unfortunately so, for it might have helped to check up Marcel Orban's statement:

A *Suite* for piano was published after his death under the title of Sonata. He did not consider it more than a study in composition; but it is a study of real beauty. The fugue remains a monumental example of the genre.

That Lekeu in letters not yet published speaks of this sonata is clear, since Orban quotes a line from one of these (without further data) to the effect that "This passage I should not to-day write again, but the fugue is *bien.*"

In the absence of documentary evidence, I hesitate to accept Orban's story. The reverse process would have been more plausible: to change the title of sonata to that of suite, as the following little exposé will illustrate.

Lekeu prefixed these verses by George Vanor to the work as a motto (serviceable for a suite as much as for a sonata):

> Comme une mère veille auprès de son enfant,
> Elle a bercé de ses chansons ma mâle fièvre.
> La bonne fée, elle a ranimé de sa lèvre
> Ma lèvre, et rafraîchi pour moi, l'air étouffant.

The music is in keeping with these verses, although it is

music with a motto rather than "programmatic" music
in the routine sense. The "mâle fièvre" and the "air étouf-
fant" predominate, but since one has to live up to one's
motto, the "bonne fée" ultimately comes into her own.
It is music as from another world, undisturbed by market
noise or by witty fashionable gossip. Immature and
youthfully crude in spots, to be sure, but like MacDowell's
first suite, an astonishing example of adolescent genius.
It is unlike MacDowell's suite, however, in its almost
ascetic avoidance of brilliant hues, albeit full of color otherwise.   The sonata inherited its gait from Bach, its mys-
ticism from Franck and its profile (as seen through a veil)
from Wagner.

Academicians among critics will deny to the work its
title of sonata. Not without cause, for at best Lekeu
wrote a sonata in the original sense of a piece to be played
on an instrument, and certainly not a sonata in the modern
sense of the term: the first and last of the five movements
excepted—practically a prelude and an epilogue—the
composer revels in a series of strictly contrapuntal fugal
movements with just a trace of the so-called sonata-form!
Combine this fact with the *fin de siècle* harmonic boldness
of the work and its somewhat morbid program, and an impression is produced as if Sweelinck or some other forerunner of Bach had returned to earth, had listened to our
modern ways of making music, and had retired to some
organ-loft to improvise an organ phantasy in the "modern"
style.   Not without clinging to the idea of *thematic unity*
(so characteristic of archaic suites and sonatas), for Lekeu
in this "study in composition," too, as in his other chamber-
music and in the footsteps of his master, César Franck,
dedicated himself wholeheartedly to a revival of that
maxim of composition.

The nobly harmonized prelude gives the mood of the
entire sonata: climaxes interrupted by mystic echoes from
the beyond, produced by the simple device of a change in
pedals, and at the end a simple motif obviously announc-

ing the chanson of the good fairy. With slight alterations the main theme of the prelude reappears immediately
after the prelude as a fugue theme. A *bona fide* four-
part fugue seems to follow, but the movement impresses
me more like a fugato variation of the prelude, the prelude
theme, the chanson motif, with the mystic harmonic interruptions and syncopations playing the same rôle here
as there. In working all this out as if in a choral phantasy for organ, the chanson motif is used partly in canonic
imitation for the preparation of a mighty climax, after
which the main theme reënters majestically with a kind
of basso ostinato leading to the end in almost literal repetition of the closing bars of the prelude. To the student
of composition this movement is particularly interesting,
for the apparent experiment in utilizing fugato as a technical contrivance, while adhering *sub rosa* to the sonata-
form. The third movement, with the chanson motif again
as ethereal thematic adjunct, is also a fugato movement in
which the first theme seems to have germinated from the
basso ostinato of the second movement. The fourth movement in very much slower tempo shows the same contrapuntal style and the same thematic material, though it is varied
to fit the story of the movement: a feverish starting up as
if haunted by tender calls, a sinking back into despair
after a tremendous struggle, yet now with rays of hope
breaking through darkness. Obviously, the composer is
preparing us for the poetic essence of his motto; and indeed, from the last movement, the epilogue, the "suffocating
atmosphere" has been dispelled. The thematic material
is the same as in the fourth movement, but the underlying
mood is more joyful, and, though passionate, calm with
the calmness of the soul after a conflagration. Unfortunately, the idea of this epilogue is better than the music,
which is somewhat banal.

Whatever one chooses to call Lekeu's "Sonate pour
piano"—a sonata, a suite, a theme with variations, an
organ fever-phantasy transcribed for the pianoforte—it

is on the whole a noble work of youthful genius reaching
with outstretched arms for ideals peculiarly his own.
But like so much of Schumann's music, it seems to have
been sung to the composer's own soul or to a few intimates,
and not to a listening crowd. With all its thundering
climaxes the sonata is music for the chamber, not for the
concert-hall, and it is perhaps impressive rather than effective. For that reason all but a few independent con-
cert-pianists will naturally hesitate to introduce Lekeu's
sonata to our audiences, so accustomed to the sterility of
"effective" pianists' programs.

In the middle of June, 1891, Lekeu informed his friend
Kéfer that he had accepted Vincent d'Indy's advice to
embark on the adventure of trying to capture the Belgian
prix de Rome:

> I obey him and so also satisfy my parents, who at present
> dream of nothing but to see one of these days this supreme and
> governmental prize allotted to me.
>
> However, I must confess candidly how disagreeable it would
> be not to be admitted to the final test; and yet from a strictly
> materialistic standpoint (I mean the time for jotting down the
> notes) I dread the preliminary more than the final competition.
> For the latter they accord us 27 days *en loge,* whereas for the
> preliminary test we have but 72 hours—3 days for the composi-
> tion of the four-part fugue and the complete score of the chorus
> with orchestra.
>
> I have never been able to make a fugue in less than six days
> and, as regards the chorus with orchestra, when I tried to com-
> pose one in as short a time as possible, it took me 8 days. . .
> However, if I can finish these two affairs in three days and the
> jury then pronounces them too bad for my admission to the
> final competition, I shall be vexed indeed. . .

This letter was followed by one *en loge* to his mother in
the first flush of victory, half an hour after Gevaert on
July 25, 1891, had pronounced him "premier admissible"
for the final test. As Lekeu was the youngest competitor,
it had fallen to his lot to draw a fugue theme from the
urn. The theme drawn was of the poorest, and so unfit

for vocal treatment that Gevaert immediately charged the competitors to use it for organ and string quartet accompaniment. Lekeu felt satisfied with his "sane, sonorous" chorus and attributed his preliminary victory to his careful instrumentation ("one is not a pupil of d'Indy just for nothing"). His fugue horrified him as "raw as iron and void of all musical interest." He did not hesitate to say so afterwards to Émile Matthieu of the jury, who replied with Gallic esprit: "Well, Monsieur Lekeu, you see that our opinion was quite different from yours." The letter continued:

I might now perhaps by sawing wood like a deaf man unhook a second honorable mention, but I hope that my two old friends [his parents] will not get a swollen head and figure out that the *premier admissible* thereby becomes first in the real competition. To write and finish such a complicated cantata as demanded here one needs an experience and a flow of ideas which one cannot have at 21 years. Perhaps in two years I could win the second prize and in four the first. However, that is a beautiful dream and nothing else.

In his letter to Kéfer of July 30 he voiced similar sentiments:

You appear to think that I shall split the drum with the first blow. At 21 one does not triumph so easily, particularly not in competition with chaps of 26, 28, and 29 years, of whom one, M. Paul Lebrun, harmony professor at the conservatory of Gand, already twice has carried off the first second prize. . . The prize will go to him who is the first to complete the sketch of his cantata and who has more time than the others to instrumentate with care. This rapidity of workmanship I am far from possessing. Shall I ever have it? . . . To be perfectly frank, I attach little importance to that bizarre faculty of completing a work of art in quick-step, and I consider it rather strange that precisely that faculty is asked of the future musician.
All this in order to tell you that perhaps by sawing wood conscientiously I may gather in the Rome prize in four years. Here I play the rôle of an *amateur* rather than of a competitor, and though I am not lying exactly on a bed of roses, my life

is not altogether disagreeable. Our subject is Andromède [the text was by Jules Sauvenière] and is burdened with three situations:

1. Ethiopia is devastated by a monster: religious scene for the purpose of asking Ammon if a sacrifice can free the country. The god answers that it is necessary to sacrifice the princess Andromeda by chaining her to a rock. Object: to reduce the affront to the Nereïdes whom Andromeda conquered in a beauty contest. The people seize the virgin without listening to her supplications.

2. Andromeda alone, her grief; the Nereïdes, playing on the waves, taunt her without pity.

3. Perseus (who, without doubt, was promenading in those parts) frees Andromeda; they marry, the people (who have turned their coat . . . why?) yell to Hymen. . . Hopes that they will have lots of children. Harps, etc. . .

My work progresses without foolish haste or exasperating slowness. To-morrow I shall have finished the first scene (the longest of the three by far). It comprises a good old religious march. Scene of invocation, the Devil incarnate and his entourage.

I see clearly that in 21 days, when I shall leave here, I shall be completely wiped out physically. Also, I have abandoned entirely my original intention of forcing a hearing of my cantata on the jury at the piano, with chorus and soloists. . .

To Kéfer, August 10, 1891.

. . . my cantata is completely composed and even the orchestration is well advanced: the seventy-fifth page of score begins to look black. To-morrow at noon without doubt, I shall be through with the first half of the text. The second, I hope, will progress with the same rapidity.

In other words, my cantata will be finished on time between now and August twentieth unless I fall sick. But that is impossible, because I have felt marvelously well since my entry *en loge*. Of the result of this contest I have not the slightest idea. Yet I can promise you that the orchestration will be good from the first to the last note. I have worked a lot during the last year and a half; I had the good luck of hearing music of mine at Angers and I begin to feel a sure hand in the polyphonic treatment of the orchestra.

Having finished the composition of the cantata in advance of the date I had fixed for myself, I shall be able to devote more time to the instrumentation. . .

Is it good? Or is it not? Who knows? It is done and settled: *voilà* the main point, finish the job at whatever cost. Such a cantata never is good from beginning to end; even the best show numerous defects. Now one lacks the time to retouch these dark spots, and for that reason this competition business is diametrically opposed to artistic work, sincere and comforting. On certain days (yesterday for example) I feel satisfied with my work. Everything looks solidly constructed; of a good, expressive musical cohesion of parts, the whole ensemble dramatic and above all sincere. In brief, I am satisfied with myself. On other days (this afternoon for example) everything looks like a failure and then I pass hours not exactly gay. This evening my spirits are higher again. I heard fragments of cantatas of two of my competitors. Verily, without wishing to be conceited, I may affirm that my own work is better than what they played to me; for truly and without doubt their productions are but vast exercises. . . powdered over with Wagnerian reminiscences; not one cry of expression, not one gripping chord, nothing of those things that come from and go to the heart.

Of such things, possibly only one or two occur in my own cantata, but at least I have the certain consolation to have felt and written in spots something sane, honest and human. But this certainty perhaps (indeed probably) will be but a doubt in the minds of the jury, and I have not much hope of getting anything out of this business. Possibly the extreme care bestowed on the orchestration will gain me a second honorable mention. But I had better not count on that. . .

But when this clairvoyant auto-prophecy actually came true, did Lekeu break forth into a *chant de triomphale délivrance?* Far from it! He proved that after all he could not only be a "serious young gentleman," but also at times a foolish young gentleman like the rest of us. The contrast in tone between the last letter quoted and the following to Kéfer, end of August, is really amusing:

Since Sunday I have passed horrible days, and still more horrible nights. And this because of a foolish, senseless, wild and perhaps unpardonable step.

But you know me and you can see me when I heard the name of S . . . come before mine. A foolish rage seized me, my teeth chattered and (so I was told afterwards) I had the expression of a maniac. Without realizing what I was doing, I re-

fused to enter the jury's room. The next day I was still so
much in the grip of this atrocious impression that I wrote a
note of protest to the *Indépendance Belge* which had published
the verdict without mentioning my refusal.

He then felt utterly crushed by his acts of "childish
folly," but by the middle of September, it appears from
a letter to Vincent d'Indy, he had calmed himself sufficiently to reach the conclusion that, everything considered, he had acted wisely! Commenting on the fact that
Oscar Roëls' cantata, "a very interesting composition, of
exquisite charm and of absolutely extraordinary formal
perfection," was thrown out of court, he leaves no doubt
that his dream of winning the coveted Rome prize in four
years had completely vanished and that he had thrown
behind him any design of further competition:

The Rome competition is not at all what I believed it to be
and I do not even feel justified in feeling proud of my victory
in the preliminary contest. With one exception I had to do
only with old conservatory pillars, who do not know even the
most elementary part of their craft and have absolutely no ideas
in their heads. However, the contest was not between them
personally, but between the *Belgian conservatories.*
I have seen the six works submitted to the jury. Four of
them do not *exist* by reason of absence of every emotion and
because of poverty of harmonic invention. As for polyphony, a
dead letter for these people; they hardly know it by name. . .
As for myself, I had the rare good chance of being moved by
my subject and of having felt during the 25 days *en loge* better
disposed for work than ever. I have composed the first work
with which I really have felt satisfied. Most certainly I shall
have to concede numerous weak spots, but I may say to you as
to my best and most sincere friend, that I have written pages
of music worthy of a pupil of Franck and in which an impartial
musician must recognize immediately that I have listened to
your counsel with attention.
I had not a single vote for the first prize. Without hesitation
the jury disregarded me, and M. Lebrun of Gand received the
prize with four against three votes for M. Smalders of Liége,
who received five votes against two for the second prize.
Roëls received nothing; he was put out of court without cere-
mony. And without doubt the same fate would have been in

store for me, had I not studied your scores (the Scène Cévenole and Wallenstein); but the jury apparently feared that I might get my work performed, and therefore offered me the second-second prize.

The cause of my and Roëls' downfall is the same old jealousy of musical academies of modern music; but for me the case became more complicated on account of the fact that my whole education was received at Paris and outside of any conservatory.

Parts of Lekeu's luckless "Andromède" were performed a few months after his refusal of the second-second prize at a "Concert des XX" at Brussels; the whole work then on March 27, 1892, at the conservatory of Verviers under the ever loyal Louis Kéfer. The reception accorded was indeed different from that by the prize jury, and this difference—it goes without saying—is strikingly reflected by the following letters written to his father.

February 27, 1892.

I must tell you about the concert of the *XX* at which a part of my *Andromède* was played. To put it briefly, it had a big success. In the first place, the performance was ideal. All the instrumentalists had become passionately fond of this music and reproduced it down to my very last intentions. After the last note, the applause exploded in the whole large hall. Mlle. de Haene stepped forward to bow to the public, but when she left the stage, the applause continued to increase; all the musicians tapped on their instruments and from every part of the hall came shouts "composer, composer." I had to show myself and the tapping became louder. When I sought to retire, the musicians would not let me and I had to bow my acknowledgments again to the public. And when at last I could reach the foyer, while Crickboom, Gillet, etc., were surrounding and hugging me, I still heard the audience applaud. To be perfectly candid, that number on the program interested the public most; I am immensely pleased with the reception, since I was just a little nervous about a public so different from that at Verviers.

But what filled me with more joy than anything else, beside d'Indy's praise, was Ysaye's conduct toward me. At the end of the concert he mounted the platform and took me, figuratively speaking, into his arms by saying aloud that my *Andromède* was the work of an *artist* and of a *great musician* and that he had never before listened to a work by so young a man *wise* and

impassioned at the same time. . . An hour later I was at the
Conservatory. . . Ysaye when introducing me to his pupils
began by bombarding me with compliments, for instance:
"Here is a pupil of Father Franck; alone of composers of to-
day, he composes music which is not an imitation of Wagner—
whom he knows by heart."

Then he asked me if I had composed chamber-music. When
I answered in the negative, he asked me to let him have all
the chamber-music which I might write in the future. He
assured me of a performance on every suitable occasion, and
more particularly he asked me to start off with a Sonata for
violin and pianoforte. Well, I call that a soft snap, to hear
one's self played by Ysaye! . . .

To-day at 11 o'clock (from 11 to 2) the first general rehearsal.
Last Thursday evening I had heard the orchestra rehearsal with
chorus and soloists. I had been quite satisfied from beginning
to end; without any weak spots it sounded excellent, but to-day
still better. The horribly difficult choruses go as if sewed together, the attacks are firm and all nuances duly carried out.

They sound splendidly; in the first part as if smitten with
affliction, lugubrious, then tragic and wild; in the second part
they overflow with life, with abandon, triumphant sonority; one
really feels that the world has been saved for ever; "that radi-
ates," as Kéfer said.

The orchestra, on the other hand, marches like one man,
disclosing the most secret sentiments of Andromeda, of Perseus,
and the crowd surrounding them. Above all, it sounds intense.
Throughout one feels the influence of the old man César Franck
more than that of Wagner; hardly at all, or not at all, that of
d'Indy: his orchestra has an entirely different sound.

I am happy beyond words, because I appear to be able to
adore the work of my master and most loyal friend without
imitating him in the slightest. Perhaps one day I shall be
able to do as well as he, though in a totally different *genre* of
sonority.

Without humbug, this work is very much more solid than the
Chant lyrique. That work still gave me somewhat the impression of a very lucky accident. But *Andromède* is the work of
a manipulator of orchestra and chorus very sure of his craft.
One feels that I can draw adequate effects from the orchestra
whenever I shall wish. I feel myself in possession of a solid
brain—I know my business. Now back to work!

In 1904 *Andromède* was again performed at Brussels,
conducted by Huberti, a member of the *prix de Rome*

jury.   According to Marcel Orban, the public gave it a
demonstrative reception, thus flaying the stupidity or partiality of the jury in 1891.   This may be true, but if
Orban sees in Lekeu's *Andromède* "melodic invention of
incredible richness, the whole work astonishing in mastery
of craft and expression," I feel inclined to argue that the
success was not wholly due to esthetic but partly to the
political reasons advanced by Orban, and that he greatly
exaggerates the merits of the work.   Of course, I have not
heard it in its orchestral garb, on which Lekeu bestowed
such care, and I realize that it is easy to do an injustice
to modern works seen through the medium of a vocal score
only, but even a vocal score will show "incredible richness of melodic invention, etc."—provided it really is to be
found.   Exactly that I am inclined to deny.   *Andromède*
is in Lekeu's typical manner, but notwithstanding this
transparent individuality, the cantata lacks a convincing
character.   Mainly because the two principals, Andromeda
and Perseus, do not stand out in proper musical relief,
though Andromeda's lament is impressive enough.   On
the whole, they betray that lifeless stiffness and strained
vitality in their utterances which one would be surprised
not to find in *prix de Rome* cantatas or in similar prize-
bouquets of artificial flowers.   The first part of the Cantata is decidedly better than the second.   It is logical,
organic, full of vigor and color; in short, it illustrates again
the curious fact that composers often bestow more inspiration and sympathy on monsters, ghosts, goblins than on
their victims.   Had the second part maintained the level
of the first, *Andromède* might be called an effective work
in spite of Andromeda, but unfortunately it is incoherent,
bombastic, and runs from bad to worse, ending with a
rather empty and insipid outburst of joy.   This weakness
of the second part in my opinion will defeat further
attempts to win a permanent place for Lekeu's cantata
in the concert-hall.   With all its undeniable merits, Lekeu's
Andromède is not a great work of art, though, of course,

very much better than many a choral work which conductors persist in inflicting upon the dear public's ears.

There is in these letters but the one brief allusion to the *Fantaisie symphonique sur deux airs populaires angevins* quoted below under date of November 2, 1892. Yet, with the violin sonata and the unfinished quartet, it forms the trio of Lekeu's works that has carried his name and fame farthest. The last page of the original score reproduced in facsimile, in Octave Séré's book, shows the dates "Mai, 1891, 28 Mai, 1892." In other words, Lekeu began work on this phantasy before his painful experience *en loge,* and did not finish it until shortly before the violin sonata occupied his mind. The first performance of the work with orchestra appears to have been delayed until October 21, 1893, at Verviers under Lekeu's own direction. After that Vincent d'Indy, Chevillard, Colonne and other French and Belgian conductors stood sponsors for the work, until, so we are told by several French authors, it has become fairly fixed in the French and Belgian repertoires. One handicap to a more rapid circulation must be seen in the tardy publication of the full score—not until 1909. In America the *Fantaisie* appears not to have attracted the attention it deserves. Properly placed on a program, the score cannot fail to release that spontaneous applause with which it has been greeted elsewhere. Nor is that hard to explain. As Lekeu justly remarked after the Verviers performance in a letter quoted by Orban, "the orchestra purls with enthusiasm and sonority. There are in the piece certain trombones fairly *Jérichotiens."* Furthermore, by virtue of the fact that he based the *Fantaisie* on two captivating folk-songs of Anjou (the first of an infecting jollity), the work is bathed in sunshine far more than any of his other works. Unfortunately, Lekeu's programmatic note prefaced to Samazeuilh's not very happy arrangement of the score for four hands has been omitted from the published full score. This omission places conductor and

audience at a decided disadvantage, since it robs them
of the key to the structure of the work. Until I discovered that discrepancy between full score and arrangement,
I was puzzled by the hesitation of a very distinguished
American conductor (who estimates Lekeu's talent at its
true value and considers Lekeu's *Adagio pour quatuor
d'orchestre* on Georges Vanor's line, "Les fleurs pâles du
souvenir," very beautiful—and it *is* a gem, as Vincent
d'Indy first proved to Parisians), to perform the *Fantaisie*
on the ground that "it is good in spots, but is very detached
and to my mind ill-formed."

I cannot but question the soundness of this stricture if
the score be examined and tested in public with the indispensable aid of Lekeu's programmatic key:

Note de l'auteur.

A la tombée du soir, les couples enlacés bondissent et tour-
billonnent; c'est le bal de l'"Assemblée" et la danse toujours
s'accélère aux crix joyeux des gars, aux rires éperdus des filles
rouges de plaisir, pendant qu'éclat, dominant la fête et sa folie,
la voix souveraine de l'Eternel Amour. . .

Vers la plaine, où l'ombre s'approfondit, paisible et mys-
térieuse, l'Amant a entraîné l'Amante. . .

Il résiste à la voix aimée qui lui demande de retourner à la
danse, et, rieuse, par les champs silencieux, va répétant les
rondes toujours plus lointaines; il sait implorer et dire sa
tendresse.

Dans le décor d'une nuit d'été lumineuse, étoilée et pleine du
parfum de la terre endormie, la scène amoureuse déroule sa
passion grandissante, et les amants s'éloignent au frais murmure
de la rivière qu'argente le clair de lune.

For one thing we should feel thankful to the jury of
1891: their verdict aroused a storm of protest among
Lekeu's friends, of whom Eugène Ysaye was the greatest,
and so indirectly gave birth to Lekeu's violin sonata, "a
masterwork which for breadth of ideas and melodic inspiration need not fear comparison with *père* Franck's violin sonata." Praise higher than this is impossible.
Whether or not he indorses fully these words of Destranges

in his "Consonances et Dissonances" (1906), every un-
biased critic will have to admit that of violin sonatas
composed since Brahms and Franck, Lekeu's is inferior
to none. Since Eugène Ysaye, to whom, of course, it is
dedicated, launched the work, it has steered a triumphal
course throughout the musical world and is to-day, or
ought to be, in the repertoire of every violinist capable of
playing and understanding it and not addicted to atrophy
of taste and ambition.

Commissioned, we have seen, by Ysaye in February,
1892, the Violin sonata was not finished until some time
in the fall of 1892, as appears from the context of the
following two letters, the first written by Lekeu to his
mother, the second to his father:

[Fall 1892.]

. . . I shall see Kéfer at Verviers and I shall acquaint him
with my Sonata for piano and violin which I (in parenthesis)
finished copying to-day. I merely have to extract the violin part
and shall then definitely be rid of that big job. I now commence
to bother my head with new things: simultaneously germs of
themes for *Paysages d'Ardennes* [where he had been with
Kéfer] and the *Conquête du bonheur*. . . and bits of verse,
rimed or not, for this last-mentioned work. Let us hope that
something good will come of all this. Fortunately I have
advanced since July last, for I already see how I could have
improved upon what I did in my sonata (this is a sure and
mathematic means for observing progress in one's ideas: to
feel the weakness of what one has done and to reason it out).
This does not mean that I shall rewrite this or that passage
in my sonata; no, the true way of correcting a work is to write
one better.

To his father, Heusy, November 2, 1892.

At Brussels yesterday morning I was put into a cheerful
mood by the exhibition of enthusiasm and friendship which
Ysaye, etc., have shown me.

If I arrive at composing the Quartet which Ysaye demands
of me, Maus is fully inclined to give at Brussels (at the *XX*)
what he calls (be it understood!) a *Séance Lekeu* ! ! ! ! ! ! !
at which one shall hear the *Sonata* for violin and piano, the
Quartet, and my three songs impatiently awaited by two or
three singers of Brussels.

Perhaps even my *Fantasy on two Angevin airs* will receive a hearing in the transcription for piano 4 hands which Monday morning at Sèthe's excited unbelievable transports of enthusiasm.

Saturday evening, Ysaye played my sonata at his home. According to all present (pupils and friends who hear him constantly) Ysaye surpassed himself.

In Crickboom's opinion, it is this sonata which Ysaye interprets with a maximum of style, either of passionate abandon or of absolute calm, as is, for example, so necessary in the second movement.

Lekeu's violin sonata (in G minor) was first played in public by Eugène Ysaye, to whom it is dedicated, but the exact date is unknown to me. At Paris it was brought out by Paul Viardot and Bertha Demanton in 1899; at Boston in 1902 by Karel Ondricek and Alice Cummings. Essentially different from the pianoforte sonata, the violin sonata, too, cannot deny its descent (for instance melodically) from César Franck. Though much maturer than the pianoforte sonata, it does not lack the flavor of a study in composition, since certain experiments in thematic developments and form seem to have occupied Lekeu's mind when composing the sonata. Instead of dissecting, doubling, telescoping, breaking up his themes and juggling with their component parts—a procedure so unendurable in the imitators of Beethoven and Brahms—Lekeu preferred to leave his themes more or less intact and sought to make the thematic narrative more convincing by repetition of important phrases at different pitches. We know this procedure of sequence from Liszt's symphonic poems. Those who criticize Liszt for following it will also condemn Lekeu. Yet the principle of sequence as a lever for development of motive power is perfectly sound in itself. The artistic test lies merely in its application. If Liszt, the pioneer, applied the principle of sequential leverage still somewhat crudely and primitively, that does not necessarily bar later composers from succeeding where he at times failed. If then Lekeu in his violin sonata, as

also in his unfinished quartet, is seen after a few bars
to have no intention to indulge in the traditional thematic
contortion and anatomical dissection, he has a divine
right as an artist to choose his own method of expression.
If we are anxious for critical battle, the only fair thing
to do is to follow the artist, meet him on his own ground
and challenge the solution of his self-imposed problem.
Hence, it is one thing to criticize Lekeu for having adopted
in his violin sonata the principle of sequence at all, quite
another to insist—and correctly so—that he failed to solve
his problem completely, since there still adheres to the result an element of experiment: unfortunately, Lekeu's thematic blocks are not so skillfully cemented as always to hide
the crevices, which is the main danger a composer faces in
that process. However, between this admission and the
verdict of incoherence occasionally rendered against
Lekeu's sonata there lies a wide gulf. Moreover, the
charge of incoherence will be put across the path of every
artist who dares to break with formal traditions, and need
not be taken seriously.

While the Lekeu "sigh," or "wail," is not wholly absent
from the sonata, it bubbles over with the freshness and
joyousness of youth, though of youth meditative, not flip-
pant. In the second of the three movements, by way of
contrast, sadder chords are touched; and also by way of
contrast to the second movement, which the composer
wished played with utmost calm, the two outer movements revel in bold, biting dissonances. No poetic program or motto prefaces the score. This fact at least per-
mits the inference that the composer had no underlying
poetic idea in mind when he composed his violin sonata
as a modern of moderns and not as a student of archaic
forms, as in the pianoforte sonata. Furthermore, the
themes of the violin sonata show a remarkable lung capacity. They possess a breadth which is just as characteristic of Lekeu as are for instance choppy themes of
the later violin sonatas of Emil Sjögren. On the other

hand, Lekeu's themes in this sonata cannot be claimed to be very original; but what they lack in this respect is atoned for by their clear, bold curve, their intensity, their driving power and their inherent fitness for application of the ideas of thematic unity. The dullest ear cannot fail to notice that the opening theme of the sonata dominates the whole work. Indeed, even the secondary themes of the first movement seem to render homage to the main theme, and we notice how a phrase of merely incidental appearance, that helps to build the bridge for the second theme, assumes vital importance in the third movement. In this last movement Lekeu either blends with surpassing contrapuntal skill the several themes of the sonata or he increases the rhythmical interest by their bold juxtaposition. To these devices Lekeu obviously owes the irresistible swing and the necessary accumulation of expansive force for the almost spectacular end of the last movement. In my opinion, however, its artistic beauty is somewhat marred by the amalgamation into one theme of a distinctly Russian dance motif and an upstarting chromatic phrase somewhat in the style of the later Wagner or Richard Strauss. The second movement is a revery. It opens in the usual $\frac{7}{8}$ rhythm, is written in the simple A B A form with section B in the "character of a folk-song," and gains additional charm by having reminiscences of the first movement dreamily interwoven in its texture.

The *Quatuor inachevé* for piano and strings was first performed at Brussels, Salle Ravenstein, on October 23, 1894, by the quartet of Crickboom, Angenot, P. Miry and Gillet, with the assistance of Miss Louisa Merck at the piano. Inasmuch as its composition was not prompted by a *premonition of death,* but was *bestellte Arbeit* by Eugène Ysaye, it goes without saying that it was dedicated to him. Presumably and precisely because this work was commissioned by his great compatriot, Lekeu took such infinite pains with it: in little less than a year he finished but little more than the first movement.

One studies this priceless torso of what probably would
have become the longest quartet on record and marvels
at Lekeu's wealth of inspiration, his emotional intensity
and the ingenuity and madness of his methods. No established pattern seems to fit the first movement; at any
rate, the classic quartet form is adhered to only as if in
a frame. To be sure, we hear two predominant themes,
they change place in the tonal structure and all that sort
of thing, but Lekeu does not stop there. At times his
bridge-work assumes prime thematic importance, or he
gives free flight to his fancy in improvising on his main
theme before he rushes into the working-out section. Furthermore, we have not one peroration only, but several, and
all this thematic strife is repeatedly interrupted, as it were,
by an armistice. It follows readily that by thus interrupt-
ing the climax—and the working-out idea is inherently the
embodiment of climaxes—Lekeu obtains a cragged, hence
bolder and more effective curve. One begins to suspect
that formal considerations alone did not prompt these
interruptions. The whole movement is to be played
throughout "Dans un emportement douloureux. (Très
animé)." This indication is prefixed to a short introduction full of Lekeu "sighs," and this introduction reappears in the thematic woof toward the end of the movement. Furthermore, this phrase "lent et passioné" played

by the first violin solo precedes the second movement. It
will not be found in the first movement, nor does it reap-
pear in the second movement so far as completed. Yet
this phrase must have had some function. And this phrase
was not a new one! Lekeu simply quoted himself: it is
the chanson motif of the *bonne fée* that plays so important
and poetic a rôle in his pianoforte sonata.

Studying the movement minutely many years ago, I reached the conclusion, as would every other student, that all these curious details of form could be understood and appreciated only (with corresponding profit for performer and audience) on the assumption that the structure of the movement followed an underlying poetic idea which was withheld from the published score or was not known. It is with a certain satisfaction, therefore, that I later found Lekeu's letters quoted below to bear out my assumption fully. I do not mean so much his letter to Crickboom, in which he says, "I have essayed a translation into music of the last eruption of Mount Ætna"—that may or may not have been a jocular remark not to be interpreted literally, but the letter of February 7, 1893, to his mother, in which he calls the first part of his quartet an "expressive chaos" and the "frame of an entire poem of the heart, where a thousand sentiments clash, where cries of suffering yield to long appeals to happiness, where there is strife and insinuation of caresses, seeking to calm sombre thoughts, where cries of love follow blackest despair in the effort to conquer it, and on the other hand eternal grief endeavors to crush the joy of life."

What rôle the second and third movements were to play in this poem of the heart, unfortunately we are not told. Hence, I must content myself with the dry statement that the second movement is not as nervous, impetuous or despairing as the first, but like most slow movements of sonatas and symphonies presents itself as a song without words written in simple A B A form. In its first part, perhaps influenced by Tschaikowsky, it soon develops into a genuine Lekeu. But, alas, just when the young master in a beautiful interlude for the pianoforte was preparing to pour out his very soul in adoration of Beauty, death checked his hand and the movement comes to a sudden halt with a painful anti-climax. Vincent d'Indy, when he revised and prepared the manuscript for publication, reverently contented himself with bringing this stump of a severed piece of music to a playable end.

No doubt there are those who will decry in Lekeu's quartet the absence of a "true" chamber-music style, will denounce it as "too orchestral," and so forth, but such pedantic or shallow objections really ought to be muttered under the breath, if at all, in view of the amazing contrapuntal resourcefulness and display of tone-color with which Lekeu gave life to the ensemble of the individual instruments. That does not mean that the quartet is so perfect as to defy criticism, but I think that legitimate criticism will have to steer clear of such *clichés* as "too orchestral" and will have to content itself with observing, for instance, that Lekeu might better have avoided a too frequent unison of the violoncello with the piano bass and, on the other hand, a too frequent display of the violoncello in its upper registers.

Lekeu's letters to Mathieu Crickboom record for us the time of practically the last stroke of his pen given by Lekeu to his marvelously beautiful swan-song. He wrote in August, 1893:

. . . The first movement of my first Quatuor for piano and strings—not an indication that a second one will emerge later— is finished since July 16, 1893, six P. M. The peroration, in which I have essayed a translation into music of the last eruption of Mount Ætna, is just barely playable.
Nevertheless, it appears very logical to me. I am now ruminating the second movement, which, I feel, will be very superior to the first, while I am recopying conscientiously what I have done since December.
I have become scared, in recopying my infernal Quartet, at the quantity of sharps and flats with which it is bristling. How, if I suppressed them altogether?

And in a letter from Angers, September 20, 1893:

The first half of the second movement of my first Quatuor for piano and strings is *confectionnée:* weight 1463 grains. .

We are equally well informed of the inception of the work and its slow progress from letters written, the first

to Kéfer, the others to his "chère petite maman," with
which this essay fittingly may end without further comment:

[*To Kéfer.*] *Angers, December 31, 1892.*
Since I left you I put the finishing touches to my *Trois
poèmes* pour chant (Soprano and piano), and I have begun work
on my quartet for piano and strings.

The first movement is started, but gives me a dog's pain. I
tremble when the idea forces itself upon me that if I wish
to adhere strictly to my plan, the second and third movements
will be still more difficult to write. I do not believe that I can
possibly get through by March and so satisfy Ysaye and Maus.

[*To his mother.*] *February 7, 1893.*
My brain is in a turmoil; my work progresses extraordinarily.
I have a thousand things to write, I am actually loaded down
and I walk the streets as one with hallucinations. After a good
many days of reflection, of criticism, of despair even, I saw
day before yesterday a long passage of the first part of my
quartet sketch itself, and since then an incredible fever of work
has seized me.

Unfortunately, for there is an unfortunately, I am just as
full of distress as of happiness. For the reason that what I am
doing is so distant from what has become customary in chamber-
music that I fear to appear to my friends and interpreters (for
the public, of course, I care not) as one tainted with the most
extraordinary madness.

And yet, everything duly considered, I must walk a straight
path and write what I feel without paying attention to others.
Instead of having, as is the sacred habit, a piece rolling on a
single sentiment, mood, color, line, the first part of my quartet
is for me the frame of an entire poem of the heart, where a
thousand sentiments clash, where cries of suffering yield to
long appeals to happiness, where there is strife and insinuation
of caresses, seeking to calm sombre thoughts, where cries of love
follow blackest despair in the effort to conquer it, and, on the
other hand, eternal grief endeavors to crush the joy of Life.
Joys of childhood, visions of dawn and of Spring, the melancholy of fall and tears; and I do not shrink from piercing cries
of pain, put into my music with all my might, with my whole
soul.

But this expressive chaos must also be harmonious, and at

the moment when I write the loveliest phrase, I must foresee the development of grief which is to follow. Hence, this is not merely a terribly difficult work to write on account of the transitions of mood, but murderous for any attempt to grasp its total structure.

However, come what may, I labor and want to carry this "work" to a successful end. Already I can affirm that in comparison with what I am now writing, my violin sonata is a mere trifle, worth two sous. And that makes me fear a little the day when Ysaye and his friends will read my Quartet for the first time. But what's the difference! If they do not understand it, so much the worse for me. Above all, I want to write down what passes in me without ulterior thoughts.

February 22, 1893.

. . . You can hear me, from morning to evening, making an infernal noise on my unfortunate Erard, for I strive with all my might to finish at Angers the first movement of the Quartet. Let us hope that it is not a crazy dream. What in this business supports me and at the same time fills me with despair is that I feel clearly how with my plan of moods a true artist could compose a masterwork: one of those unforgettable *machines* which send shivers up and down the spine, which grip you amidst tremblings of admiration, leave you breathless, exhausted, ravished, enchanted, all in one.

I am playing for a big stake. If what I am doing is good, if my interpreters (for I work only for them and myself), if Ysaye, Van Hout, Jacob and my dear Mathieu Crickboom comprehend my work, that will give me courage vertiginous and as soon as possible I shall install myself in the *Paysage d'Ardennes* or the *Légende éternelle,* or take up any other of a dozen or fifteen projected works (yes, O Lord, not less than that; I drew up a list just for the sake of curiosity), and I can say that I wrote a beautiful work, unless . . . *cré nom de chien,* my profession is after all not a soft snap! However, just at present, I have the courage of a devil and I could apply the admirable verses of Baudelaire to Théodore de Banville, then at the beginning of his career, to myself. You do not know them, these verses. Read and re-read this magical French:

> Vous avez empoigné les crins de la Déesse
> Avec un tel poignet, qu'on vous eût pris à voir
> Et cet air de maîtrise et ce beau nonchaloir
> Pour un ruffian terrassant sa maîtresse.

April 30, 1893.

. . . Last evening I recommenced work on my Quartet, which slumbered for almost three weeks. Good news! So far everything in it appears to me to sound well and full of expression. It is, I believe, of much more solid workmanship than the violin sonata. Verily, if I can carry to a successful end this big, very big job, it ought to become a beautiful work. All my melodies are laid out. To-morrow I shall embark on the peroration section, which will bring about the return of the principal theme, enlarged, stronger, and still more beautiful. For a piece of music should grow while expanding. All this, of course, with regard to the first movement. The second and third will give me less trouble, I hope . . .

More and more clearly I see and feel that I need your presence for my complete happiness. The future absolutely must reunite us and I wish that my life might end as it began, in the cradle of your love.

See how tender I become; it is the best proof that I am well prepared to resume my work. *Allons,* dear, adored mother; courage, perfect health and then tell yourself often, always, that your *Sidoüm* is and always will be he whom you so well know.

That is my pledge for life. To you I owe everything.

"CARACTACUS" NOT ARNE'S CARACTACUS

(Sammelbände der I. M. G., 1911)

SEVERAL years ago the Library of Congress acquired an anonymous score entitled "Caractacus," which I, as others had done before me, attributed to Thomas Augustine Arne. Later we instructed our agent to locate for us, if possible, a copy of Bishop's "Caractacus." A few months ago he reported a copy at a reasonable figure, and we promptly ordered it. Of course, I was delighted, but my amusement and disappointment may be imagined when this long-looked-for copy turned out to be merely another copy of the anonymous "Caractacus." The dealer himself must have had his misgivings, because (with the slang motto in mind, "pay your money and take your choice"), he had written in pencil on a fly-leaf this legend: "Bishop (H. R.) London (1806)—Bach (J. Chr.) London 1767." Now Bach's "Carattaco" was a *bona fide* Italian opera and has as much to do with this anonymous English "Caractacus" as Bishop's "Grand ballet of Caractacus," performed at Drury Lane on April 22, 1808—in other words, absolutely nothing. I could but meekly put this *canard* down as a second copy of "Caractacus." In so doing I examined the volume more closely than I had done before, and my observations developed into rather unexpected conclusions.

The anonymous "Caractacus" contains 2 p. l., 4, 76 p. fol., no imprint and no real title-page, merely the ornamental, calligraphical title. On the second preliminary leaf appears an undated and unsigned dedication. Then

come four pages of "General instructions for the performance of the music of Caractacus." After these follows the
score, paged 2–76, the first page being blank.

The collation of the second copy—2 p. l., 6, 76, 3,
1 p. fol.—showed that it was not really a duplicate. Nor
could it belong to a later edition or issue, because the
pages common to both (i. e., everything that appears in
the first copy) bear the watermark 1794. The two additional pages of the preface and the three additional pages,
or the one page mentioned in the collation of the second
copy, are merely supplements, and the whole simply represents a copy of the original issue of "Caractacus" with supplements for insertion! As these supplements are printed
on the same kind of paper, on plates of the same size as
those of the body of the volume, and are printed or
engraved in the same style, it stands to reason that the
supplements cannot have been issued long after the body
of the volume.

That the supplements were really intended for insertion into copies of the original and only edition, and that
a separate issue of the body of the work did not accompany
these additions, appears further from the facts that the
bindings and the leather title labels on the front cover are
absolutely the same in both our copies, that the uncut
margins of the supplements protrude beyond the margin
of the binding and that, as stated above, the watermark
throughout the two bound volumes is 1794. On the other
hand, the watermark of the *first two supplements is 1796,
that of the third 1797*.

As pp. 5–6 of the preface have been added "General
instructions for the performance of this music with respect
to quickness and slowness," with "Additional general
instructions for the instrumental music." The second
supplement, headed "Corrections," contains three numbered pages of score marked "No. 5." as substitute for
the original No. 5 and (with the watermark 1797), headed
"Corrections," the (one-page) third supplement contains

a substitute for the original No. 14.   That this third supplement was in turn an afterthought, appears conclusively
from the remark engraved on the lower margin of the
plate of p. 3 of the substituted No. 5, "At the beginning
of the symphony No. 26 . . . "

Nor did the unlooked-for attractions of this second
copy, a veritable bargain, stop here.   It contains numerous
manuscript corrections, not only of obvious misprints,
but significant changes of rhythm, harmony, accompaniment, time-signatures, expression-marks, instrumentation,
words and even punctuation in the dedication.   For
instance, in the substituted number 14, "Andantino" is
changed to "Spiritoso"; Nos. 5 and 14 are crossed out
in the original with the remark "see the correction"; and
as to the instrumentation of No. 29 it is remarked: "This
Symphony had perhaps better be performed by the Clarinets, Bassoons, and Serpent only; one of the Bassoons to
play the Tenor part."   All corrections and changes are
accompanied by marginal cross marks and the great majority of the numbers is preceded by the indication "This."
Finally, the anonymous dedication is headed "To the
Rev. W. Mason."

All these corrections and revisions are of such a nature
as to force the conjecture on us that they were made by the
person most concerned, namely, the composer, with the
object either simply to dedicate to the Rev. W. Mason,
the undisputed author of the *"libretto,"* an absolutely
correct and final copy of the anonymous volume with its
supplements, or to prepare the score for performance or
for the printer for a new edition.   The second possibility
is improbable, because even the composer, preparing the
score for performance, would hardly have troubled himself with the correction of the punctuation in the dedication; and the third possibility is not very much more
probable, as the composer had just gone to the trouble of
issuing supplements.   This much, I believe, may be conceded: nobody except the composer would have dedicated

this particular and peculiar copy to the poet *during the lifetime of the composer.*

With such a minute examination the bibliographer's interest in the volume would ordinarily stop, but now the musical historian's interest is awakened. Upon turning the leaves of this curious work he reads this engraved dedication:

Sir:

As the contents of the following pages took their rise from your work, it is but just that I should dedicate to you what you are in some measure the Author of. I have in them endeavoured to restore to Music its ancient and long neglected office of handmaid to Poetry. Poetry is the language of enthusiasm and passion. Music the suitable enunciation of that language: while therefore the latter subordinately coöperates with the former, it acts in its proper sphere; but when, quitting this dependent situation, it arrogates to itself independence of, nay dominion over, its powerful directress; it loses sight of the end of its nature and becomes justly reprehensible.

Whether this offspring of my labours may be considered altogether as a suitable enunciation of the lyric poetry of *Caractacus,* I know not: perhaps it does not entirely correspond to what might be produced by a continually spontaneous exertion of energetic Fancy: but not being always able to do what we would, we must sometimes be satisfied with doing what we can: such as it is, however, I hope it will be found not entirely unworthy of the original: whatever are its merits or its faults, to a considerable share of the former I consider you to be justly intitled, the latter I must as justly take entirely upon myself.

I am Sir
with the respect
due to your age and character
the Author.

The esthetic creed of our anonymous can hardly be called sound, but it surely is radical and, though by no means absolutely new, this doctrine of music as the "handmaid to poetry" had not often been expressed with such one-sided matter of fact boldness. One begins to suspect that the author had been infected by the melodramatic-programmatic bacillus of Rousseau's and Benda's era, and is no longer taken by surprise when reading under the head of "General instructions for the performance of the music of Caractacus":

The design of this Music is to represent, by corresponding Sounds and Rhythms, the Ideas expressed, and those alluded to, in the Drama, principally in its lyric parts: the former is attempted to be done by the Vocal; the latter by the Instrumental Music.

The Vocal Music professes to represent the Expressions and the Metre of the Lyric Poetry: for the former purpose I have endeavoured to accommodate the Melody and Harmony to the general sense of the phrase, yet so as to express also particular emphatical words:—for the latter I have, 1st. in general measured every syllable by one note of nearly corresponding length—2dly. I have marked the accented syllable by the Downstrike, leaving the unaccented ones to the Upstrike—3dly. I have marked the end of every line with a short rest, unless where the sense requires a longer one.

The Instrumental Music professes to represent that to which the Drama in different parts refers, *viz.* Symphonies, or that which may be expressed by Symphonies: the words therefore which precede or follow will often sufficiently point out the nature of each: but as there is no such guide for the Overture and some others, and as several of the rest are very generally referred to, I shall subjoin a particular explanation of such as I think require it.

The Overture consists of two parts: the first (No. 1) is intended to represent the Spirits of Snowdon lamenting the approaching fall of *Mona:* the second, (No. 1a) the souls of the departed Druids, personified by the Harp, interceding to avert the impending danger; the first continuation of No. 1 a reluctant denial of their request: the continuation of No. 1a. a second attempt of the Druids to avert the danger: the second continuation of No. 1 which concludes the Overture, a reluctant but final denial.

The Symphony, No. 2 is intended as an introduction of the Druids in a manner suitable to their character: the first four Bars are more particularly meant to regulate their steps: each interval between note and note in the Base Cliff to be one step. The remainder of the Symphony may either mark the progress of the procession, (in which case there will be two steps for every Bar), or it may be played the Druids standing still.

Then follow brief explanations of the other thirty-four numbers of the score. Their quotation would serve no useful purpose, except the instructions for No. 26, which are amazingly pretentious:

From the bar where the Bassoons enter, to the end of No. 26 I have endeavoured to represent by the notes allotted to that instrument, the act of dying of a man such as alluded to in the words; the upper part, which may be considered as a continuation of the Symphony, being intended to soothe him in his last moments. Having now, at the end of 26. breathed his last, his Spirit is endeavoured to be represented, in the first 26a. as "stealing from the earth," and beginning to approach a Chorus of blessed Spirits, represented as at a distance by the first 26b. —The Spirit continuing to raise itself from the Earth in the second 26a. The Chorus is heard a little nearer in the second 26b.—the Spirit continuing to raise itself in the third 26a. at length approaches the Chorus, which now breaks out in full Symphony in the third 26b.—the fourth 26a. is intended as a still nearer approach to, and final junction with, the chorus in the fourth 26b. which is then supposed gradually to recede from the audience, until lost "in the bright fount of day."

All this sounds promising, once one has become accustomed to the antiquated phraseology, and one certainly feels the presence of an ambitious man. He seems to stand above his subject, he seems to have calculated nicely the exact effect of his ideas and to be unwilling to leave the desired results to mere chance. One wonders by what novel or at least unusual and bold means he accomplishes his purpose. Turning to his "General instructions for the performance of the instrumental music," the first disappointment awaits us. He simply says: "The band should be large" and "There must be three Trombones for the symphonies of the last act." Two more instructions follow, but they are so insignificant as not to deserve quotation. Nor are the two "additional general instructions" of much consequence, though the remark "By *bases* in the symphonies I mean Double Bases and Violoncellos; by *base* Double Bases alone," at least is a helpful clew to the user of the score.

The author calls for a large band. This is the instrumental apparatus which he employs: String quintet, 2 flutes, 2 clarinets, 2 bassoons, 2 trumpets, 3 trombones, serpent, harp, organ, kettle-drum. Save for the absence of oboes and horns, such an orchestra would, historically speaking, be quite capable of uncommonly expressive effects, but this rather modern apparatus is never employed *in toto* in "Caractacus." Generally the string quintet only bears the burden of the message. In several numbers the harp only is active, in a few it is combined with the string quintet or, as in No. 7, it forms part of this odd combination, *flutes, bassoons and harp*. In No. 8 the author even perpetrates the combination *bassoons and harp* without any further support. As to the organ, where it is employed, it meekly plays in unison with the basses. In No. 31 the instrumentation is clarinets, trumpets and bassoons; in the final symphonies, where the composer's insistance on three trombones leads us to expect massive orchestration, we are greeted by trombones and harp only and, indeed, the nearest approach to a band, much less a large band, is in the (original) No. 29 with its clarinets, violins, tenors (violas), bassoons, violoncellos, double basses and serpent.

At the very best one can concede that the composer deliberately discarded the orchestra of his time and sought to replace it by unusual instrumental combinations. Whether or no he succeeded with his esthetic experiments, will appear later; but first we must quote from the "General instructions for the performance of vocal music" so much as is necessary for the purpose of this article:

The voices for which the above music is composed are Base and Tenor; either single, in Unison, or in parts: it is single only in the Arch-Druid's musical part, in the answers of Cadwall and Brennus, and in the words, "Mona on Snowdon calls," to be pronounced by one of the Chorus: The rest is sometimes in Unison, sometimes in two, three, or four parts; all equally intended for the whole Chorus.—To ascertain, with certainty, the exact proportion of each kind of Voice, is, at present, impossible; but I think that six Bases and six Tenors, or, if it be thought worth while, twelve Bases and twelve Tenors . . . will sufficiently produce the effect intended . . .

From the Composer's "General instructions . . . with respect to quickness and slowness" I shall quote only two as typical:

No. 1, which is in common Time and marked *Largo,* may be played at the rate of one bar to five seconds . . . No. 9, which is likewise in ¾ marked *"Spiritoso,"* may be played at the rate of one bar and one third of a bar to three seconds . . .

This, then, is the literary preface to a score which is commonly attributed to Thomas Augustine Arne. For instance, such an eminent authority as William Barclay Squire had this to say of the anonymous "Caractacus" in his Arne article, written many years ago for the "National Biography":

The latter work [Caractacus] was published in 1775, with a preface and introduction in which Arne shows a curious insight into the relationship between dramatic poetry and music. He expresses opinions on the subject, the truth of which, though couched in the stilted language of the period, is only beginning to be recognized at the present day. The overture to the same work is a singular attempt at program music, and the minute directions as to the constitution of the orchestra and manner of performance almost forestall the similar annotations to be found in the works of Hector Berlioz. During the latter years of Arne's life he achieved but few successes.

Another authority, Mr. J. S. Shedlock, holds practically the same view in an attractive article on "Dr. Arne's Caractacus" in the "Musical Times," February, 1899, pp. 88–89; and, of course, the new Grove follows suit. It may seem foolhardy to question the authority of these two scholars in such purely English matters, and yet I have come to have the gravest doubts about Arne's authorship, doubts that for me amount to the certainty that Arne is not the author. It might be suggested that a comparison between this "Caractacus" and Arne's autograph score would immediately settle the question of his authorship, but unfortunately the score is believed to have been destroyed in the conflagration of Covent Garden in 1808 (*see* "National Biography").

* *
*

The title of the first edition of William Mason's "Caractacus" reads:

Caractacus, a dramatic poem: written on the model of the ancient Greek tragedy. By the author of Elfrida. London, J. Knapton . . . and R. and J. Dodsley, 1759.

The poem met with such success that a second edition was published in the same year, a third at Dublin in 1764, a fourth at York in 1774; and it was translated into French, Italian, even Latin and Greek. Such was the popularity of a poet of whom a little more than a hundred years later the "National Biography" remarks:

Mason was a man of considerable abilities and cultivated taste, who naturally mistook himself for a poet. He accepted the critical canons of his day, taking Gray and Hurd for his authorities, and his serious attempts at poetry are rather vapid performances, to which his attempt to assimilate Gray's style gives an air of affectation.

Mason's "Caractacus" is, as the title says, a dramatic poem, not a dramatic play. It is written on the model of the ancient Greek tragedy in so far only as the poet has indulged in "Odes," and introduces the "Chorus" as one of the

Persons of the Drama

Aulus Didius, The Roman General
Vellinus ⎫
Elidurus ⎬ Sons of Gartismandua
Chorus of Druids and Bards
Evelina, Daughter to Caractacus
Arviragus, Son to Caractacus

Scene, Mona

The dramatic part of the Chorus is supposed to be spoken by
the Chief Druid, the lyrical part sung by the Bards

Beyond this, music had no voice in "Caractacus," nor
did the poet consider it necessary to tell us where in a
"Chorus" or a "Semichorus" the "dramatic," i. e., the
spoken part, ends and the "lyrical," the sung part, begins.
The Chief Druid is never introduced by name or rather
by title, and even the "Odes" are anonymous—their lines
are given to nobody in particular, so far as I can see, but
that they were to be spoken, not sung, is obvious. Thus,
without acts and scenes or clearly defined stage business,
the poem in its original form could not possibly have been
performed as a play, nor, to be just, was this the intention
of the author; but he, too, aspired to theatrical laurels,
and the result was a dramatized version of "Caractacus."
In 1772 Colman had dramatized, without the poet's consent, Mason's "Elfrida," constructed on similar lines to
"Caractacus," and Colman performed it at Covent Garden. Presumably this high-handed procedure opened
Mason's eyes to the theatrical possibilities of "Caractacus," and he set himself the task in 1776 of altering his
dramatic poem for the stage. He fully realized the difficulties of this task and particularly of a proper union of
poetry and music.

Quite accidentally, I ran across contemporary testimony
to this effect. Antonio Peretti in his libretto for Angelo
Catelani's "Carattaco" (1841) speaks of a letter from
Algarotti to Agostino Paradisi, in which Algarotti says
that Mason informed him how he found

una difficoltà insormontabile a potersi mettere il suo Carattaco sulle scene per l'abbondanza dei cori che di necessità
esigono di essere accompagnati della musica, la quale a' suoi
tempi non la credevi egli capace di rivertire degnamente una
poesia grave e dignitosa.

Furthermore, in a letter to Thomas Harris, manager of

Covent Garden, partly quoted by Mr. Shedlock in the
"Musical Times" article, Mason, though having curtailed
his dramatic poem, fancied "it may still be too long for representation." "If therefore," he continues, "upon rehearsal
with the music, you should find this to be the case, I will
send you a second copy, in which several other lines and
passages shall be marked with inverted commas, which
you may either omit, or retain, as shall then seem expe-
dient." Mr. Shedlock, always believing Arne to be the
anonymous composer of "Caractacus," adds:

The poet, therefore, looked upon the musician as an ally, as
one who was trying to strengthen his drama.

Quite naturally so; but that Mason's letter, at least
so far as quoted by Mr. Shedlock, contains any allusion to
melodramatic, programmatic music, I, at least, fail to see.
Whatever Mason may have thought of Colman's dramatization of "Elfrida"—presumably not overly much, as
he himself redramatized it in 1779—he cannot have had
serious scruples about collaborating with the composer who
had set the "Elfrida" choruses in 1772, namely, Thomas
Augustine Arne, one of whose very last musical works for
the stage was exactly the incidental music to Mason's
"Caractacus." The first performance took place at
Covent Garden on December 6, 1776 (not Dec. 1, 1776,
as in the "National Biography" under Mason), and Genest
("Some Account of the English Stage") records fourteen
performances of the play, as also a revival on Oct. 22,
1778. The "National Biography" (under Mason) says
that the success of both "Elfrida" and "Caractacus" was
"very moderate," but this statement is not quite in harmony with contemporary criticism. At any rate, the
editor of "Caractacus" in Bell's "British Theatre" (v. 31,
1796) remarks:

The commendation bestowed on Elfrida and Caractacus in
their original form, have been seconded by an equal degree of

applause since they were adapted to the stage. The first is perhaps the most finished, the second the most striking performance,

and Mr. Shedlock's quotation from the New Morning Post, or General Advertiser, December 7, 1776, further shows that Mason and Arne's joint labors had been appreciated. The town is congratulated "on the acquisition of so fine an entertainment" as "Caractacus," "where poetry and music unite their fascinating powers."

Quite an extensive review, with synopsis of the plot and compliments to the cast, I found in the London Chronicle, Dec. 7–10, 1776, wherein is said:

The performers did great justice to their respective characters . . . Dr. Arne's music is certainly good, and the choruses are correct in point of harmony, and fine through all the accompanyments.

The three following Airs gave great satisfaction to the Audience:

Air.   Mr. Leoni and Mrs. Farrell.

Welcome! welcome! gentle train
Mona hails ye to her plain!
Here your genial dews dispense,
Dews of peace and innocence!

Air.   Mr. Leoni.

Change! my harp, O change thy measures!
Cull, from thy mellifluous treasures,
    Notes that steal on even feet;
Ever slow, yet never pausing,
    Mixt with many a warble sweet,
In a ling'ring cadence closing.

Air.   Mr. Leoni.

Radiant ruler of the day,
    Pause upon thy orb sublime!
Bid this awful moment stay,
    Bind it on the brow of time!
While Mona's trembling echoes sigh
To strains that thrill when heroes die!

The British Museum possesses "The lyrical part of the drama of Caractacus, etc., 1776"; but the fact that its "Caractacus, a dramatic poem . . . altered for theatrical representation," bears the date of imprint 1777, might lead to a belief that the whole play was actually not published before 1777. That the publication really took place simultaneously with the production, appears from the following advertisement in the London Chronicle, Dec. 7–10, 1776:

This Day was published, price 6d.
The lyrical part of the drama of Caractacus, as altered by the author, and as spoken and sung at the Theatre Royal, Covent Garden. The music by Dr. Arne.
Printed for R. Horsfield . . . and J. Dodsley . . . and sold by J. Wilkie . . . Where may be had, price 1s. 6d. the whole dramatic Poem, as altered by the Author.

Curiously enough, the dramatized version of "Caractacus" was not incorporated in Mason's collected works, which every library possesses in one edition or another. As the publications of 1776 are extremely rare, a comparison between the dramatic poem and the drama "Caractacus" would have been attended by unusual obstacles, but, fortunately, John Bell included in his most useful collection "The British Theatre," in v. 31 (London, Printed for George Cawthorn 1796. front., 106 p.), not the dramatic poem, but the five-act drama, though it is still called "Caractacus. A dramatic Poem. Adapted for theatrical Representation, as performed at the Theatre-Royal, Covent Garden . . ." The speaking characters have remained the same as in the original poem, but we now notice

Persons of the Chorus

Modred, the Chief Druid. . . .Mr. Aickin
Mador, the Chief Bard. . . . . Mr. Hull
Second Bard . . . . Mr. Leoni
Third Bard . . . . Mrs. Kennedy
Fourth Bard . . . . Mr. Reinhold

Scene, the consecrated Grove in the Island of Mona, now Anglesea.

Those parts of the Odes which are distinguished by *double* inverted commas are meant to be performed musically; the rest to be recited by the Chief Bard. The parts omitted in the Representation are distinguished by *single* inverted commas only.

Since Modred and Mador appear among "the persons of the Chorus," it might be surmised that they are singing characters. Such is not the case. Both are speaking characters; indeed, Modred has become one of the main constituents of the plot. The music is entrusted entirely to a Chorus, which still occasionally has a collective voice in the proceedings, and to the second, third and fourth bards as soloists. Mason's main difficulty in adapting "Caractacus" for the stage had not been the breaking up of the monologues and dialogues of Caractacus, Evelina, etc., into acts and scenes, which was easy enough, but to vitalize for theatrical purpose his "Chorus" and "Semichorus," modeled, though poorly enough, after the "ancient Greek tragedy." Genest quite correctly summed up the difference between the dramatic poem of 1759 and the play of 1776 by saying:

Modred spoke a great deal of what in the first edition is attributed to the Chorus.

To my knowledge, Arne's actual coöperation with Mason has not heretofore been the subject of an article, and it will therefore be interesting to see just to what extent and in what manner Arne was called upon to exercise his powers as composer. That incidentally the following remarks will strengthen the object of this essay, goes, of course, without saying.

Repeatedly the direction "Symphony" is printed, but never except in scenes when the "Persons of the Chorus" appear and only at the end of the play was Arne invited to employ an independent piece of music, where he fur-

nished "A Dead March: during which Caractacus, Evelina
and Elidurus are led off by Romans." Nor did the
Chorus, though present in almost every scene, assume other
functions than those of a silent mob, except in the six
scenes planned entirely or in part for musical treatment.
In these scenes Modred or Mador, or both, speak more
or less, whereas the three other Bards sing Airs, and the
generally silent mob joins in choruses. Of ensembles
there are only two, a "Duet by the second and third Bard"
("Welcome, welcome, gentle train") scene 6, act I, and a
trio of Bards second, third and fourth ("Radiant Ruler:
hear us call") in scene 6, act V. Thus, Arne's collaboration was neither very extensive nor difficult. On the whole,
it must be said, this dramatized version of "Caractacus,"
far from being modeled after the Greek drama, is a strange
and hybrid mixture of spoken drama and opera.

Quotations from three of the six musical scenes will
render this perfectly clear, if the note following the
"Persons of the Chorus" be kept in mind—that the parts
distinguished by double inverted commas were to be "performed musically," the rest to be "recited." I select first
the fourth scene from the first act.

The Chorus, preceded by Modred, the chief Druid,
descend to a solemn Symphony.

Modred

Sleep and silence reign around;
  Not a night breeze wakes to blow;
Circle, sons, this holy ground;
  Circle close, in triple row:

Chorus

Druid, at thy dread command,
When thou wav'st thy potent wand,
See, we pace this holy ground
With solemn footsteps soft and slow,
While sleep and silence reign around,
And not a night breeze wakes to blow.

Modred

'Tis well.   And now, if mask'd in vapours drear,
Any malign or earth-born spirit dare
To hover round this sacred space,
Haste with light spells the murky foe to chace.

Chorus

Lift your boughs of vervain blue,
Dipt in cold September dew;
And dash the moisture, chaste and clear,
O'er the ground, and thro' the air.

Modred

Now the place is purg'd and pure.
                    (*A short Symphony*)
Brethren! say, for this high hour
Are the milk white steers prepared?
Whose necks the rude yoke never scar'd,
To the furrow yet unbroke?
For such must bleed beneath yon oak.

Chorus

Druid, these, in order meet,
Are all prepar'd.

Modred

                    But tell me yet,
Cadwall! did thy step profound
Dive into the cavern deep, etc., etc.

Second Bard

Druid, these, in order meet,
Are all prepar'd.

Modred

                    But tell me yet,
From the grot of charms and spells,
Where our matron sister dwells, etc., etc.

Third Bard

'Druid, these, in order meet,
Are all prepar'd.

Modred

Then all's complete.
(Symphony repeated)
And now let nine of the selected band,
Whose greener years befit such station best,
With wary circuit pace around the grove, etc., etc.

The Ode in scene 4, act IV, shows this disposition:

Mador

Hark!   *(Symphony behind the scenes)*
  Hark!   *(Symphony louder)*
    Hark!   *(Full symphony)*
Hark! heard ye not yon footsteps dread,
That shook the earth with thund'ring tread?
'Twas Death, etc., etc.
I mount, your Champion and your God, etc.

Full Chorus

'He mounts, our Champion and our God.
His proud steeds neigh beneath the thong;
Hark! to his wheels of brass, that rattle loud!
Hark! to his clarion shrill, that brays the woods
    among.
(Here one of the Druids blows the sacred trumpet.)

Mador

Fear not now the fever's fire,
Fear not now the death-bed groan, etc., etc.
(Four nine-line stanzas!)
Swiftly the soul of British flame, etc., etc.

Full Chorus

The godlike soul of British flame
Animates some kindred frame,

Swiftly to life and light triumphant flies,
Exults again in martial ecstasies,
Again for freedom fights, again for freedom dies!

While this is practically a Chorus Ode, the Ode in scene
4, act II (after a monologue by Modred) is one for the
soloists only.

Air

Second Bard

Hail! thou harp of Phrygian frame!
In years of yore that Camber bore
From Troy's sepulchral flame:
With ancient Brute, to Britain's shore
The mighty minstrel came.

Recitative Accompanied

Fourth Bard

Sublime upon thy burnish'd prow,
He bade thy manly words to flow:

Air

Britain heard the descant bold,
She flung her white arms o'er the sea;
Proud in her leafy bosom to enfold
The freight of harmony.

Mador

Mute 'till then was ev'ry plain,
Save where the flood o'er mountains rude
Tumbled his tide amain; etc., etc.

Second Bard

Change! my harp, oh change thy measures,
Cull, from thy mellifluous treasures
    Notes that steal on even feet,
Ever slow, yet never pausing,
    Mixt with many a warble sweet,
In a ling'ring cadence closing.

Mador

Now the pleas'd pow'r sinks gently down the skies,
And seals with hand of down the Druids' slumb'ring
        eyes, etc., etc.

After this long monologue, which is interrupted three
times by a "symphony," the Third Bard sings:

Wake, my lire! thy softest numbers,
Such as nurse ecstatic slumbers,
Sweet as tranquil virtue feels
When the toil of life is ending,
While from the earth the spirit steals
And on new-born plumes ascending,
Hastens to lave in the bright fount of day,
Till Destiny prepare a shrine of purer clay.

Modred (waking, speaks). It may not be. Avaunt,
        terrific axe! etc., etc.

It will be admitted that the construction of such simple
scenes did not even require considerable constructive technical skill, much less involve the solution of difficult
esthetic problems such as really might induce once in fifty
years an experienced composer to put on paper such elaborate instructions as are found in the anonymous "Caractacus" score. Be this as it may, this much is clear, if the
anonymous "Caractacus" was by Arne and was used at
Covent Garden on December 6, 1776, it must agree absolutely with the "libretto" and its demands.

Accordingly, I now return to the anonymous (corrected)
"Caractacus" score. It so happens that I open the score
at the end, where one expects to find the "Dead March"
called for by the libretto. Instead, one finds a four-part
chorus without even an instrumental postlude! We turn
to the first of the musical scenes quoted above, and the eye
is greeted by this:

No. 2.

Grave.

Sleep and si - lence reign around Not a night breeze wakes to blow.

Cir - cle, sons, this ho - ly ground. Cir - cle close in trip - le row.

No. 3.   *Andante.*   I.   II.

1st.
Violins.
2d.

Tenor.

Harp in unisono with the upper parts.

Bases.

Grave.

Druid, at thy dread command, When thou wav'st thy potent wand,

See, we pace this holy ground With solemn footsteps soft and slow, While

sleep and si-lence reign a-round. And not a night breeze wakes to blow.

'Tis well!   And now,   if mask'd in   va-pours drear,

A - ny ma-lign   or earth-born spi - rit dare   To ho - ver round this

con - se - cra- ted space, Haste with light spells the murky foe to chace.

No. 6.   *Andantino.*   *Usual pitch.*

                                                               Snowdon

Bases and   *Tutti piano.*   *Diminuendo.*
Organ in
unison with
them.

mark

          Piano.   *Crescendo un poco.*

                              'Tis ma - gic', hour!

     Diminuendo.   *Piano.*

     Crescendo un poco.

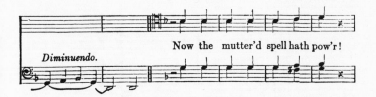

and so forth. The "solemn symphony" of the libretto indeed opens the scene, and the choruses are in their proper places, but note the discrepancy between Modred's lines in the libretto and in the score. There they are "recited," here they are "performed musically"; in fact, repeatedly in the course of the score Modred *sings,* though his part in the libretto is plainly a speaking part. Still, Arne may have had a special dispensation from the poet to treat music thus as the handmaid to poetry. I therefore proceed to the second scene quoted, the Ode in scene 4, act II. After twenty-five bars of preluding by the harp the *chorus* falls in with

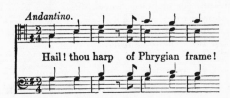

and after a short instrumental interlude the *chorus* continues with

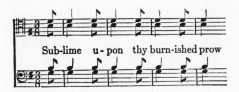

and the *chorus* still continues with

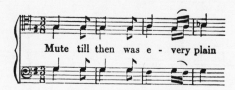

Mute till then was e - very plain

Such discrepancies cannot be explained away by any argument of musical expediency. Mador is supposed to *speak* the words "Mute 'till then was ev'ry plain," and here they appear in a four-part chorus which also comprises the texts which in the libretto distinctly figure as "Airs" for two different soloists, one, moreover, preceded by a "Recitative accompanied." And that there be no misunderstanding of the anonymous Caractacus composer in this connection, I again quote from p. 3 of his General Instructions:

The Voices for which the above Music is composed are Base and Tenor; either single, in Unison, or in parts: it is single only in the Arch-Druid's musical part, in the answers of Cadwall and Brennus, and in the words, "Mona on Snowdon calls," to be pronounced by one of the Chorus: The rest is sometimes in Unison, sometimes in two, three, or four parts; all equally intended for the whole Chorus.

If we finally compare the Ode in scene 4, act IV, with the music of No. 29 in the score, the discrepancies crowd each other so, that one does not know where to begin. The Ode is supposed to begin with a "Symphony *behind the Scenes,*" becoming louder until we have a "full" symphony. In the score, "Clarinets, Violins, Viola, Bassoons, Bases and Serpent" start in "tutti forte" and remain so without modification, and this notwithstanding the fact that the composer was elsewhere profuse in the demand for "piano," "forte," "un poco forte," "diminuendo," "crescendo un poco," "fortissimo," "tutti diminuendo al pianissimo," and other such dynamic shadings—indeed, so profuse, that the score might well attract the attention of a historian of musical dynamics. Furthermore, Mador's spoken words are again sung in four-part chorus, which makes it utterly impossible for a full chorus, as demanded by the libretto, to take up his words as a chorus refrain; and finally, where *one* of the Druids is to blow the sacred trumpet, the clarinets, trumpets and bassoons perform this pleasant duty!

A comparison of the play with the score still further strengthens the inevitable conclusion: The *music of this anonymous "Caractacus" cannot possibly have been used for the production of Mason's play at Covent Garden on December 6, 1776, and after.* Consequently, the score cannot possibly be *identical with Arne's score as then played and sung.*

Only one possibility remains, in view of the claim that this anonymous "Caractacus" is by Arne and that it was published in 1775: perhaps Arne composed the score as published, but utterly revised it for theatrical production. I shall now proceed to show how very improbable such a possibility is. In the first place, why such a futile and useless attempt at mystery at the end of a distinguished career?—futile and useless, because a composer of Arne's talent and individuality could not, for any length of time, have hidden his authorship. And what sense would there have been in keeping "Caractacus" anonymous in view of the fact that the music for Mason's pendant to this work, "Elfrida," had been published with Arne's name as composer! Furthermore, the anonymous author ends his dedication with the phrase "with the respect due to your age & character." Even a broad-minded Catholic might avail himself of a polite reference to the clerical "character" of the Protestant clergyman Mason, but I doubt very much that Arne (1710–1778) would address a phrase like "with due respect due to your age" to Mason (1724–1797), who was by fourteen years his junior and in 1775 surely was not yet an aged man. It stands to reason that the phrase would more likely have been addressed by a comparatively young man to Mason in his old age. Moreover, the anonymous author, on p. 3 of his instructions, says in italics: "If this should ever be performed." What an absurd doubt in the mind of a man of Arne's calibre and fame! Granted that towards the end of his career his successes became fewer, Arne never found much difficulty in obtaining performances, and he surely never was *persona non grata* to the extent of being justified in using such an ominous "if."

All this is circumstantial, external evidence against Arne's authorship. We have more direct internal evidence in the fact that the composer of "Artaxerxes," of "Rule Britannia," of the "As you like it" music, of so many charming songs and pieces, cannot possibly have composed such poor music as has been quoted above, even in his weakest moments. Imagine the man who, almost alone of English composers of that age, withstood the aggression of Händel's hypnotizing influence, guilty of such dry, stiff and uninspired stuff, which is by no means the worst in the anonymous "Caractacus." Dr. Cummings has recently told us (in the "Sammelbände") that Arne, too, rarely employed the full orchestra of his time and preferred unconventional instrumental combinations, with an apparent predilection for the horns; but imagine Arne experimenting, absolutely without horns, so childishly and unskillfully with the bassoon and harp, etc., as was shown above of the composer of the anonymous "Caractacus."

If this score cannot possibly be Arne's work, what remains of the tradition? The unsupported statement that the score was published in 1775! Just when this date was introduced into historical literature, I am unable to say. At any rate, it does not yet appear in the Arne article by Mr. William H. Husk in the first edition of Grove, 1879. On the other hand, Busby, whose "Anecdotes" (1825) the "National Biography" enumerates among the sources for Arne's life, distinctly says (v. 2,

p. 62) that the "music of Caractacus was never printed."
No modern historian will rely blindly on statements by
Busby, but his denial of publication becomes significant
in this connection.   I may add that I have looked in vain
for contemporary evidence for the date 1775 in the form of
newspaper advertisements in the London Daily Advertiser
and in the London Chronicle.

The absence of documentary evidence of any kind will
force us to rely on conjecture, if we wish to date the anonymous "Caractacus."   One point is clear: The text of the
score, as comparison will prove, contains nothing—slight
verbal changes excepted—that does not appear in the dramatized version; whereas it contains lines which will not
be found in Mason's "Caractacus" as originally published.
Furthermore, the instructions on pp. 1–2 of the "General
Instructions" on how "to regulate the steps of the Druids
circling the holy ground," the reference on p. 3 to
"Modred's speech" (also not mentioned at all in the original version), and the reference on p. 4 to "the fourth
Scene of the Second Act," leave no doubt that our author,
no matter how unskillful he was and how readily he dis-
obeyed the libretto (four-part choruses, when Airs should
have come from his pen!), composed his music with the
dramatized version of the poem at hand.   This dramatized
version did not appear in print until December, 1776.
Consequently, if our anonymous published, and (let us
assume) composed this score in 1775, he cannot have done
so without having had access to or a copy of Mason's
manuscript in 1775 at the latest.   This, however, is
practically impossible, for the simple reason that, as we
have seen, Mason, when corresponding with the Covent
Garden manager about the performance of his "Caractacus," had not yet put the finishing touches to the manuscript, and he is not known by any of his biographers to
have undertaken the dramatization of his "dramatic poem"
before 1776.   And now the watermarks 1794, 1796, 1797
in the paper of the score and its supplements which caused

me to investigate this whole matter of "Caractacus," assume the importance of clews in a positive and safe direction! In the absence of any evidence for an earlier date, the only plausible explanation of these watermarks would be, that the score was published not earlier than 1794, and two of the supplements not earlier than 1796. That the third supplement was published not later than about April 7, 1797, may be surmised from the fact that Mason died on this day and that the author of the anonymous "Caractacus" must naturally have believed Mason to be still alive when he dedicated to him that peculiar revised and annotated copy of his work which is now in the Library of Congress.

In closing, I may be permitted to quote a few lines of a letter which I received, after completion of this article, from Mr. Squire under date of October 17, 1910, in answer to my request for information on the date 1775. Just having recovered from a severe operation, Mr. Squire was unable to comply with my request, but he wrote:

> Cummings had already drawn my attention to the probability that the anonymous music was not Arne's, but he did not know about the watermarks, which are certainly strong evidence against Arne's authorship. The music, too, seems hardly possible by him—but whose can it be!

Well, I think that the employment of the organ and the serpent point in the direction of some English organist, whose skill, experience and talent as a composer did not measure up to his ambition, his interest in esthetics, and his unbalanced doctrine of music as the handmaid to poetry.

A DESCRIPTION OF ALESSANDRO STRIGGIO AND FRANCESCO CORTECCIA'S INTERMEDI "PSYCHE AND AMOR," 1565

(The "Musical Antiquary," October, 1911)

THE origin of opera remained an open problem for many years, because historical attention was concentrated too exclusively on the experiments of Count Bardi's Neo-Hellenic laboratory. Gradually historians persuaded themselves that the whole chromatic movement, the long established practice of interspersing plays with music, the revival of lyric monody, the well-developed *intermedi,* the various ballet entertainments, and so forth, might have an evolutional bearing on the origin of opera. More and more information of this kind accumulated, and an avalanche of essays was heaped on us when Angelo Solerti, coming from literary history, diverted part of his energy into the channels of musical history. This whole movement may be summed up in the paradoxical title which Romain Rolland gave to a brilliant essay in his *Musiciens d'autrefois* (1909): 'L'Opéra avant l'opéra.' There is some danger at the present time that we may be led to an underestimation of the efforts of the Florentine Camerata. They sought Greek drama and found opera. And whether or not they, consciously or unconsciously, utilized the traditional or progressive elements of their time, no historical subtleties will ever succeed in proving that opera really existed before the Florentine Camerata stumbled on it. All the undercurrents of their time might have been converging towards opera, yet of themselves they would not have led to opera without the new and distinguishing element of dramatic musical speech.

If that be clearly kept in mind, then a conclusion which Solerti reached in his essay "Precedenti del melodramma" (*R. M. It.,* 1903, p. 470) still retains its proper significance: "dalla tragedia, dalla favola pastorale e dagli intermedi proviene l'opera seria; dalla commedia dell'arte l'opera buffa; dalle mascherate e dagli intermedi le veglie e i balletti."

It will be noticed that here the *intermedio* contributes to two kinds of theatrical performances with music, but it will also be noticed that one kind is not mentioned: the pantomime. Perhaps Solerti, following our rather loose terminology in such matters, includes pantomime in ballet, but, as a matter of historical and esthetic fact, ballet and pantomime are no more synonymous than are opera and ballet. True, from the beginning the various species of musical theatrical performances had certain features in common, but it will not do to throw them all into a common historical melting-pot. An opera may contain a ballet, and a ballet operatic arias; still, the lines of distinction are easily discernible. On the other hand, I admit, the distinction between a ballet and a pantomime is difficult of definition for us moderns, but it exists, as everybody will testify who has waded through thousands of old-time librettos. A pantomime may contain a good deal of dancing and a good deal of singing (the "speaking pantomime"), and still the pantomime, if representative of its genre, is not a ballet, much less an opera. It may be likened, notwithstanding such ingredients, to living pictures, moving or not, the appreciation and understanding of which depend on ready symbolical association and ready solution of allegorical puzzles. Exactly because the ballet, from mere danced symbolical action, developed almost into a danced pantomime, it becomes difficult to keep the two apart for historical purposes.

We have been so much fascinated by the history of

opera, that we have quite overlooked the possibilities of evolutional histories of the other genres, the ballet and the pantomime. Existing books notwithstanding, they remain to be written, and it is imperative also for problems connected with the history of opera that they be written soon with acumen and patient research: particularly a history of musical pantomime during the latter part of the sixteenth century. Not until then, perhaps, will the obscure points in the origin of opera proper quite disappear, so far, at least, as the relationship between the *intermedi* and the first opera is concerned. The first operas dealt, like most of the *intermedi,* with mythological subjects, but they dealt with them as plays and as such bore their message to the audience through the words of the libretto and a more or less developed psychological plot. While a familiarity with Greek mythology was helpful for the appreciation of the first operas and increased their enjoyment, it was, strictly speaking, not necessary. The *intermedi,* on the other hand, dealt with mythological episodes not as vehicles for dramas, but for allegories. Their puzzles were not dramatic. In other words, for a ready understanding of the innumerable and often involved allegorical and external symbolical allusions to Greek mythology in the *intermedi* an intimate familiarity with the details of Greek mythology was absolutely indispensable—a familiarity, indeed, which would be quite beyond our mixed modern audiences, but for which the aristocratic audiences of the Renaissance period were abundantly trained.

To come to the real point of these introductory remarks, the *intermedi* were pantomimes. While they had some features in common with the first operas and perhaps even affected their origin, their real importance, beyond their own historical significance, attaches not so much to the history of opera as to that of pantomime. Indeed, it looks to me as if Caccini's *Il Rapimento di Cefalo* was much more closely related to the *intermedi* than his or

Peri's *Euridice* or their respective settings of *Dafne*. This is, of course, a thesis, not necessarily a new thesis, yet one not generally accepted and not acceptable until a discriminating, exhaustive history of Renaissance panto-mime has proved its correctness.

However, whether this thesis be correct or not, the problem of the origin of opera will not find a perfect solution until, on the basis of literary history, the musical history of the *intermedi* has advanced far beyond its present, more statistical and chronological than evolutional stage. Solerti and others have repeatedly referred to Ubaldo Angeli's *Notizie per la storia del Teatro a Firenze nel secolo XVI, specialmente circa gli intermezzi* (Modena, 1891), in which, with one exception, all important *intermedi* down to 1569 are mentioned. Unfortunately, this book has not been accessible to me, but if it enumerates not less than fifty works before 1569, and if we consider that the genre continued to flourish for decades, surely Angeli's book offers food for thought to us musical historians. The conclusion is inevitable—and how inevitable even a rapid glance into Creizenach's history of the drama will prove—that the *intermedio* with its musical ingredients was a fully developed form of art, long before opera came into existence. That it was largely pantomimical, allegorical, and that it was undermining the interest in drama, for this we have abundant esthetic contemporary testimony. It is not surprising that reference is made in recent historical literature to this encroachment upon comedy and tragedy, and a quotation of the poet Antonio Francesco Grazzini's (called *Il Lasca*) madrigal, "La Commedia che si duol degli Intermezzi," is made to do useful service, but it is amazing how very little comparative research has been centered on the *intermedio* for purposes of musical history. Certainly, only such comparative research can fully establish the extent and scope of the participation of musical art in these entertainments.

In what the *intermedio* technique of a Corteccia or a
Striggio consisted cannot surely be fully revealed except
by exhaustive comparison. In other words, a history of
the *musical form* of the *intermedio* is badly needed, a
history which would treat methodically of monody as
employed therein, of the part the chorus played, of how
solo voices and chorus alternated or were combined, how
their numerical proportions were balanced, how instrumental music was employed either for purely instrumental purposes or for those of accompaniment, how this
accompaniment differed if used for solo voices or for
ensemble scenes, how the composers utilized their orchestral resources for purposes of variety, of color, of deliberate grouping and differentiation. That much information
of this kind is to be found in our books, I know very well,
but it is more or less disconnected, not methodical, and
it is based principally on the later *intermedi,* particularly
Malvezzi's and others' celebrated *intermedi* of 1589 at
Florence, published 1591. And even they were not pene-
tratingly treated before Goldschmidt in his splendid essays
on early opera brought some analytical-synthetic order out
of chaos. For the earlier period, we have practically not
got beyond Kiesewetter, who in his *Schicksale und Be-
schaffenheit des weltlichen Gesanges* (1841) dealt in a
cursory way with the *intermedi* composed in 1539 by
Corteccia, Festa and others for the marriage of Cosimo de'
Medici and Leonora of Toledo, those composed (1565)
by Corteccia and Striggio for the marriage of Francesco
de' Medici and Giovanna of Austria, and finally those of
1589. Not even Rolland, in his book on opera before
Lully and Scarlatti, considered it worth while to let an
investigation of his own supersede that of Kiesewetter.
Indeed, if we add Leichtentritt's translation, in his revised
edition of Ambros's fourth volume (1909), of Baldinucci's
description of the festivities of 1569 (correctly as on p.
245, not 1565, as incorrectly on p. 265) with Striggio's

unfortunately lost *intermedio* music for the comedy of
L' amico fido, we have nearly reached the end of accessible
historical resources.

It may be that not many descriptions of the numerous
intermedio entertainments exist which would enlighten us
musical historians as to the part music played, thereby
consoling us somewhat for the loss of most of the music;
but that would be the very reason why the few should be
made fully available. Of what earthly use, for instance,
can it have been to those who followed Kiesewetter without retracing his steps, that he, in commenting on the (first
only of the) *intermedi* of 1565, naïvely gives this inventory:

Die Instrumente, welche verschiedentlich zur Begleitung der
Gesänge, oder zu Zwischenspielen verwendet wurden, sind bei
jeder Nummer genannt. Sie waren schon damals sehr zahlreich:
2 Gravicembali, 4 violoni, 1 leuto mezzano, 1 cornetto muto (?),
4 Tromboni, 2 Flauti diritti, 4 Traversi, 1 Leuto grosso, 1 Sotto
Basso di Viola, 1 Sopran di Viola, 4 Leuti, 1 Viola d'arco, 1
Lirone, 1 Traverso Contralto, 1 Flauto grande Tenore, 1 Trombone Basso, 5 Storte, 1 Stortina, 2 Cornetti ordinarii, 1 Cornetto
grosso, 1 Dolzaina, 1 Lira, 1 Ribecchino, 2 Tamburi.

Probably because of Kiesewetter's hurried and slight-
ing comment, later historians did not consider it worth
while to bestow attention on the *intermedi* of 1565 which
drew their inspiration from Apuleius's tale of Cupid and
Psyche, yet their published description turns out to be,
at least musically, one of the most instructive we possess.
The complete reprint as it follows here will surely further
a more correct understanding of the art-form of the *intermedio* in all its aspects, and, if nothing else, at least prove
that we may yet hope to rediscover the music, generally
considered not published, since the remark on p. 18 of the
Description makes it clear that Corteccia's and Striggio's
music was in press in 1565. Kiesewetter quoted Giunti's
fourth [*sic*] edition, of 1566, entitled:

Descrizione dell'Apparato della Commedia ed Intermedii d'essa, fatta in Firenze il Giorno di S. Stefano l'anno 1565.

The copy from which I quote is that printed with and attached to the Library of Congress copy of

La Cofanaria. Commedia di Francesco d'Ambra. Con gl'Intermedij di Giovambattista Cini. Recitata nelle Nozze del Illustrissimo S. Principe Don Francesco de' Medici, & della Sereniss. Regina Giouanna d'Austria. Di nvovo ristampata. In Firenze, per Filippo Givnti. M D XCIII.[1]

The comedy is evidently a reprint of the original edition, since Alessandro Ceccherelli's prefatory dedication with its reference to the "eccellente Musica" is still dated "Di Firenze il dì 15. di Gennaio 1565"; but that the *Descrizione de Gl' Intermedii* as edited by Il Lasca—the same Il Lasca who had a playwright's grievance against the whole genre—goes far beyond the description originally published, will immediately become clear.

[1] This is the same edition which G. Giannini used for his quotations (*Propugnatore*, 1893, pp. 251-3) from the *Descrizione*, in his essay *Origini del dramma musicale*. It is a splendid essay, but to my way of thinking Giannini lays too much stress on the origin of opera from the *intermedio*. Besides the *Descrizione dell' Apparato*, Il Lasca issued a *Descrizione degl'Intermedii* in 1566, which is practically identical with the edition of 1593: but its text is rather better, and Il Lasca's Dedication is different. The text of 1593 has, however, been consistently retained here. With a slightly different orthography it may also be found in Vol. V of "Il Teatro Comico Fiorentino," 1750, where it follows the reprint of "La Cofanaria." In "The Musical Antiquary" I reprinted the original Italian without a translation. Here I have dispensed with the original in favor of a translation by Dr. Theodore Baker. The Arabic figures refer to the pages of the original to facilitate comparison.

1

DESCRIPTION/ OF THE INTERMEDII/
REPRESENTED/ WITH THE COMEDY/

At the Nuptials of His Most Illustrious and Ex-/cellent Highness the Prince of/Florence, and of Siena.

IN FLORENCE,/
By Filippo Giunti./ mdxciii

3

TO HIS MOST ILLUSTRIOUS,/AND EXCELLENT/
HIGHNESS D. FRANCESCO/ MEDICI

Prince of Florence, and of Siena,/ AND TO THE MOST
SERENE, and noble Queen Giovanna of Austria/ my most
exalted Lieges.

The Intermedii which were produced with the Comedy at your
Most Regal Nuptials having been published in haste by other
persons and, consequently, with insufficient care, and based on
a simple description supplied to you before the representation by
the author at the instance of His Highness to promote His more
pleasurable appreciation of the same :—induced by Him and by
you to make up for the apparent lack of care, I have undertaken
to extend them considerably and to reduce them to the form
hereinafter to be seen. And to present them as something
belonging to and made for you. Grant them,/ therefore, a
gracious reception, inasmuch as they were prepared by the
Author with singular devotion, and are presented by me with
all reverence, in the hope that they may meet with your favour
in some small degree.

Your most humble and obedient servant,

Il Lasca.

5

ALL the Intermedii—which, for the sake of greater per-
spicuity, are not intermingled here with the Comedy—were
taken from the story of Cupid and Psyche, so pleasingly related
by Apuleius in his romance, "The Golden Ass"; and we proceeded by selecting the parts which appeared to be the leading
ones, and fitting them to the Comedy with all the skill at our
command, with the intention of making it appear as if that
which is enacted by the Gods in the fable of the Intermedii, is
likewise enacted—as it were, under constraint of a higher power
—by the mortals in the Comedy.

4

Accordingly, a brief space after the descent of the curtains which conceal from the eyes of the Spectators the Perspective of the concave Heavens of the opening scene, there is seen to appear a second, most ingeniously contrived Heaven wherefrom, little by little, a Cloud is perceived approaching, in which there is set with singular ingenuity a gilded & gem-encrusted Car, recognized as that of Venus, because it is seen to be drawn by two snow-white Swans, and in which, as Mistress and charioteer, is most majestically seated that loveliest of Goddesses, entirely nude, engarlanded with roses and immortelles and, reins in hand, adorned with the beautiful girdle called Cestus by the ancients.

In her train follow the three Graces, likewise recognizable by appearing wholly nude/ by their brilliantly blond tresses falling free over their shoulders, but still more by the manner in which they hold each other's hands.

And the four Horæ with wings in exact resemblance of butter-flies, distinguished according to the four seasons, as follows:

The first with flowers in her headdress and in her shoon, and with robes of changing colour in imitation of Spring blooms.

The second, Summer with her garland, and with shoon bedecked with lavender, and with a yellow robe betokening maturity of the grain.

The Third for Autumn, crowned and shod with apples, with ivy, and with vineleaves, and with a russet robe indicating similarly their maturity.

And the last for Winter with a Turquoise robe all beflecked with snowflakes, and also wearing shoon, and with tresses all behung with hailstones and icicles.

All these were to be seen as in the train of Venus, and as following the Car and seated in charmful grouping on the afore-mentioned cloud, the which, descending little by little, seemed to leave behind it in Heaven Jove, Juno, Saturn, Mars, Mercury, and the other Gods, from whose midst was nevertheless heard to issue a Harmony passing sweet, seemingly a thing divine rather than human, while the entire great, dark Hall was filled with the sweetest and most precious odours.

At the same time there was seen at one extremity of the perspective, as though walking on the earth, Cupid approaching/ with wings and quite nude as he is described by the Poets, in whose company were seen his four principal passions, as described, whence flow all the difficulties that so frequently dis-turb his Kingdom; as follows:

Hope, all clad in green, with a spray of flowers in her hair.

Fear, recognizable by the Hares in her headdress, and on her shoon, and by her pale robe.

Joy, in a robe of white and orange with a thousand other beautiful colours, and with a flowering branch of borage in her tresses.

And Sorrow, all in black, and with every symbol of grief, and weeping.

Of whom, in the guise of servants, Some bore the Bow, Others the Quiver, and the Arrows, Others the insidious Nets & Others the Torch, from which was seen issuing inextinguishable flame.

All these having come near to the car, which in the meantime had reached the ground, halted, while the Horæ and the Graces slowly descended from the Cloud and, gathering around Venus, who had risen to her feet and gracefully turned about, seconded her in singing the first two stanzas of the following ballatetta; The Horæ continually holding astrain the circumstanding garlands composed of thousands of divers flowerets; all which having been carried out, & all returned to their places, the Cloud, the Car, & the Swans were seen to return little by little into the Heavens whence they had arrived and which then closed in a moment without/ a vestige remaining to show where the Cloud and so many other things had entered or whither they had betaken themselves.

In the meantime Cupid, crossing the Stage with his companions, who seconded him in a sort, proceeded to the last stanza of the Ballata, the while he let fly numerous arrows into the crowd of onlookers, whence it might be gathered that the Lovers, moved thereby to the following discourses, originated the ensuing Comedy.

VENUS

To me, so quite neglected and alone,
> No longer vows nor altars now are raised,
> But unto Psyche all devoted,
> To her are given—she usurps them.
So if thou e'er didst love me, or still love me,
> Take up thine arms, my son,
> And all this rabble fire
> With vilest love of mortal man.

CUPID

Then, Mother, let us go: who gives me the Bow,
> The arrows who? that I,
> With courage mounting high,
> All hearts may conquer, bind, pierce, & inflame.

The first Act being finished—following, as will always be the case, the introductory fable—there is seen issuing, from one of the four passageways left between the scenes for the use of the actors, a tiny Cupid gracefully bearing in one arm the counterfeit presentment of a swan, whereto is most skillfully attached a bass viol of no great size, from which latter, with a willow wand held in the other hand and concealing the Bow fixed beneath it, he, as it were with playful art, drew sweet sounds.

When he had reached his predetermined station, there were seen approaching by the four passageways, and at the same time, the following:

Zephyr, the wind of love, all in blue, and recognizable by his wings, and his flower-crowned youthful head and smiling countenance, and by his robe and shoon all woven with Flowers, and with his lap full of the same, tossing them in great profusion among the bystanders.

And Musick, likewise readily to be recognized by the harmonic band which she wore on her head, and by her rich robe all bestrewn with her various instruments, and with divers charts whereon were inscribed all the notes and all the measures of the same, and by the large and handsome bass Lyre, on which she played while advancing.

From the other two passageways appeared, on the one hand, Pleasure, and on the other, Laughter, in the guise of two tiny Cupids.

Behind these, and ere they had arrived at their proper stations, there were seen to enter all at the same time / four more Cupids, who advanced playing on four profusely ornamented lutes; and after them four others, two with apples in their hands and disporting together, and two who with bows and arrows were shooting at each other with a certain affectionate grace.

All these, now formed into a choir, most sweetly sang and played the following madrigal:

> Oh, we have seen the new, sublime miracle,
> But who doth live, that doth believe on it?
> That Cupid, taking arms 'gainst love,
> Should fall a victim to himself, and Psyche?
> Therefore to Psyche be awarded
> The palm for loveliness and worth
> By every other beauty: withal that from the fear
> Her Prisoner inspires, she still is grieving.
> But let us follow on the way we started:

Come, Pleasure, come too, Laughter,
Come, O sweet Harmony of Paradise,
Let us allay the torments that she feels
With strains of musick soft, that soothes and heals.

While Cupid is bent on another task, namely, the inflaming
of human hearts, it appears at the end of the second Act as
though the floor of the stage were rising up into seven small
Hillocks; whence were seen to issue gradually, at first seven,
and then seven other Deceptions. These were readily to be
recognized as such, because every one / wore as a headdress, each
in a different and graceful attitude, a Wolf, forming indeed a
pleasing and diverting spectacle for the audience; having,
furthermore, their busts all mottled and spotted in the sem-
blance of Leopards, & the rest of the body, and the legs and
tails in the guise of serpents. Some held in their hands Nets,
Others Fishhooks, & Others having Paws with Claws, beneath
all of which were concealed small Cornets. And when those
who had sung at first, had then sung and played the following
Madrigal, they took their most orderly departure by the four
passageways on the Stage.

If Cupid, bound and vanquished, has forgot
His Bow, and blazing torch,
A fresh desire to mystify his Mother
Now spurs him; and if Psyche plays him false,
And if the impious and faithless pair
Of envious sisters, fraud and foul deceit,
Think only this: Who is there in the World
To-day, who would withhold from Us the Kingdom?
Therefore let all the wise enjoy the fruits
Of fraud; and if some other hope they cherish,
Soon indeed that hope shall perish.

Offense resulting from the Deceptions, and dissensions with
a thousand other ills from the offense, after the third Act, instead of the seven Hillocks which had been seen to appear
upon the Stage in the second Intermedio, / now engulphed as it
were in the Ground, there came to view seven small Craters,
whence issued at first a dark smoke, followed gradually by
Discord, symbol in hand, as the leader, recognized by her
arms, and motley and disordered raiment, and disheveled locks.
Anger, likewise recognizable, besides by her arms, by shoon
in the guise of paws, and by a Bear's head in place of a helmet,
from out of which issued smoke and flame.

And Cruelty with a scythe in her hand, known by her helmet in the shape of a Tiger's head, and by shoon resembling the feet of a Crocodile.

And Rapine with Pruning-hook in hand, and with the rapacious Bird on her helmet, and with feet like Eagle's claws.

And Vendetta, with a bloodstained cornet in hand, with shoon and helmet all fashioned of Vipers.

And two Anthropophagi, or Laestrygones, whichever one may please to name them, who, blowing two trombones in the form of ordinary trumpets, seemed as though they would excite the spectators to combat.

Each one of whom was placed between two Furies provided with Drums having iron drumsticks, and with divers arms, beneath the which were hidden divers instruments.

The aforesaid Furies were identified by the wounds wherewith their entire bodies were covered, out of which it seemed as if flames of fire were issuing, by the snakes wherewith they were engirdled, and by the broken chains hanging from their legs / and arms, and by the fire issuing from their headgear:— all of whom together sang and played the following Madrigal while executing, in the excitement of combattants, a new and extravagant Moresca, at the end of which, rushing hither and thither across the stage as if in confusion, they fled in simulated terror from the gaze of the spectators.

Flee in blind haste, ye vile
Deceptions; in the World to-day are known
Anger alone, and Madness; ye bold and tricksy sprites,
Approach to prove your valour,
For as, if by this light Love now doth Languish,
We are not willed that theirs shall be the Kingdom.
Up, then! Let every dauntless heart
Beat high: and let our warlike song
Be War, war! and our only cry be Arms, arms!

In sequel to the Fourth Act the wretched Psyche, given over to desperation, provides the theme for the fifth Intermedio; she is seen—after having been sent by Venus, as the fable hath it, to the Infernal Proserpine—approaching by one of the passageways in deepest dejection, accompanied by malign Jealousy all pallid and doleful, recognizable like the others who follow by her four heads and her Turquoise robe all bestrewn with eyes, and ears.

By Envy, likewise known by the Snakes which she is devouring.

By Brooding, or Care, or Solicitude, however/ one may choose
to call her, known by the Raven which she wears on her head,
and by the Vulture preying on her vitals.

And by Scorn, or Disdain (to apply the feminine name[1]),
who reveals her identity by the Owl she wears on her head,
and by her ill made, ill fitting and disordered raiment.

Now, when these four, while beating her and urging her on,
were arrived at the intended spot, the Earth suddenly opened
with fire and smoke, wherefrom were marvelously seen to
appear four Serpents, the which they seized, however they
sought to prevent, and, lashing them right and left with the
thorny rods they held in their hands, under which were hidden
four little bows, they finally seemed to disappear into the en-
sanguined gorge, and immediately there was heard issuing from
the interiors (Psyche singing the ensuing Madrigal) a mourn-
ful, yet wondrous suave and sweet harmony, for that within the
Serpents there had been set with singular ingenuity four bass
Viols, & she then sang, with such sweetness that one saw the
tears drawn from the eyes of more than one.

When this was ended, each one taking her serpent on her
shoulder, there was seen—to the no small affright of the watching ladies—a great opening in the ground, whence issued smoke
and a vast and continuous flame; & in a moment one beheld
the three heads and heard the fearsome baying of the infernal
cerberus, to whom Psyche is seen to toss one of the/ two cakes
she held in her hand; and soon thereafter there is seen to
appear, with divers Monsters, Charon with his Skiff, into which
the despairful Psyche, entering, was borne offensive and dis-
pleasurable company by her four aforesaid harassers.

> Fled is my every hope,
> And fled nevermore to return:
> Only thou, who destroyest
> All my peace: who sendest to remain
> Envy, Jealousy, Care, and Scorn,
> With me within the dim Inferno,
> Where lives eternally my torment sore.

The entire sixth and last Intermedio was joyous; for when
the Comedy was finished, there was seen to rise all at once out
of the flooring of the stage a small, verdant Mount all adorned
with Laurels and divers flowers, the which, bearing on its
summit the winged Horse Pegasus, was directly perceived to
be Mount Helicon, whence little by little was seen descending

[1] In Italian.—ED.

that charmful band, already described, of Cupids, and Zephyr,
and Music, and Cupid, and Psyche held by the hand and all
joyous and in festal mood, now that she had returned safe from
the Inferno, and through the intercession of Jove, moved by the
prayers of her Husband, Cupid, had won pardon and grace from
the offended Venus, as may be read more in detail in the fable,
and with these was Pan, and nine other Satyrs with divers
Pastoral instruments in their hands, under which various
other musical instruments were concealed,/ all of whom, descending from the aforesaid Mount, conducted with them
Hymen, The God of Nuptials, and playing and singing in his
praise, as in the following canzonets, executing during the
second a new & most vivacious dance, they formed a graceful
close to the festival.

> From beautiful Mount Helicon
>   Behold god Hymen, who descends
>   And straightway lights the torch, and crowns himself.
> With Marjoram he crowns himself,
>   Odorous and sweet,
>   And all gray care from Earth he banishes.
> So, Psyche, banish thou, too,
>   Thy keen and cruel sorrow,
>   Give joy alone a welcome in thy breast.
> Cupid within his breast
>   Then gives thee happy refuge,
>   Consoles thee with a thousand sweet attentions.
> No less may Jove console thee
>   For thy past weeping,
>   But welcome thee to Heaven with smiles and songs.

Canzonet the Second

> Hymen therefore calls to one and all:
>   Hymen, full of charm and fair bedight:
>   Ah, how glad and fair a day
>   Hymen bringeth back with thee.
> Hymen heareth for his goddess,
>   For his very soul, Giovanna,
>   How from either bank of broad Rhine
>   Sounds sweet musick on and on.
>   And no less on sparkling Arno
>   For th' illustrious, well-belovèd,
>   Kind Francesco, all are thronging
>   There to sing the praise of Hymen.
> Hymen, etc.

> Gladsome Flora, happy Arno,
>   Humble Arno, kindly Flora:
>   Ah, what happier lot was ever
>   Seen of men, or ever heard of?
>   Fortunate and favoured country,
>   Land so near and dear to Heaven,
>   Unto whom so rare a blessing
>   From benignant Hymen floweth.
> Hymen, etc.

> Then bring Laurels, Palms & olives,
>   Crowns & Scepters now, and Kingdoms
>   For these twain thrice happy souls.
>   Thine be only Flora's portion,
>   May whate'er is vile, unworthy,
>   Hold aloof; may true Peace only,
>   And Delight, & Springtime flourish
>   Everlastingly within thee.
> Hymen, etc.

18   For the Satisfaction of curious Musicians, should these lucubrations fall into the hands of any such, we shall add that as the Hall, besides being marvelously beautiful, was of a singular magnitude and altitude, and perhaps the greatest of which we have knowledge to-day, it was necessary to make the Concerts of Musick very full, and therefore

The first, from which emanated that exceeding sweet harmony in the open Heavens, was formed

> By four double Gravicembalos
> By four Bowed Viols
> By two Trombones
> By two Tenor Flutes
> By one soft-toned Cornet (Corneto muto)
> By one Cross-flute
> And by two Lutes

Which, the Musick (now in press) being placed, as will be seen, with the most admirable discretion, allowed due space for the descent of the Car, and for the Horæ, and for the Graces, that betook themselves to their assigned stations.

The Musick for the first two stanzas of the Ballata of Venus was in eight parts: only sung on the stage by voices, and accompanied behind the scenes, a feat of singular difficulty, calling for ingenuity,

By two Gravicembalos
By four Bass Viols
By one Medium Lute (Leuto Mezano)
By one soft-toned Cornet
By one Trombone
And by two direct Flutes (Flauti diretti)

Then the last stanza of Cupid was likewise sung by voices
throughout in five parts, on the stage, and accompanied behind
the scenes
By two Gravicembalos
By one large Lute
By one deep bass Viol adjoined to the parts
By one soprano Viol, also adjoined
By one Flute, similarly adjoined
By four Cross-flutes
And by one Trombone.

And this was in the first Intermedio.
The second was in four parts sung on the stage by four
voices, and played
By four Lutes
By one Bow-Viol
And by one bass Lyre
    And off-stage
By three Gravicembalos
By one large Lute
By one soprano Viol
By one alto Cross-flute
By one large Tenor Flute/
By one bass Trombone
And by one soft-toned Cornet, which played a Fifth addi-
    tional soprano part.

The third Intermedio was played in six parts and sung all on
the stage, viz.:
By five Serpents
By one soft-toned Cornet
And by eight voices, doubling the sopranos and basses.

The Musick of the Fourth was also similarly sung in six parts
and played throughout on the stage, doubling all the parts in
the voices, and adding thereto
Two Trombones
One tenor Oboe (una Dolzaina)

> Two ordinary Cornets
> One large Cornet
> And two Drums.

In the fifth, in five parts, one solo soprano voice was accompanied on the stage
> By four bass Viols
>   And behind the scenes
> By one bass Lyre
> And by four Trombones.

The last was in four parts *allegrissimo,* and most fully / quadrupling all the voices. And adding thereto
> Two soft-toned Cornets
> Two Trombones
> One tenor Oboe
> One small Serpent
> One bass Lyre
> One Lyre
> One small Ribec
> And two Lutes

Playing in the first Canzonetta, and all singing.

In the second, where they danced, the lines were sung by only eight voices, and the Lyre and bass Lyre played, but in the refrain, refreshing as it were the spirits of the auditors, all were heard joyously singing and playing together with a certain renewed delight.

The arrangement and the words of the Intermedii were by M(esser) Gio. Battista Cini, and they were staged under his supervision, as well as the Comedy, and all the rest appurtenant to the same.

The machinery for drawing aside the Heavens and operating the traps in the flooring according to the directions of Messer Giovan' Battista was the work of Bernardo Timante, the imaginative Painter, and in no little favour with his most Illustrious and Excellent Highness, our Lord the Prince.

Messer Alessandro Strigio wrote the Musick for the / First, the Second, and the Fifth Intermedios. That for the Third, the Fourth, and the last was furnished by Messer Francesco Corteccia, Maestro di Cappella to their most Illustrious Excellencies.

THE END

(The "Description" translated by Theodore Baker.)

MUSIC IN OUR LIBRARIES

("The Art World," 1917)

Poets and other generous souls have extolled the charms of music until the emotional superiority of music over other arts has become a dogma too venerable for doubt. Possibly the emotional appeal of music *is* more intense than that of other arts, but the account is squared by several obstructions in the path of that appeal. Chief among these (with all the inherent consequences) is the inordinately complex and costly apparatus required for performance of musical works in the larger forms, such as symphonies, oratorios, operas. The composer faces a second disadvantage in the necessity of recording his thoughts with the help of symbols which can reach the sense appealed to, the ear, only by way of another sense, the eye. Furthermore, comparatively few music-lovers possess the imagination or the training to transform such visual impressions into the corresponding aural impressions. The accomplishment of "reading the score" of a modern opera, for instance, is an accomplishment indeed, and of truly deterring difficulty. Yet on this very accomplishment of those interested in him every composer sooner or later depends for his intercourse with contemporaries or posterity whenever the performer, the intermediary between composer and public, chooses not to perform a composer's works.

A minimum of reflection will show how under the circumstances, without the hospitality of libraries, composers are in danger of being shut off from posterity. But there his musical thoughts lie practically buried alive, encap-

suled in books of mute hieroglyphics. It is the best the world can offer him until that time when we shall have not merely musical libraries but "museums" of music, where in sundry feasible ways the public appeal of works of musical art will be made to endure, in effect similar to the permanent and ever-direct appeal of paintings, sculptures, etc., in museums of the Fine Arts. A fantastic dream? Not at all; but my present purpose does not permit of unfolding my ideas on this solvable problem of art-conservation and presentation.

If works of musical art, then, must fall back gradually on the hospitality of libraries—from the very nature of music virtually the hospitality of a mausoleum—has the best been made of the situation? Hardly. Musical libraries that are reasonably representative of the mighty growth of musical culture in our country, culture that springs from tender but healthy roots two hundred years old, are too few and far between to suggest a different answer. Perhaps the librarian profession still hesitates to recognize in music intellectual elements not less worthy of attention than genealogy or fiction. Perhaps we suffer from a dearth of expert musical librarians whose authority might compel a more hospitable attitude of mind. Perhaps musicians and music-lovers in musical communities are still too indifferent, or too unaware of their power of concerted action to have the rights of music as a cultural and therewith civic factor more adequately respected in libraries. Perhaps American libraries are richer in good will than in funds; perhaps the cost of music, comparatively much greater than that of literature, works as a handicap. Whatever the reason or reasons, the fact remains that music is deplorably underfed in the great majority of our libraries. Otherwise cities like New York, Philadelphia, Chicago, St. Louis, Cincinnati, San Francisco, Minneapolis and half a dozen others of our musical centres would not lag so far behind Boston in the possession of a municipal musical library of which all citizens may feel proud. They would not be able to emulate certain unique features of the late Mr. Allen A. Brown's munificent gift to the city of Boston, but if they had started in time and had persevered, they would now, as they ought, possess musical collections fairly equal to his in extent and merit.

In any ambitious community a library without the complete works of Shakespeare, Goethe, Dickens, Ibsen, Molière, Balzac, Dante, Longfellow, Poe—or without various serial works published to embrace a comprehensive selection of representative and historically important literary masterpieces, such as Johnson's 75-volume edition of English writers, would very properly invite scornful criticism. Apply a similar test with reference to the great masters of music. Does your local library contain the more or less complete editions of the works of Palestrina, Orlando di Lasso, Bach, Händel, Purcell, Rameau, Grétry, Haydn, Mozart, Beethoven, Schubert, Schumann, Mendelssohn, Berlioz, Liszt, Wagner, Verdi? Does it contain such historical publications as the *Denkmäler der Tonkunst* in Austria and Germany, the *Paléographie musicale, Les Archives de Maîtres de l'Orgue, L'arte musicale in Italia, Les maîtres musiciens de la Renaissance française,* the series of volumes of the Musical Antiquarian Society or the other similar undertakings designed to rescue from oblivion and to revive, at least for the student, masters of the past? If by way of excuse the answer be that there is no demand in a particular, supposedly musical community for such publications; that too much of the music is of "purely antiquarian interest" and of too little "musical interest to modern ears," then my counter-argument is: first, that the community is not yet as musically cultured as it thinks it is, or ought to be; second, that the tendency to appoint prevalent fashion or taste a complacent judge of art-values of the past is damnable and is more likely than not to lead to a conservatism hostile toward pioneers of the future; third, that "purely antiquarian interest" is not more of a crime and not less of a virtue in music than in other fields of human endeavor represented for that very reason in libraries. My fourth is, that much, very much music pleasing to the modern ear is already too dead even for antiquarian interest, hence might be denied asylum in libraries on special principles; my fifth, that a librarian ought not to content himself with giving to the public what it happens to want, but ought to help create a demand for what the public needs; my sixth, that no self-respecting library can afford to be without certain cultural documents, whether they be consulted frequently or seldom. Do you ask for more? then my seventh: that the needs of one solitary scholarly specialist should weigh with librarians just as heavily as the wants of a hundred "general" and generally superficial and unproductive readers.

After all, it is not the frequency of use that counts, but the use to which a book is put. A costly and rare book consulted only once in ten years, but then by a man of far-reaching research or codification of research, has justified its acquisition just as much as an inexpensive, commonplace book consulted every day for mere receptive information.

If the absence of works of "antiquarian" or "modern" interest be explained on the grounds of expensiveness, the explanation will carry weight. For it is a regrettable fact that chamber music, orchestra music, opera scores and so forth entail an expenditure which acts as a barrier to the comprehensive acquisition of meritorious music. And when the prices of foreign works of musical art are Americanized, a librarian may well despair of his ability to satisfy the needs of a musical community. When scores of the type mentioned above run in cost anywhere from four to two hundred and fifty dollars, the difficulty of assembling a representative collection of music becomes obvious, not to mention a moderate indulgence in bibliographical rarities or in autograph scores.

On the other hand, however, by no means all desirable and necessary music is beyond reach of even poor institutions. In every country music publishers have sought to meet the situation by issuing the standard works by standard composers for a moderate price. By surveying such editions any librarian with a modicum of expert knowledge may assemble a collection of indispensable works of musical art and of books on music. Indeed, respectable publishers have tried to facilitate his task by forming for him just such collections at a price which, of course, keeps pace with the character, extent and scope of the purchases *en bloc* suggested. Strange to say, either for lack of confidence in the interested disinterestedness of publishers— or for lack of interest or knowledge or ability to resist the temptation of wasting one's meagre funds on favored composers and alluringly advertised expensive publications— or for other reasons, it would appear that the movement has not been an unqualified success. True, many small libraries have embraced the opportunities offered, but just as many have neglected them, with the result that the number of reasonably well-equipped public musical libraries seems to be abnormally small in our country.

There is something fundamentally wrong somewhere in the situation if, for instance, a prominent publisher could sell to private music-lovers many thousand single volumes, but to public libraries only about fifty complete sets of a remarkable publication (now nearing the hundredth volume) which will form a comprehensive musician's library in itself, costs less than two dollars a volume, and for merit belongs to that type and class of publication which ought to be not in fifty, but in a thousand public libraries.

Precisely such serial publications, in a way encyclopedic publications, ought to form the basis of every public collection. It is the centre from which the concentric method of library development can best find its outward impetus; and no other method, provided it be not employed too rigidly or pedantically, will produce equally satisfactory results. Without it the collections will soon become unbalanced; they will suffer from obesity here and from anemia there. Nor is this all. Such publications, planned as libraries within libraries, lend themselves to bibliographical treatment for reference purposes more readily and more fruitfully than collections formed by picking out this or that work from catalogues. And paradoxical as it may sound, small libraries, with contents of such publications analytically catalogued, will often be in a better position to supply a sudden demand for specimens of work by an out-of-the-way composer than large libraries with an operating force too small or administrative machinery unsuited for proper analysis of collective publications.

Occasionally I have been asked to estimate the annual outlay necessary to form a good musical working library satisfactory to readers esthetically and historically as well as pedagogically inclined.

The question is a rather dangerous one to answer, because such estimates are hardly ever better than guesses or expressions of personal judgment not necessarily in harmony with that of colleagues. Having thus invited criticism of my estimates, I would say that an annual appropriation of three hundred dollars for the purchase of good music and good books on music is the *minimum* expenditure from which to expect results of substantial benefit to even small musical communities. This estimate applies merely to reference libraries, not to circulating libraries with branch offices. Moreover, it takes into account only the acquisition of printed music and does not concern itself with a collection of talking-machine records or player-piano rolls, so useful and desirable for purposes of *vulgarisation,* as the French would say. The larger a community is, or the more it bubbles over with musical activities, the more inadequate such a small annual appropriation as the above naturally becomes. If we pass on to our musical centres, or would-be musical centres, even one thousand dollars will prove insufficient if music really is meant to find a place in the public library in keeping with the community's interest in music.

In my humble opinion the public libraries in cities like those mentioned above would deserve no *ordre pour le mérite* for exceptional services rendered, if their annual appropriation for music and books on music reached or exceeded two thousand dollars. They would really be doing their duty only (and not more) toward music and its devotees by spending that sum every year. Even so, they would soon discover that the intelligent annual expenditure of two thousand dollars will not nowadays cover the field of legitimate ambition and that their musical collection will retain at that rate the characteristics of a good "working library" on a fairly large scale, but will never develop into a really first-class library of international importance for antiquarian research or the study of modern music.

These estimates will come as a shock to hard-pressed librarians and library trustees. I tender my sympathy; yet I must adhere to my estimates, since they are based on our experiences at the Library of Congress. There we have spent each year since 1902 vastly more than two thousand dollars on music and books on music. In fact, in one year necessity or opportunity, as one might prefer to call it, compelled us to spend not very far from ten times that amount. Nor do the more than 80,000 "pieces" (so-called in bibliographical jargon) purchased since 1902—and representing about one-tenth only of the entire collection —tell the whole story. The other nine-tenths consist of the American musical copyright deposits that have accumulated since about 1820 and the European deposits since 1891. Blessèd are they who do not come into contact with the bulk of this music; but of the about 25,000 publications drawn from the Copyright Office at the Library of Congress into its Music Division every year, perhaps one-fifth is music which any library might care to purchase if it could afford it. If one considers that these 5000 publications include hundreds of scores of expensive chamber and orchestra music, and opera scores by composers of standing or promise, the estimate of a market value of five thousand dollars certainly must be conceded to be very conservative.

With such a steady influx of material by way of copyright deposits or purchase (not to mention valuable gifts of autograph compositions by American composers) the collections in the custody of the Music Division of the Library of Congress *in their totality* cannot help surpassing not only in quantity (mere numerical superiority would be of little moment) but in quality and scope all other American collections by far and, within certain limits, rivaling and even excelling the foremost collections abroad. But this is not the deduction from the above excursion into statistics here intended. The plea is for a very much more enlightened, for a very much less philistine and stingy consideration of musical art in American libraries. Perhaps the financial burden suggested will be borne more cheerfully and more willingly if it be considered that even the unprecedented financial support that music finds in the Library of Congress does not by any manner of means put us in possession of "all the music published in the world," as vocal Baedekers have it on sight-seeing automobiles. We do not harbor the ambition to suffer from such a horrible affliction. The few library experts who really know how much or how little music cast in certain forms of art is preserved in famous libraries, also know the difficulty of assembling enough of the entire literature to form a collection of preëminent importance and usefulness.

The Library of Congress may have reason to believe that it now houses collections of operatic music, orchestral music, chamber music, books on music old and new, and so forth, second to none for purposes of serious art-study; that it can now place on exhibition an accumulation of musical rarities sufficient to force the blush of emotion in even the most blasé of connoisseurs; but no more than any other library can it claim completeness for special fields. While it may claim absolute superiority in some respects over all other institutions, on the other hand it must acknowledge an inferiority in other respects to certain institutions abroad that is pathetic; for instance, in the matter of autograph scores of great masters or of codices illustrating medieval music. Their cost and scarcity simply prohibit any attempt at rivalry. Hence it was the part of easy wisdom to curb ambition where ambition would have been ludicrous.

Which is a convenient way of insisting that even the Library of Congress is too poor for rendering a national service musically on a scale befitting the National library of the United States. Advisedly I say "a national service," because many visitors still entertain the strange belief that the Library of Congress is a local institution for the exclusive benefit of Washington! In that case its musical collections would have become by this time a grotesque anomaly.

A PREFACE

This preface was written in December, 1915, when I had practically completed the manuscript of a "Catalogue of Full Scores of Dramatic Music" at the Library of Congress. Publication of that work, which may easily run to a thousand pages, was delayed because I wished to enter and analyze certain important scores recently purchased abroad but not deliverable on account of the war. By the time I resigned as Chief of the Music Division of the Library of Congress—in August, 1917—publication of such an extensive work by the Library of Congress had become an inopportune expenditure. With the return of normal conditions I hope that it may still be my privilege to see through the press (with the few necessary additions) a catalogue which bids fair to be helpful not only to librarians, bibliographers and collectors, but also to the student of operatic history in a manner similar to my "Catalogue of Opera Librettos published before 1800."

It so happened that the preface came to the notice of scholars interested in the subject, and they urged me to publish the preface in advance of the whole work because, in their opinion, it sheds light on certain bibliographical and historical problems, neglected or misunderstood even by many historical writers not really familiar with the world's available, or rather non-available, operatic literature. Incidentally the contention was that it would do no harm and might do some good if the American student of operatic history were stimulated by way of a more attractive route than a government publication to make a pilgrimage to the Library of Congress and revel there in operatic treasures available nowhere else in such bewildering, though nicely ordered, profusion.

Not being averse to doing a very unconventional thing occasionally, I accepted the suggestion, but not without first having obtained the permission of my friend and former *chef,* Herbert Putnam, Librarian of Congress.

*

* *

Of late years considerable research has been devoted to the forerunners of opera—"l'opéra avant l'opéra," to quote Romain Rolland's *mot*. It may be doubted that further research can now add much to our knowledge of the musico-dramatic elements in the *Sacre representazioni, Maggi, Canti carnascialeschi,* dramatic madrigal cantatas, *favole pastorali,* and other types of spoken drama with incidental music, *intermedi,* allegorical and mythological pageants, pantomimes, ballets, and other forms of art, spectacular or not, running counter or parallel to or intersecting the first tender roots of opera proper. But it may also be doubted that this historical movement has brought to light in recent years much that is essentially new. Its main importance would seem to consist in the final harvest and sifting of data for the rather old chapter on how, towards the end of the sixteenth century, the soil was prepared for the germination of opera, a vague term used then as now to label a very definite thing. To accept the doctrine of "l'opéra avant l'opéra" literally, leads to historical nonsense. It is one thing to reduce the novelty of the hellenistic experiments started in the musico-dramatic laboratory of Count Bardi's Florentine *camerata* (*ca.* 1580 to 1590) to a reasonable minimum; quite another to deny or, with historical sophistry, to underestimate the novelty, a mistake which at any rate Angelo Solerti, the greatest of scholars who have investigated the origin of opera, did not permit himself to make.

Presumably Vincenzo Galilei, Emilio de' Cavalieri, Ottavio Rinuccini, Jacopo Corsi, Count Bardi, Jacopo Peri, Giulio Caccini and their comrades in esthetic arms were just as conversant with the music of their time, including "l'opéra avant l'opéra," as we are. Presumably, also, they knew just as well as their somewhat later champion, Giov. Batt. Doni, that "at all times it was customary to join to dramatic action some kind of *cantilena,* either in the form of intermedi between acts or merely within an act when something suitable occurred in the represented subject," but "one should know that such melodies are very different from those of our time composed in the generally so-called recitative style . . . and that they have nothing in common with good and true music for the theatre." This is but one of the clear-cut critical opinions of the time which saw in Emilio de' Cavalieri's pastoral scenes "Il Satiro" and "La disperazione di Fileno" (1590) and (more elaborate) "Il Giuoco della cieca" (Florence, October 29, 1595), then in Corsi's and Peri's "Dafne" (1595 *or* 1597), and finally in Cavalieri's "Rappresentazione di anima et di corpo" (Rome, February, 1600) and in Peri's and Caccini's settings of "L'Euridice" (Florence, October 6, 1600) the dawn of a new art. The ideas of these composers soon found an echo in the mind and heart of great masters like Marco da Gagliano and Claudio Monteverdi, and before long quite a literature had grown up in eloquent testimony to the novelty of their "nuove musiche." Discount the excesses of partisan propaganda and the naïve notion—not shared by Peri—that these pastoral dramas in music constituted at last a rediscovery of Greek drama, enough remains to compel acquiescence in the contemporary verdict that the novelty of opera was revolutionary, not merely "evolutional" or reminiscent of earlier attempts in the same direction and of the same kind.

Indeed, the very fact that Ingegneri and other keen minds of the age, in Florence, Ferrara and elsewhere, busied themselves with the problem how music should be set to the words of a drama to form real musico-dramatic speech, would tend to support Doni's contention that the usual music in dramatic performances was considered as of a different type. And well it might, for it was different in character from that evolved by Emilio de' Cavalieri, Peri and Caccini after persistent experiments. It was lyrical and melodic or chanting rather than dramatic and *parlando,* and remained so, to judge from the few extant specimens, notwithstanding the probability that many a composer instinctively or intentionally would seek to invent musical phrases in keeping with the dramatic sense of the words. In opera neither the musical setting of an

entire text nor monody itself constituted the real novelty
(they had existed for centuries) but a far-reaching new
technique of monody for purposes of dramatic recitative—
as Angelo Grillo (1608) formulated it, "un cantar senza
canto, un cantar recitativo." The idea was, in supposed
imitation of the Greeks, to so adjust musical values of
pitch, intervals, rhythm, accent, emphasis, melodic phrase
and design to the psychological and poetic values of the
text of the drama that the result would be a musical speech,
not less natural than that of the spoken word and not
detrimental to the values of the text, but moulding its subtle or obvious meaning in clearer relief, framed by sugges-
tive harmonization and appropriate instrumental accompaniment. "Absolute" music played no part in this scheme
of things; the composer stood at the command of the dramatist, and gladly sacrificed his freedom as a musician to
render homage to the dramatist.

So completely did, for instance, Peri succeed in thus
subordinating music to drama that the structural weaknesses in Rinuccini's text are amusingly and distressingly
mirrored in his music; much of the monotony in his recitative is to be credited to the poet. On the other hand, so
thoughtfully and skillfully does he put the structural
resources of music at the disposal of Rinuccini, that one
is tempted to smile at those who perceive in these earliest
recitatives but infantile awkwardness and primitive
stammering. Primitive they are, as is all really new art,
and if they often sound awkward in modern interpretation
it is largely because we have only lately rediscovered some
of the secrets of their proper performance. And if Peri's
contemporaries be taken to task for insisting on the new-
ness of this art of "un cantar recitativo" because this or that
modern historian fails to hear characteristic differences between this and other, also earlier, types of monody, the
argument is not exactly sound. It suffers from the same
anachronistic perspective as that which would deny to
the polyphonists of the age a difference in atmosphere

between their sacred and secular music simply because many of us to-day hear none. The truth cf the matter is, that in all ages sacred and secular music sprout from a common ground; to the ear of contemporaries characteristic differences between the two stand out much more clearly than to later generations, for the same reason that different objects will melt more and more into a common background the farther from them our point of view recedes. For music-lovers of three hundred years hence the differences in expression between our own secular and sacred music will have become just as elusive as are for us the differences in expression between a sacred and secular madrigal of Palestrina.

The members of the Florentine *camerata* and their followers had ushered in a new type of art indeed with their experiments in musico-dramatic speech. That it was imperfect detracts nothing from the novelty of the underlying principle. Nor that it required the general musical genius of a Monteverdi to perfect it into something vital, nor that recitative fairly soon became conventional and more or less sterile, nor that within fifty years strict recitative found itself woven into the fabric of opera together with free melody, with polyphony and all other resources of music, just as Emilio de' Cavalieri, the real father of opera, seems to have foreseen.

At first glance such historical considerations would appear to overstep the boundaries of the legitimate professional interest of a librarian. They do, if he is content to act as a guardian of books, a recorder of bibliographic details, a servant of readers; they do not, if a larger view of the public's needs embraces the function, circumstances permitting, of developing the collections entrusted to his care organically, and not haphazard.

A special collection requires a definite radius of action with a definite point of departure, and both are determined by specialized historical considerations. In the case of opera, then, the librarian will have to choose between opera and "l'opéra avant l'opéra." In the Library of Congress, for the reasons stated above, the choice has been opera as dating from about the year 1600. This does not mean that "l'opéra avant l'opéra," so far as the music is extant and accessible to collectors, has escaped attention, but it does not form part of our collection of opera proper. When the problem becomes one of dramatic music, i. e., music for works acted on the scenic stage, in general, as represented by this catalogue, then of course the forerunners of opera must be comprised in the plan of organic development. But even then a limited radius of action, if only for purposes of a workable classification, is preferable to one unlimited. Thus "l'opéra avant l'opéra" would form (and forms) part of our collections as here represented only if its bearing on modern opera, ballet, opéra-ballet, incidental music for plays, was felt to be direct instead of indirect, problematical or too remote. Thus *moralities, sacre representazioni,* miracle plays, dramatic madrigal cantatas and the like are excluded from this Catalogue but, of course, the "Balet comique de la royne" (1581; publ. 1582) is included, as would be the *intermedii* of Alessandro Striggio and others, and as might be Germi's music for Poliziano's "Orfeo" (1471), if they were extant or accessible.

This last condition leads to a consideration more practical than theoretical or historical. What is the situation confronting the collector of opera? Organic development of a special collection obviously does not mean to collect indiscriminately every available work, but for purposes of illustration be it assumed that an enthusiast with ample funds had ventured on the enterprise of collecting as many operas as possible regardless of any intrinsic value, artistic, historical, bibliographical, or other. He would encounter obstacles not ordinarily suspected even by historians, critics, or librarians, and known in their full extent only to a few disillusioned collectors and bibliographers.

More than thirty-five thousand operas of every description have been performed since about the year 1600. This estimate does not account for the thousands of ballets, etc., performed since then, nor for the thousands of operas that never reached the footlights of a theatre. All these works—perhaps a total not far from fifty thousand—must once have existed in the composer's original manuscript score. Most of them have been swept into the débris of time; perhaps not more than five thousand full orchestral scores of different operas, etc., have been preserved, inclusive of those not in the composer's own but in some copyist's manuscript score. (A sufficient warning, it would seem, for composers to bequeath their manuscript scores to libraries, if they care to see them reasonably protected against utter disappearance.)

As might be expected, these manuscript scores are scattered through the libraries and opera archives of Europe in a very limited number of copies. Indeed, the majority of the works thus represented exist but in one, two or three copies. Furthermore, they are by no means evenly distributed. Certain libraries, particularly those at Brussels, Naples, Parma, Modena, Berlin, Paris, London, Vienna, practically have a monopoly of the works of certain composers, and at the same time lack manuscript scores of certain other composers who are just as important. This decentralization of extant operatic literature naturally militates against the comprehensive study of operatic history in any one city, while it may facilitate the specialist's study of a given composer. Thus the total of perhaps five thousand different manuscript scores becomes in general effect still more feeble than in fact it is. From the standpoint of the collector these library copies, of course, do not exist. Unless he gain permission to have transcripts made of them for his own or his institution's use, he is dependent on the relatively few manuscript scores that find their way to the market, where other bidders may successfully block his ambitions.

How ungently time has dealt with manuscript opera

scores might be illustrated interestingly by a number of examples. Here it will suffice to offer one striking illustration with a reason. In his able essay on "Ensembles and Finales in 18th century Italian Operas" Edward J. Dent says:

"Considering the popularity of comic operas in the first half of the 18th century, the number of works that have survived is small, but we must remember that they were regarded even then as trivial, and in most cases were of purely local interest. Moreover, it was seldom that a more widespread celebrity was conferred upon them by any singer of European fame." Dr. Dent then proceeds "to make out a chronological list of such scores as are now available for study."

His list of comic operas runs from 1718 to 1760; it tests the fifteen European libraries where such scores are preserved; the census is startling in its negative results: *only thirty operas by ten composers!*

If we turn to published operas, etc., we must distinguish between full orchestral scores and vocal scores with arranged pianoforte accompaniment. The latter are a relatively modern form of publication; generally speaking, they date in any noticeable number from about 1750. Before that time scores, if printed or engraved at all, would be published either in full or in compressed orchestral score, preferably the latter, since then as now a publisher would prefer that form of publication which would ensure the widest circulation. As the orchestra employed by composers increased in volume, the possibilities of compromise between a full and a compressed or skeleton orchestral score became fewer and fewer. The latter, for reasons of popularization, rapidly were superseded by scores in which the complicated orchestral accompaniment was frankly arranged for pianoforte only. The number of operas thus published in vocal score with pianoforte accompaniment increased enormously; whereas, not only because of the by far greater cost of publication, but because very few persons can possibly be expected to read a complicated modern orchestral score, the number of published full scores correspondingly decreased. Of course, stage success or at least expectation thereof remains to this day, as a rule, the premise of publication of even vocal scores, but in this arranged form presumably about ten thousand operas, etc., are available, the great majority published since the end of the eighteenth century. (This estimate is based on the fact that the Library of Congress possesses at least seven thousand vocal scores.)

With reference to operas, etc., published in full orchestral score the situation is entirely different. Probably not more than twelve hundred works, if that many, have been published in the composer's original full orchestral score, or, as was the rule in earlier times, in compressed orchestral score! At that, this meagre total is reached only after inclusion of the scores of older masters published within recent years in historical editions! It is exceeded by a few hundred, if, as in this catalogue, the "Favourite Songs" in full or compressed score with which principally Walsh and Bremner of London flooded the market in the eighteenth century are taken into consideration.

The above estimate will sound incredible to those who are not really familiar with the subject. Here, then, is corroborative evidence. The following list represents all the Italian operas, etc., published in full or compressed score in Italy and elsewhere from 1600 to about 1815. The list may show a few gaps, but it surely is not far from complete. (The works with asterisk are in the Library of Congress in the original editions, those with double asterisk we have either in transcript or in modern editions.)

OPERAS, ETC., IN ITALIAN PUBLISHED IN FULL OR COMPRESSED SCORE
FROM 1600 TO CA. 1815

(Orazio Vecchi's "L'Amfiparnaso," 1597, and similar dramatic
madrigal *cantatas* by Banchieri, Torelli, etc., not here
entered. *See* Vecchi's "L'Amfiparnaso" in the Catalogue.)

**C. Malvezzi, L. Marenzio, E. de' Cavalieri, etc.: Intermedi
et concerti fatti per la commedia rappresentata in
Firenze. . . . [La pazzia, 1589.] Venetia, Vincenti, 1591
(Part-books)

**E. de' Cavalieri: "Rappresentazione di anima et di corpo,"
Roma, Mutii, 1600 (L. of C. has also the 1912 facsimile)

**G. Caccini: "L'Euridice," Firenze, Marescotti, 1600 (1601)

**———— ————, Venetia, Vincenti, 1615

**J. Peri: "L'Euridice." Fiorenza, Marescotti, 1600 (1601)

**———— ————, Venetia, Raverii, 1608

*G. Caccini: "Il rapimento di Cefalo." (Allegorical ballet.)
Only fragments were printed on pp. 19-24 of his "Nuove
musiche," Firenze, Marescotti, 1601 (1602)

**A. Agazzari: "Eumelio," Venetia, Amadino, 1606

**C. Monteverdi: "L'Orfeo," Venetia, Amadino, 1609

**———— ————, Venetia, Amadino, 1615

*Marco da Gagliano: "La Dafne," Firenze, Marescotti

G. Giacobbi: "Dramatodia overo Canti rappresentativi
sopra 'L'Aurora ingannata,'" Venetia, Vincenti, 1608
(Intermedi)

D. Belli: "Orfeo dolente," Venetia, Amadino, 1616 (Intermedi; in parts, not in score)

G. B. Boschetti: "Strali d'amore," Venetia, Vincenti, 1618
(Intermedi)

**S. Landi: "La morte d'Orfeo," Venetia, Magni, 1619

*F. Vitali: "L'Aretusa," Roma, Soldi, 1620

**———— "Intermedi per la commedia de gl'Accademici Inco-
stanti" ["La finta Mora"], Firenze, Cecconcelli, 1622

**F. Caccini: "La liberazione di Ruggero dall'isola d'Alcina,"
Firenze, Cecconcelli, 1625

*D. Mazzocchi: "La Catena d'Adone," Venetia, Vincenti
[1626]

Marco da Gagliano: "La Flora," Firenze, Pignoni, 1628

**G. Cornachioli d'Ascoli: "Diana schnernita," Roma, Ro-
bletti, 1629

*S. Landi: "Il S. Alessio," Roma, Masotti, 1634 (one issue
    with plates, the other without)
*M. Rossi: "Erminia sul Giordano," Roma, Masotti, 1637
**C. Monteverdi: "Il ballo delle ingrate." (*In his* "Madrigali
    guerrieri, et amorosi," 1638)
** ——— "Il combattimento di Tancredi e Clorinda." (*In his*
    "Madrigali guerrieri, et amorosi," 1638)
**L. Vittori da Spoleti: "La Galatea," Roma, Bianchi, 1639
*M. Marazzoli: "La vita humana, overo Il trionfo della pietà,"
    Roma, Mascardi, 1658
  G. A. Bontempi: "Paride," Dresda, Berger, 1662
*Doletti: "Les ariettes du Joueur," Paris, Mᵉ Boivin, [etc],
    [1752?] (*Same as* "Il Giocatore" by Orlandini or Vinci)
*G. B. Pergolesi: "La serva padrona," Paris, Aux addresses
    ordinaires [1752 *or* 1753]
* ——— ———, Londra, Bremner, 1777
* ——— "Le maître de musique" (= Il maestro di musica),
    Paris, Boivin [1753]
* ——— "Tracollo," Paris, Aux addresses ordinaires [1753]
*Rinaldo di Capua: "La Bohémienne," Paris, Aux addresses
    ordinaires [1753] (*Same as his* "La Zingara")
  Maria Antonia Walpurgis, of Saxony: "Il trionfo della
    fedeltà," Lipsia, Breitkopf, 1756
* ——— "Talestri, regina delle Amazzoni," Lipsia, Breitkopf,
    1765
*G. Sarti: "Ciro riconosciuto," Copenhagen, n.publ. [1756]
*C. W. v. Gluck: "Orfeo ed Euridice," Parigi, Duchesne, 1764
* ——— "Alceste," Vienna, Trattnern, 1769
* ——— "Paride ed Elena," Vienna, Trattnern, 1770
*G. F. Händel: "Acis and Galatea," masque, London, W.
    Randall [1770?]
  A. Tozzi: "Il Rinaldo," Venezia, n.publ. [1775]
*F. G. Bertoni: "Orfeo," Venezia, Alessandri e Scattaglia
    [1776]
*G. Sarti: "Giulio Sabino," Vienna, n.publ. [1781]
  G. Millico: "La pietà d'amore," Napoli, Porcelli, 1782
  N. Jommelli: "L'Olimpiade," Stuttgard, L'imprimerie de
    l'Académie Caroline, 1783
*A. Salieri: "La grotta di Trofonio," Vienna, Artaria [1785]
*J. F. Reichardt: "Brenno," Berlin, L'Autore [1789]
*G. F. Händel: "Agrippina" and "Teseo" [Dr. Arnold's his-
    torical ed., London, 1789-1797]
*J. Haydn. "Orfeo e Euridice." Lipsia, Breitkopf e Härtel
    [*ca.* 1806] (Contains only eleven numbers)

*W. A. Mozart: "Il dissoluto punito ossia Il Don Giovanni,"
    Lipsia, Breitkopf & Härtel [1801]
*D. Cimarosa: "L'Impresario in angustie," Paris, Sieber
    [1802] (Secco recitatives replaced by French spoken
    dialogue; Italian text added to the French in the arias)
*G. Paisiello: "La pazza per amore," Paris, Pleyel [1802]
*W. A. Mozart: "Idomeneo, rè di Creta," Bonn, N. Simrock
    [ca. 1805]
*V. Fioravanti: "I virtuosi ambulanti," Parigi, Mme Duhan
    & Cie. [1807]
*W. A. Mozart: "La clemenza di Tito," Leipzig, Breitkopf &
    Härtel [1809]
*——— "Così fan tutte," Leipzig, Breitkopf & Härtel [1810]
*——— "Il flauto magico," Bonn, N. Simrock [ca. 1810]
*——— "Le nozze di Figaro," Bonn, N. Simrock [181-?]
*D. Cimarosa: "Il matrimonio segreto," Paris, Imbault
    [1813?]
*——— "Gli Orazi e i Curiazi," Paris, Imbault [1813]
*G. Weigl: "Il ritorno d'Astrea," Milano, Ricordi, 1816
    (Publ. by Gaetano Melzi)

Barely sixty operas published among the thousands
performed; and not a single opera by Cavalli, Cesti, Luigi
Rossi, Legrenzi, Scarlatti, Caldara, Conti, Leo, Bononcini,
Hasse, Piccinni, and other masters of early Italian opera!
Händel is represented only in a post-mortem edition.   To
be sure, his operas were published during his lifetime,
but practically with omission of all recitative,[1] in which he
so often excelled as a dramatic composer.   As to Hasse, he
had prepared his scores for publication, but the bombard-
ment of Dresden in 1760 and the consequent destruction
of the manuscripts put an end to his plans.   Possibly the
enterprise would have miscarried anyhow, as did Jommelli's plan of publishing his Stuttgart operas by subscription, since only his "L'Olimpiade" (1783) was able to
reach the public.
    The list also reveals the fact that Italian publishers
showed unqualified reluctance to engage in the publication
of Italian opera scores from about the time that opera

[1] The Library of Congress possesses practically a complete file of such
editions.

ventured forth from the courts and appealed to the public in general. This reluctance lasted until the end of the nineteenth century! Indeed, it persists to-day. Though the firms that now hold the destiny of Italian opera in the hollow of their hands not infrequently print full scores of the operas under their control, they do not publish them, i. e., they will loan or perhaps sell them to the theatre performing the work, but they dislike to sell them to private or public libraries. In effect, the scores remain just as scarce or unavailable as in the days when the vast majority of Italian operas, including even those by composers like Bellini, Donizetti, Rossini, Verdi, existed in manuscript copies only, made either by some individual copyist (by authority or surreptitiously) or in the *copisteria* of an opera-producing firm of publishers.

The question of exercise of control and of self-protection against piracy helps in part to explain the paucity of Italian opera scores printed or published in Italy during the last two hundred and fifty years. But there are other reasons for this paucity, which is the more noticeable because of the few scores by Peri, Caccini, Paisiello, Rossini, published after 1860 by Guidi of Florence, the pioneer publisher of orchestral scores in pocket editions. Before the advent of the Ricordis, Italy could not boast much progressiveness, organization and enterprise in the music-publishing business. Then again the very fertility of Italian composers, some with a hundred or more operas to their credit, militated against publication of their works. To this must be added the instability of the works themselves, the pasticcio tendency inflicting alterations on them in their course from one theatre to the other—obviously not an element of attractiveness for publishers. But, whatever the reasons and explanations may be, the fact stands out that it is an impossibility to study the development of Italian opera since 1650 by way of published full scores; and of those actually available, most left

German and French presses, not Italian, before the recent (by no means comprehensive) enterprise of the house of Ricordi to do justice to the towering genius of Giuseppe Verdi in their memorial edition of his operas.

No more striking contrast can be imagined than between this state of affairs and that prevailing in France. True, French publishers, in common with their Italian and with certain German colleagues, print but rarely sell their scores to the public. True also, that nearly a century elapsed before the publication of the "Balet Comique de la royne" in 1582 was followed by the publication of another musico-dramatic score; but, on the one hand, the anti-public "en location" system mentioned is a comparatively recent French practice, and on the other, when Christophe Ballard did in 1671 begin the publication of full scores of operas, he set an example unhesitatingly followed ever since by French music publishers.

Thus it is entirely feasible to-day to study the development of French dramatic music comprehensively and with but few serious gaps. This statement requires modification only with reference to the (as a rule hopelessly mediocre) ballets proper in the répertoire of the Paris Opéra, numbering, until the publication of Lajarte's fine catalogue of the "Bibliothèque musicale du Théâtre de l'Opéra" in 1876, about one hundred and ten. Most of these remained in manuscript, but also—principally preserved in the elder Philidor's collection of transcripts —the characteristically French "Ballets de cour" of Louis XIV, including even those by Lully. That is regrettable, for in the opinion of competent judges Lully's genius as displayed in his court ballets—how they evoke the memory of Molière!—fully matches that in his many operas, all of which were published by Ballard. If we except one or two modern full scores of his ballets, the statement in the "État des opéra en musique par Monsieur de Lully" in the "Fragments de Monsieur Lully" (Paris, Ballard, 1702) that none of his twenty-three ballets had been published, is still true to-day. Yet there must have been a demand for them, since "Foucault, Marchand" advertised in Lacoste's "Aricie," 1697, "les anciens ballets de M. de Lully en six volumes in folio écrits à la main." A further modification of the above statement is perhaps also applicable to the period just prior to Gluck, when the fortunes of the "Académie royale de musique" were at a rather low ebb, and to the first years of the French Revolution (which is easily understood); but on the whole French *opéra* and particularly *opéra comique* in full score has fared wonderfully well at the hands of French music publishers.

With the exception of Russia, Germany and England, other countries are a negligible quantity in this connection, though even America has a few printed scores to its credit, as this catalogue shows. In Russia the enlightened and patriotic liberality of publishers has placed freely at the public's disposal a considerable number of Russian operas, from Glinka to Rimsky-Korsakow.

Germany stands somewhere between Italy and France in the matter under discussion. The first periods of German opera, i. e., including Hiller's "Singspiele" and Benda's melodramas, are barren of published full scores, for even the great Reinhard Keiser had to content himself with a few selections of arias. Vocal scores became fairly numerous in print, but the honor of being the first full-fledged orchestral score of a German *grand opera* would seem to belong to Holzbauer's "Günther von Schwarzburg," performed 1777 but not published until *ca.* 1783. For almost a century German music publishers then contented themselves with the issue of vocal scores, and their efforts to publish full scores of successful German operas remained rather sporadic, if we except Mozart, Weber, Beethoven and Wagner. For instance, Marschner, Spohr and Lortzing had to wait until the firm of Peters in Leipzig honored their memory by the publication of a few representative scores. Since then the spell has been broken and the younger generations of German opera composers have often had the satisfaction of seeing their operas in print and, until very recently, available to the purchasing public, even though their stage life has frequently been short.

In the musical life of Great Britain English opera has been the Cinderella for a good many years. It is therefore not surprising that full scores of English operas have received but scant courtesy at the hands of publishers. The case of Arthur Sullivan is one in point. Had he labored in France, the scores of all his delightful operas would be available in print, instead of as now two or three, including "Amor an Bord," a German version of "H.M.S. Pinafore." Sometimes one cannot help thinking that English opera might have fared better, had Händel and Mendelssohn exercised a less compelling influence on the musical life of England. However, with the passing of Matthew Locke and Henry Purcell the fortunes of *grand opera* in English by Englishmen fell, and therewith disappeared automatically the incentive to publish full scores of operas, mere selections of arias in more or less compressed scores or vocal scores finding favor with the publishers. The very thing that is characteristic of opera, the recitative, is held to have been abhorred in England on the stage; and it is very instructive to find that, contrary to current belief, the recitatives were *not* printed in the full score of Dr. Arne's otherwise successful "Artaxerxes" (1762). In other words, the one element that made his attempt to transplant Metastasio to the English stage so bold—English recitative instead of spoken dialogue—was suppressed in the published score of "Artaxerxes."

But general deductions from this rather startling fact should be avoided, for Arne's two-act pastoral opera "Thomas and Sally" called throughout for recitatives instead of spoken dialogue (as in *opéra comique*), and the compressed full score was published in 1761 with all the recitatives. In fact, the same observation applies to William Boyce's two-act pastoral operas "The Chaplet," published in 1749 or 1750, and "The Shepherd's Lottery," published in 1751. Decidedly more frequent than the publication of full scores of English *operas* was the publication of English *masques* during the first half of the eighteenth century. Does not this fact perhaps have its value as a hint in the right direction, whenever the stale problem whether or not dramatic music to English words is foreign to British instinct, taste and genius, arises for discussion?

This survey of actual conditions, of difficulties in the path of the collector of operas, will facilitate a fair and intelligent judgment on the unrivaled resources of the Library of Congress in this particular field. The historian may point to the absence of this or that published and historically important score, as for instance Nessler's musically unimportant "Trompeter von Säkkingen," and the bibliophile may miss a copy of some coveted edition, as for instance one of the fifteen autolithographic copies issued of the first edition of Wagner's "Fliegender Holländer," but both will remember that our collection is comparatively very young. While the Library of Congress has been favored in a good many instances by unusual luck, some scores which are to be found in other, older music collections have stubbornly refused to turn up in the market during the last fifteen years. Other and normally rarer scores would be offered at a reasonable price, but our competitor's distance from them would be shorter and his purse longer than ours. Then again certain very rare scores, like Peri's "Euridice," could have been acquired, but at a price so prohibitive that we preferred to content ourselves with a transcript; or scores by important composers were held by the family and were not accessible. Also certain publishers persisted in their traditional policy of refusal to sell their scores, even if printed, or they attached conditions of sale so irritatingly beyond the customary obligations of a publisher's "Revers" that dignity forbade further negotiations. Moreover, certain scores have become indeed *introuvables*, though for many years collectors and second-hand dealers have endeavored to ferret them out. It would be expecting too much of the Library of Congress to succeed where they failed. Finally, a grim consolation attaches to the fact that of certain published opera scores only one copy is known to exist. For example, the score of Landi's "La morte d'Orfeo" at the British Museum would appear to be unique: as long as no second copy finds its way into another library, the Library of Congress as a collector derives a certain (negative) satisfaction from the existence of such scores, without being troubled by memories of the fable of the sour grapes.

After all is said, the Library of Congress aims less at an unbroken series of operatic rarities than at a representation of available scores comprehensive enough to lay bare the development of dramatic music at all periods and in all countries. Though "special" in fact, our collection of full opera scores is "general" in principle. Viewed from this angle, the statement that *only about ten per cent. of the published scores of operas, etc.,* are not represented in our collection takes on its proper significance. Perhaps the estimate is not absolutely accurate, but it cannot be far from correct, since it is based on a final list of *desiderata*, of scores not in our collections but known to exist. Indeed, the author of this catalogue himself did not quite realize the strength given by him to the collection by organic development until he had compiled said list. Then it was found, for instance, that the Library of Congress possesses all of Lully's published operas except his "Pourceaugnac," 1715. Not less of a surprise was the discovery that of Ballard's list of sixty-five "Opéras modernes" advertised by him as published from Lully's death to 1721, we possess all but five. Studying Lajarte's catalogue of 1876 it was further found incidentally that of the works in the répertoire of the "Académie nationale de musique" (the Paris Opéra) until then, the Library of Congress had accumulated ninety published scores more than were (in printed copies) then in the archives of that world-renowned institution, thus putting before the American student of French *grand opera* until 1876 more than two hundred seventy of the about three hundred published full scores in a répertoire of about four hundred and eighty-four operas.   And since attention was drawn above to Mr. Dent's census of only thirty preserved scores of Italian comic opera from 1718 to 1760, it may not be improper to remark here that the Library of Congress possesses, by way of transcript, twenty of these thirty scores; the Royal Conservatory at Naples comes next with ten, the British Museum with five, and other famous libraries with less than five out of the thirty.

This last remark leads conveniently to a brief consideration of our manuscript scores.   Though the market be favorable, it is obviously impossible to overcome the natural obstacles in the way of collecting manuscript scores by direct purchase.   The Library of Congress would always remain under a heavy handicap as against certain older national or governmental libraries in Europe which have received by transfer or contain *eo ipso* the manuscript scores of operas performed in that particular city at that particular court through the centuries, and have been further enriched by purchase and generous bequests by the crown or public-spirited citizens.   Such collections may but seldom be well balanced from the standpoint of a librarian; from his point of view quite naturally they will show an array of too many scores by one composer and of too few by another, equally important; but each and all of such collections, formed more by accident than by design, will contain many a score that is indispensable in any collection formed in the interest of the student of operatic history. As a rule, such manuscript scores are utterly out of reach, so far as the second-hand market is concerned; hence their acquisition must be accomplished differently. The only feasible methods are to acquire the scores in transcript or in photographic facsimile. Accordingly, the details of a project were worked out for the acquisition of a large number of important operas by these methods. The project in its final form enjoyed the benefit of Geheimrat Prof. Dr. Hermann Kretzschmar's authoritative suggestions, and the majority of European librarians who were approached in the matter put their treasures at the service of the Library of Congress in a scholarly spirit. It soon developed that photographic facsimiles would practically have to be excluded from the project; inexpensive as some of the photographic processes now are, the administrative machinery to avail ourselves of these processes simultaneously in half a dozen countries on a large scale proved to be inadequate. Of course, a photographic facsimile of an old score has on the whole decidedly more advantages than disadvantages for the purpose of historical study. The chief advantage is accuracy of reproduction, and no set of rules prescribed to a corps of transcribers for guidance nor any amount of carefulness on the part of the expert transcriber will remove the certainty of errors in copies made by hand and pen. As our transcribers are musicians, the errors in the music itself may safely be said to be comparatively few (in excess of those made in the score by the original transcriber of the composer's autograph score with its own errors), but some of the errors made by the transcribers in their frantic efforts to wrestle with the often barely legible foreign text are ludicrous in the extreme. It goes without saying that our transcripts, made by the hundreds, do not lay claim to that scientific accuracy which one expects of a special transcript by a musicologist for publication in the "Denkmäler." All we claim is, that

our transcript project has made about five hundred selected rare old operas available in America, and that our
transcripts are sufficiently accurate for study by scholars
with an eye trained to detect obvious errors.

As is easily understood from the survey of conditions,
the majority of operas selected for transcript are Italian
operas. Now, many of these are known to exist only in
Italian libraries—and the reluctance of Italian librarians
to grant permission for the copying of such scores has been
proverbial. In fact, the reluctance goes so far as often to
amount to an unqualified refusal, an attitude, it is but
just to remark, not shared by librarians recently appointed. Here, then, was a seemingly unsurmountable
obstacle to the complete realization of the transcript project. However, when the author had the honor to represent
the United States Government at the International Musical Congress at Rome in 1911, his mission comprised
instructions to interest our Ambassador in obtaining permission to transcribe scores preserved in libraries under
the direct control of the Italian government. Mr. Leish-
mann took the matter up and succeeded in obtaining this
permission, but unfortunately too late for action by the
author while in Italy. Then difficulties of a different kind
arose, and to our regret the transcript project, so far as
Italian libraries are concerned, is still practically in the
preparatory stage. Fortunately hundreds of historically
important Italian operas of olden times could be and were
transcribed for the Library of Congress in London,
Vienna, Berlin, Paris, Brussels, Dresden and elsewhere.

All told, our collection represents not far from three
thousand musico-dramatic works in "full" scores, printed
or manuscript, and inclusive, of course, of operas, etc.,
contained in such historical publications as the several
"Denkmäler" or the editions of the complete works of
Mozart, Grétry, Rameau, Purcell, etc., or similar undertakings acquired by the Library of Congress by subscription and as a matter of general policy. In 1902, when the

Music Division was reorganized by me, the collection consisted of only about sixty full scores deposited for copyright. When at that time the author's plans for a systematic development of the resources of the Music Division were carried into effect, opera received a considerable share of attention in preference to other special collections since developed or yet to be developed at the proper time; first, for reasons of administrative expediency; second, because the peculiar condition of opera in the United States seemed to demand that a centre of reference and research be created for the students of opera and its history.

Comparatively few seventeenth and early eighteenth century published scores conform to a literal interpretation of the term "full orchestral score." Not unlike the scores of secco recitatives printed with their mere figured basses for accompaniment by the harpsichord and some other supporting bass instrument, they often present a mere outline of orchestral forces employed (with their plucked instruments so different in basic color effect from the modern orchestra), or they compress the orchestral accompaniment into a small compass, or they so adjust to it the technique of the harpsichord, the harmonic backbone of the orchestra, that one might almost speak of vocal scores with accompaniment of harpsichord and *obbligato* instruments. Still, the differences between the various types of compressed orchestral score and their logical offspring, the vocal score with orchestral accompaniment arranged solely for the pianoforte, are generally characteristic enough to show the dividing line. It has therefore become customary among librarians to so stretch the term "full orchestral score" as to permit the inclusion of compressed scores. Nevertheless, occasionally the line has to be drawn somewhere against skeleton scores, and it will hardly cause criticism, if such publications as G. E. P. Arkwright's "Old English edition" of Campion's "Masque for Lord Hayes' marriage" (1607), or John Stafford Smith's reprint in "Musica Antiqua" of G. Mason and J. Earsden's music for the Brougham Castle masque of 1617, will not be found here.

This catalogue also stretches definitions in another direction: not only *entire* full scores are represented, but published *excerpts* in full score, like the large "Favourite Songs" output of London publishers, and unpublished excerpts in full score like those in our important Martorell Collection of favorite old arias. Exclusion of such excerpts would have barred reference to many an old opera score not preserved in any but this incomplete form. Quotations in full score (for purposes of illustration) contained in biographies and histories should not be looked for in this catalogue, unless they be excerpts in full score and complete in themselves. The fact that most of such printed full score excerpts from the old operas will be found here, offers no guarantee that all will be found. Their entry was a matter of expediency, not of principle, and was prompted largely by a desire to guide students to historical specimens available to them perhaps only in books that should be in every well conducted library. A systematic and exhaustive effort to gather references to such historical material may properly be reserved as part of a much needed work in imitation of Eitner's now antiquated but still very useful "Verzeichniss neuer Ausgaben alter Musikwerke aus der frühesten Zeit bis zum Jahre 1800." In passing, principally Gevaert's "Les Gloires de l'Italie" may be recommended as a splendid but neglected collection of excerpts from eighteenth century operas with pianoforte accompaniment.

The principle of admitting "Favourite Songs" and the like is not new with the present catalogue. It found its expression in our "Catalogue of Full Scores of Dramatic Music" published in 1908, as did certain other practices of the Music Division, now fairly well known to the professional world. But while both catalogues have essential features in common, principally as to the method of entry, the catalogue of 1908 was merely a tentative forerunner of this, and is totally superseded by it. Whoever goes to the trouble of comparing the two will find so many new features, and the old so developed, that it would really be absurd to call the present catalogue a "revised and enlarged edition" of that of 1908.

In fact, it is in most respects a new book, and where it differs from the old its preparation was governed largely by the principles prevailing in my "Catalogue of Opera Librettos," in conjunction with which it should be used for operas before 1800. To dwell on these principles here at length, is therefore superfluous. Suffice it to remark that analytical work has been restricted in the main to operas of the pasticcio age. This analytical work has been carried far in the entries of the "Favourite Songs" literature, as in operas represented by that type of publication the pasticcio craze was most virulent. And a craze it was, brought about by peculiar operatic conditions in London, since Burney lists certainly not less than one hundred and fifty Italian works which plainly were compiled and performed in London from the beginning of the eighteenth century up to about 1775 along pasticcio lines. Perhaps it was unnecessary to devote such an amount of labor for the purposes of a catalogue to tracing the ingredients of such ephemeral pasticcios; but inasmuch as the Library of Congress possesses the great majority of such publications, and since such musico-chemical analysis, as one might call it, has its fascinations and would have had to be done some day, the author succumbed to the temptation of doing it at this time. Analysis practically stopped with the more modern operas, because it would have led to research quite out of proportion to obtainable results. Furthermore, so far as pasticcio elements are concerned, there is this vital difference between operas performed before and after about 1780. In the latter a composer simply continues the old practice of occasionally utilizing material from previous works of his own; whereas in the former, if in the nature of *replicas,* heterogeneous elements from different operas not only by one composer but by several composers were mixed without warning in one opera that continued to travel under the name of the composer of the original production.   To us this practice may seem very strange, but it really is far from mysterious if one keeps in mind that the "star" shone more brilliantly than the composer in the public's eye and that the interpolated arias were often familiar favorites of the public.   Needless to say, such "anonymous" pasticcios differ greatly from those raised to a distinct, though esthetically objectionable, type of art by openly assigning the several acts to different composers, as in the case of "Muzio Scevola," or individual scenes to a host of coöperative composers, as in the case of certain French operas of the Méhul, Boieldieu, Catel and Cherubini era.

If, then, a library possesses a manuscript score of an old opera without clear proof (as for instance in the case of transcripts from authentic autograph scores) that it represents the original version of the work, a reasonable effort to establish, by textual comparison, the character of the score as either original or an altered version becomes almost a duty.   It is precisely in such special technical work that the librarian acts as a scout for the historian.

It will be noticed that dates of publication have been added comparatively seldom to the imprint when the dates of publication or U. S. copyright do not appear in the score, and this is true of most scores printed since about 1750.   This absence of dates of publication from music has been a source of complaint from Burney to Kretzschmar, and also a source of confusion from which only the music publishers can possibly have profited.   Amongst librarians, dealers, etc., the custom grew up to take the date of performance, so often mentioned at any rate in French scores, as the date of publication without further scruple.   In the majority of cases the custom did not and does not lead to serious errors of judgment, but in a noticeable minority it is open to censure. In many instances the date of performance simply cannot have been the date of publication. A closer scrutiny of the publisher's plate-numbers, a comparison of them with the actual imprint on the title-pages, the observation that "A. P. D. R." would hardly appear on works published during the French Revolution, somewhere in the volume the composer's lists of works inclusive of such performed after the date of performance mentioned in the title, the advertisement by the publisher of works not then as yet issued, these and many other criteria and tricks of bibliographic technique would and should have established the impossibility of the assumed date of publication. In other words, the custom mentioned is fairly dangerous. For this reason it has not been followed in the present catalogue. Here the rule has been to let the date of publication be *inferred* from the date of performance, whether mentioned in the volume itself or added in a note, without actually identifying the two. The date has been added (within brackets, of course) to the imprint only when available clews, criteria, and standard books of bibliographic reference, pointed to it with reasonable safety. Also, for British publications, the dates in the British Museum Catalogue were frequently accepted on the strength of Mr. William Barclay Squire's authority.

No consistent effort has been made to state the process by which the score was printed, whether from engraved copper plates, from pewter plates, from the stone, from movable type or by sundry new electrotype and other processes. Except for certain few cases in which they are necessary, such distinctions contribute little to the identification of scores. Similarly, titles and emoluments of composers given on the title-page or the names of the persons to whom the score was dedicated were copied only if that appeared advisable for reasons of bibliographic distinction.

As in the Libretto catalogue, prefaces and other introductory matter in the old scores have been quoted more
or less fully, but now and then considerations of space
interfered with this practice. In such cases a reference
to such easily accessible compilations of "sources" as Solerti's "Le origini del melodramma" has been substituted.
In fact, since the historian may prefer to turn to these
books, the usefulness of such quotations in a catalogue
may be disputed by some. Other users of the catalogue
may feel inclined to think differently of the matter, especially if they prefer consultation of one book to consultation of two books; and for the benefit of these the
practice of quotation was intended. Besides, the quotations will be as oases in a desert; the searcher after
bibliographical and historical data is not always averse to
finding a few "readable" pages in a catalogue, and those
are extremely few who can appreciate a lucid catalogue
entry as something more than a dry statement of facts, as
something to which real brainwork often must be applied
tenaciously.

No such apology, if apology it be, is required for the
many purely bibliographical investigations and "articles"
scattered through this work. They are not presumed to be
final, for with every day's accumulation of experience the
lesson has been brought home the more forcefully to the
author that infallibility may be possible in other branches
of learning, but certainly not in bibliography, where the pit-
falls are many and the few avenues of escape so frequently
blocked by unsuspected obstacles. Hence, every bit of
information added to the common stock or brought together for handy reference cannot fail to be greeted with
satisfaction by all whose profession, trade or hobby is
likely to bring them into contact with a catalogue descriptive of a collection of operas such as ours. The author's
regret is that considerations of space, time and cost did
not permit him to go more deeply into these incidental
bibliographic features of the catalogue than to reduce the

necessity of further research by other bibliographers and historians to a minimum. Moreover, it became a physical impossibility to incorporate evenly all improvements of the original plan that suggested themselves during the years of collecting and cataloguing since 1908.

THE HISTORY OF MUSIC IN AMERICA

A Few Suggestions

("Proceedings of the Music Teachers' National Association," 1916)

The title of this address is ambiguous, yet it was not chosen hastily. It may mean the *history of music* in America, but it also may have the narrower meaning of the history of *music in America*. I propose to steer my course between the two. More or less in circles that may cause wonder at the pilot. Nevertheless, the main drift of his thoughts will, I trust, be discernible from beginning to end, and will leave the impression, as it were, of a rondo with two interdependent themes.

Within the last eight years at least three general histories of music in America have been published. A comparative study would readily disclose a family resemblance between the three as to contents, method of procedure and balance of interest. The authors themselves would hardly claim their books to be works of research in the stricter sense. All three are compilations—no opprobrium attaching to this term—somewhat in the sense that Naumann's "History of Music" was a compilation. All three have their merits and demerits. All three are useful general surveys of general conditions and all three are weakest perhaps in their bibliographic data.

I shall not criticize the fact that the lists of bibliographic references include titles with next to no bearing on the subject, but I must criticize the absence of books, monographs, articles that do bear fruitfully thereon. Perhaps this absence was merely an oversight, but it is possible that the authors failed to acquaint themselves with their existence. From a more or less careful perusal of the contents of the three books, I am rather inclined to take the less charitable view of the matter.

Let us suppose that a reader has derived all possible positive benefit from the study of these books, and that his historical curiosity has been aroused to the extent of desiring to go a little deeper into special phases of musical development in America. For instance, of church music. He turns to one of us librarians and we consult the index together. Our first shock comes when we notice the absence of a reference to Waldo S. Pratt's carefully studious series of articles in the "Christian Union" (Nov. and Dec., 1888) on "Church music as it is." The omission of such a historical tool sets us thinking. Its author's name suggests by way of mental association the Proceedings of the M. T. N. A. Of the three books only one, and that incorrectly, refers at all to this remarkable set of volumes. Once we discover that omission, we are not astonished to find that one of the books does not even mention the M. T. N. A. in its historical survey of musical education in America, and the two others in a very superficial way only. That the set of Proceedings, at least as far as they contain articles on the present or past status of music in America—and they certainly do—were not consulted by the authors, now almost goes without saying. Otherwise, it could not have happened, for instance, that all three books, when dealing with the library situation (only two of them condescending to do so at all), consistently ignore the existence of the music collections of the Library of Congress, unquestionably by far the most important musical library in the country. As to the articles on music in America in the publications of the International Musical Society, they, too, have escaped the attention of our authors. A goodly number of other omissions could be mentioned under challenge, but the above will serve as a warning not to issue that challenge.[1]

Whatever the explanation of such historical negligence, any critic would be justified in repeating (with certain modifications) to-day what I wrote in the first volume of the Proceedings and Papers of the Bibliographical Society of America, 1904–05, in an essay on "the Bibliography of American Music":

But the blankest spot in the bibliography of American music has not yet been touched, and it is only with a keen sense of humiliation that I, as an American writer on the musical life of America, lead you for a moment into this "darkest Africa." What I mean is simply this: We do not even possess a bibliography of books and articles on the musical history of our country. Still worse, with exception of certain subjects . . . , not a single, separate branch of the literature relating to our own musical history has been accorded conscientious bibliographical treatment. In vain will you look for a half-way complete list of contributions towards the history of American opera, American oratorios, American national music, American musical instruction, American musical societies, and the effort to locate a comprehensive or even fragmentary list of bio-bibliographical sketches of individual American musicians will be just as futile. Yet we continue to write histories of music in America, though we know, or at least should know, that bibliography is the backbone of history.

Bibliographical work is fascinating for him who happens to be afflicted with the disease; it is stupid work in the eyes of him who is not; but it becomes useful work in the eyes of even the scoffers if circumstances compel them to depend upon a piece of bibliographic work well done. So I suggest now as then that some one with a thirst for titles (and the necessary capacity) have pity on those who write histories of music in America and devote himself to the irksome but useful task of preparing a bibliography of the literature on music in America.

[1] Of course, the "American Supplement" to Grove's Dictionary, edited by Pratt and Boyd, 1920, is not one of the three works here criticized so severely.

It is a task such as I would propose for a graduation theme in a college or a library school. The wonder is that none of these institutions seem to have given to this subject any serious attention, though it lies so close to our doors and cries out for a less amateurish treatment than heretofore.

Such a thesis would involve historical research, in the sense of a compound of investigation and codification. But patient research is exactly what the rising generation of American writers on music does not appear to relish. They are carrying too readily the technique of journalism into the writing of historical books, where it does not belong. Indeed, I contend that the older generation of our writers on music shows more power of research and more willingness to be slaves of research for the time being than they, and began to do so at a time when the facilities for historical research in our country were still more limited than now. There are notable exceptions, of course, but on the whole, books entailing the drudgery of historical research and not merely that of compilation are written in America by a well-known circle of older men who do not seem to have many successors.

It will be objected that one of the main reasons for this condition is that the older men with well-known names have a kind of monopoly on that type of books, and that the publishers' doors would be closed to younger, unknown men. That is probably true to a certain extent. Nevertheless, the objection is not altogether sound. The man with the fatal gift of research and the ambition to do research work does not give much thought to the ultimate consumers *until his work is finished*. He sees a historical problem (I allude more especially now to antiquarian subjects) and he sets out to solve it in the spirit of "das Ding an sich."

A mature, sophisticated man, weighed down by the problems of daily life, may shrink from the monotonous, boresome, slow, grinding, unremunerative labor of an extensive piece of research, but a young man never, provided he really possesses the interests and instincts of a scholar. He may be impatient of results, but he will be patient in labor. He may need encouragement because of discouraging features of the work itself, but the prospective indifference of publishers and magazine editors will not enter into his scheme of life sufficiently to deter him from further research. He may and will and ought to carry the fruits of his labor to market in expectation of a fair exchange of values which will provide him with the necessities and luxuries of life, but he will not submit to a dictation of the terms under which he is willing to labor for others as well as for himself in search of facts, effects and causes, by commercialism, that hideous curse of our age. And by commercialism I mean in this connection the creed of those who prostitute commerce, deliberately turn the temple of art into a bucket-shop of art and let every stroke of their pen be governed by the desire to do profitable work instead of good work.

Those writers on music who hypocritically hide the shortcomings of scholarly ambition and tendencies behind the broad backs of the wicked publishers and editors, may safely be left to their own devices. They will always represent a negligible quantity, whether conditions can be improved or not by mere discussion of the real reasons why only a few isolated men and women are doing historical research work in music in that scholarly spirit which so many others are displaying in musical psychology, acoustics and so forth.

In the first place, Americans do not so eagerly and consistently view life from the historical point of view as do the French, the Germans, the Italians. Our professional historians are many, true, but they do not command the same respect with the people at large as do their colleagues abroad. Americans do not as yet and as a rule, possess the passion to put world events under the historical microscope as do the Europeans. We are not, generally speaking, a people of a historical bent of mind as they are.   Indeed, the American policy of education would seem to be tending in the other direction if it be true that in many of our schools the study of history is not obligatory.   To this add in our special field of musical history the fact that practically no provision is made anywhere for training professional historians of music as we do historians of other factors of civilization and culture. There has been no demand for them.   The few men who did take up the history of music as their main profession are mostly self-made historians with limited radius of academic action and scant opportunity for producing a crop of disciples.

Should a demand for professional historians suddenly arise (which is not likely to happen), it would be difficult to supply it because so exceedingly few libraries are equipped for musical research work even of an elementary, non-antiquarian, contemporary kind.   How many libraries are there in which a student could formulate a really comprehensive historical estimate of, let us say, the roots, growth and ramification of the art of Horatio Parker and base it on the scores and not merely on books and articles already written?   (This condition of affairs, by the way, will not be remedied until the musicians and music lovers revolt against it.)   In such libraries, however, as are fairly equipped for research work of a modest kind, American library policy often stands in the way of real research work.   The American librarian takes a paternal or maternal interest in his or her clients.   He seeks to remove even the pebbles out of their path to the catalogue and the shelves, which is as it should be as regards the general reader, but when it comes to the novice in research work, the practice is not altogether wholesome. It has a tendency to leave his research-muscles undeveloped, a tendency to spare him the trouble of digging through the literature and finding or not finding by his own efforts what he needs.   Not that I decry guidance in proper methods of research, but I hold to the view that once that method has been pointed out a maximum of independent research will, other things being equal, lead to a maximum of results.   Now, there are cases on record in which a candidate for academic honors with the consent of his professor requested a librarian to furnish a list of references to the books which he *might* need for his thesis. In my humble opinion neither professor nor candidate knew what scholarship means.   At any rate, they made the fatal blunder of deluding themselves into the belief that one can do research work on the principle of "Let George do it."   In anticipation of the customary objection I contend that no one has yet become a respectable historian without having wasted much precious time on bibliographical research, if it really be a waste of time to consult literature not perhaps immediately applicable but containing suggestions for later and other use.

A further, and probably the most important reason for the scarcity of serious effort in behalf of history of music in America lies in that history itself.   Our musical past, excepting the immediate past, lies in low-lands.   No peaks commanding a far view of our country's domain in the world of music attract the esthetic wanderer.   Our share in the glories of the past is negligible.   There is little room for historical hero-worship or for the demonstration of vital riparian rights along the broad stream of musical evolution.   In consequence whereof the American is not tempted as is the European to abandon the pursuit of happiness as a chirper of song in favor of the more altruistic and sensible task of recording his country's heroic deeds and of singing the praise of artistic forebears greater than he can ever be.   Indeed, in that respect the American does not feel himself as an American at all, but as a European; or, if you prefer, musically his country interests him and exists for him only in so far as it has participated and is participating in the council of nations governing the world of music.   The proof of this we see in the fact that he has been singularly silent on his domestic historical affairs, but has on frequent occasions paid a thoughtful and searching tribute to those masters and to such historical problems as belong to and affect the whole world of music.

If such contributions but rarely partake of an antiquarian research character, and are mostly confined to contemporary music, contemporary in the broader sense of music forming our daily musical diet, that is but natural. The musical past of Europe absorbs the interest of the American musician in so far only as it wedges itself into the present and future problems of musical life in America. Chief of these is the problem of educating a musical people, such as ours is, to become an artistic people and the correlated problem of fighting for his place in the sun as an artist and of making his voice as an artist heard in the international ensemble of contending voices. For him the age is still primarily one of action, perhaps of introspection, certainly not yet of retrospection: We are still unripe for an American Romain Rolland.

If the vision of history were restricted by the esthetic horizon, historians of music in America would be in a sad plight. Fortunately, another factor presents claims on our attention. Curiosity is the mother of all knowledge, curiosity from its crudest to its most refined forms. The historical instinct, too, is one of curiosity. History but records the inquiry of the curious into the facts of the past and their logic of friction or mutual support. This type of refined curiosity is sufficient unto itself without the alluvium of esthetic, ethical, didactic or other mental deposits. Hence, the would-be historian need not feel apologetic at all if his curiosity move him to lift the veil of otherwise merited oblivion from facts that the historically non-inclined sneer at as being dry-as-dust and of no value for the furtherance of present musical art. The historian and the esthetician simply work in different mediums which may or may not converge. And speaking entirely for myself, I do think that to roam through the cemeteries of music not infrequently has more charms than to visit the noisy market-places of venders of sham art. Also, I cannot help thinking that the excavation of some forgotten fact of musical history, trivial in itself perhaps, bears at least as much on the art of music as would the snapshot of a charming primadonna brushing the teeth of her pet monkey.

I have not yet seen quite so original a publicity picture as that, but I have seen many others almost as musical. As a historian I do not resent them, for I know that they help to make our modern musical news-magazines what they are. Without these the future historian would miss not only a handy mirror of public taste but a very valuable source of information about the events of the day. Economic conditions have become so complex that an artist or teacher who wishes to reach a wide public must advertise his wares somehow. He needs publicity of some kind and it is one of the legitimate functions of the news-magazines to afford him that publicity by dwelling on his personal traits, the events of his life, his theories of art, and what not. All that makes for valuable biographical data, and incidentally for history, often sound, often unsound if it be allowed not to square with the actual facts. However, the historian, viewing things from an impersonal distance, will not be fooled so easily that he cannot determine (generally from the astonishingly unoriginal and monotonously stereotyped pattern of publicity matter) where the effort to present real personal or institutional history ceases and the effort to help musicians or institutions in their business by exaggerated coloring of the facts begins. As long as the ethics of journalism are preserved and advertising or self-advertising is done within the proprieties of good taste, no one can resent publicity in whatever form. What I personally do resent is this, that such magazines—as they should in the interest of their readers —frequently open their own columns to more or less valuable historical articles including such of an antiquarian

kind, and then poke fun at outsiders because they devote
themselves to historical subjects without "news" value in
the ordinary sense.   The editor who indulges in that kind
of criticism underestimates the intellectual and cultural
horizon of educated American musicians and is rendering
a very poor service to music in America.   And when his
attacks become unfair and vicious, he seems to forget to
reckon with posterity.   He may be able to blacken the
reputation of a man and injure him grievously for the time
being; nevertheless, the historian will have the last say in
the matter, for his books and his estimates of men and
times will be consulted long after the public will have
ceased to take an interest in any particular magazine or its
editor.

Furthermore, a singular little fact ought not to be forgotten by those who do not possess the historical instinct
and yet presume to sit in judgment over what is and what
is not fit for historical treatment: quite often an esthetically, artistically noteworthy occurrence or development
does not excite the interest of the historian, whereas one
of esthetic or artistic dullness does, just as beautiful
scenery often fascinates the painter for purposes of a
picture very much less than a tumble-down, dirty old
shanty on which Light is improvising a rhapsody in colors.   Finally, the historical instinct (and frequently more
so than the artistic instinct) draws nourishment from
the most mysteriously complex of human characteristics,
which is as natural as it is artificial, as superficial as it is
deep-rooted, as harmful as it is beneficial.   I mean pa-
triotism.   He is a sad failure as a genealogist who blushes
with shame and mortification because he has traced his
ancestor in the rôle of a goat-herder instead of that of a
son-in-law of Charlemagne.   Just so he is a sad failure
as a historian who turns his back on the humble musical
origin and growth of his own country and disdains to
busy himself therewith for that reason.   On the contrary,
dulce et decorum pro patria mori, if I may liken to suicide

the perfectly natural and laudable desire to investigate the musically humble past of our country.

After this somewhat oblique metaphor, my utterances will no longer appear cryptic. I was simply leading up to a plea in accordance with the hidden meaning of the sub-title of my address—to the suggestion that the history of music in America is not at all uninteresting or unworthy of serious consideration by the modern American musician of scholarly interests, if only it be approached in the proper spirit and from the proper angle: from that of research for the sake of research, unaffected by forethought esthetic or mercenary.

Perhaps this suggestion will not fall on deaf ears, coming as it does from one of those who may be conceded to have done their share in that detached spirit. It does not, however, embrace the plea that persons insufficiently trained for research work make historical problems of music in America the playground of their patriotic hysteria. (Of that kind of amateurish sport we have had by far too much, and it has helped to discredit the legitimate interest in such problems.) Nor is meant by research work the industry of rival editors who survey present musical activities in certain localities and inevitably shed glory on their own set of subscribers and advertisers. Such articles undoubtedly will be helpful in the future for local history, since the combination of two and two of rival brands will at least produce the sum of three. Real research is more neutral, more impartial, more disinterested—in brief, more scientific. That implies a scientific method and the appreciation of the fact that a mere chronological string of dates or names does not constitute history. They are merely the bricks with which the historical edifice is reared. In other words, the historian is not a bricklayer, but an architect, though often he will have to act in both capacities. The plea then is to apply to the investigation of our musical past, no matter how humble it may be, more of that scientific method and technique, more of that historical analysis and synthesis which still (in a degree) distinguish the best of our historians from the best in Europe. The place to foster all this is not really within the province of conservatories, be they private or collegiate. Their function is to train musicians who shall possess also requisite knowledge of the history of their art. They are not the place to train historians with the requisite knowledge of music. Once this fundamental idea is grasped, it will become obvious that historical training for research work must be undertaken by the universities very much in the same manner as we see it done in certain countries of Europe. And very much with the same object in view, too; namely, that the graduates of such courses march into the world of music not as "musicians" but as professional historical investigators, as professional teachers of musical history or as critics who realize that at any time their critical estimates may need a background of historical reasoning.

Initial steps toward this goal have been taken, to be sure, but they are too tentative and too few. The movement is as yet sporadic, not general. That ultimately it will become general, is my firm conviction. The development is likely to come about, as most reforms do in our country, either with exasperating slowness or with a rush. When it does come about, studies in the history of music in America ought not to be neglected. In the meantime individual pioneer effort, as heretofore, will have to tap the mine of subjects, though, of course, the yield cannot possibly compare with that by historical laboratories in the form of seminaries when they shall form part of our academic institutions. About individual coöperation in the shape of a historical association, as might be advocated, I personally have my doubts. The practical obstacles are too numerous. There is a surfeit of associations anyhow in our country, a veritable craze for founding societies and burying them almost as fast as they are born. For in this respect we Americans resemble the Germans: if four of them assemble, they will found five societies. The result is generally attrition by jealous rivalry.

The diffident will ask: Are there subjects enough to make this plea for an extensive and intensive study of the history of music in America more substantial and solid than so many other pleas which have turned out to be mere soap-bubbles of specialists? I had occasion to ask myself the same question when I surveyed "The musical life of America from the standpoint of musical topography" under this title for the Congress of the International Musical Society at Vienna, in 1909. My survey of the psychological and economic foundations of music in America included an analysis of the chief historical contributions. It was prefaced by this general remark:

The literature on music in America is fairly voluminous and is constantly growing, but the books and articles deal more with the history of music and musicians in America than with the history of America's musical life. For example, the scientific historical study and comparison of the German, English, Italian, etc., influence would immediately be paralyzed from a lack of such literature as can be taken seriously. Opportunities are not much better for reading up on a scientific, useful treatment of the historical vicissitudes of single masters in America (such as Haydn, or Wagner), or of the development of music in the various states and cities, of church music, chamber music, orchestral music, choral music, opera, music in our colleges, the music trades, the manufacture of instruments, the music-publishing industry, musical societies and organizations, municipal and governmental interest in and subvention of music, folk-music and a host of other subjects. Even exhaustive biographic and bibliographic literature is not impressive in quantity. Whoever seeks scientific information in any of the fields enumerated must laboriously dig it out from books and sporadic articles in magazines innumerable, not to mention newspapers in which often our best writers on music have buried their investigations alive. Moreover, a good part of all this literature does not possess the character of original research (Quellenforschung).

To be sure, since 1909, a number of permanently valuable books on several of the subjects enumerated above have appeared, but otherwise the diagnosis of poverty is just as correct to-day as it was then. At any rate, my chart of subjects not yet treated scientifically or not at all, presents a nucleus of subjects (selected at random) that will help to answer diffident questioners. Many more could have been added from the common fund of our personal experiences, for no thoughtful American musician is living whom life, travel, profession have not somehow and some time brought into contact with phenomena in our musical life which excited his curiosity. Frequently only history can give a key to the puzzle; and in such cases the "musician" will naturally turn to the historian, just as the latter will go to the musician for explanation of some technical puzzle in music. Just a few illustrations from my own experience in elucidation of this point and also as proof of the contention that our musical past embodies countless themes which are interesting from the point of view peculiar to the historian. It is perhaps the penalty of a musician who has specialized along these lines and in whose custody the vast output of American music publishers was placed that he should stumble right and left on exactly such subjects which others would naturally fail to notice.

Take "Dixie." I have reason to believe that research in the history of the song will bring to light information which probably will not alter the main history of the song, but will at least throw interesting side-lights thereon. —Or a totally different subject: Horatio Parker speaks in the volume on the Yale pageant recently published of a Beethoven society that flourished at Yale generations ago. I happen to know that it was called "Beethoven Glee Club." Mr. Parker's reference reminded me immediately of certain other Beethoven societies existing in the first half of the nineteenth century. Would it not be worth while to study the reasons why just Beethoven was selected as the titular hero of such societies? Did they or did they not cultivate his music? And, in general, when

and where did the Beethoven cult in our country originate
and how did it spread?

The book on the Yale pageant with its chapter on music
at Yale vividly brought back to my mind the studies I
made many years ago on music in our colleges during
the eighteenth century. My plan was to combine those
studies with others on our early music trades, music publishers, music instruction and so forth, for a companion
volume to my books on our Early Concert Life and our
Early Opera. The plan has been frustrated, but, at any
rate, I know positively that those subjects are full of interest not only to the investigator but to the reader. Especially that on music in our colleges. And if research
covered this particular subject through the nineteenth
century, a really fascinating book could be produced.

My studies in our early musical life took a direction
toward the secular phases because these had been neglected
in favor of our early sacred music. Yet even in that
field very much remains to be done to establish proper historical perspective. The subject will always retain the
flavor of that oddity which appeals to those who do not
really have a historical mind. But as a matter of fact
the problems involved are fairly complex and not at all
so odd if care be taken to check up historically, let us
say, early American psalmody, with the similar movement in England. Nor did sacred music in our country
consist merely of an imitation, for the worse or better,
of English psalmodists like Tans'ur. The Germans, the
Swedes, the Dutch and others made their contributions,
and a historian might well afford to look broadly and
deeply into all this instead of gazing contentedly through
a New England church window. If New England has
its William Billings, Pennsylvania has its Conrad Beissel
and his brother and sister mystics at Ephrata. A volume
has been devoted to their music by Sachse, but it was
not given to him to solve all the inherent puzzles. Again,
who has not heard of the Shakers? But does any histori-

cal treatise exist on their music? Possibly so, but certainly in that case it is not generally known. As to the music of the Catholic church, its history in our country is practically a sealed book. In these days of revival of the traditional chant I might, as a reference librarian, be asked any day questions like these: To what extent did liturgical uniformity prevail in the music of the Catholic churches in America seventy years ago? How about boy choirs? When were voices first raised in our country —and by whom—to restore Gregorian chant to its traditional purity? Who were the chief American champions of Dom Pothier and his collaborators at Solesmes? Was early Catholic music in our country adulterated by Protestant ingredients?—I should not know what to answer offhand, but for a reply to the last question at least I should refer the inquisitor to certain articles by Monsignor Henry.

Whoever has had to occupy himself with our recent histories of music in America, will have noticed the scant courtesy shown to the first half of the nineteenth century. By paraphrased repetition of what Ritter, Matthews and others knew and by utilization of a few recent monographs on special subjects, the fact is more or less cleverly concealed that we know comparatively little about the historical currents and under-currents of that period. Certain phenomena like Lowell Mason's activity or Garcia's importation of Italian opera, or the Handel and Haydn Society, stand out prominently, surrounded by the names of sundry pioneers in the realm of higher art; but a cross-section of our historical knowledge of that period would reveal a rather brittle surface. I, for one, cannot rid myself of the impression that the history of our musical life after 1850 with its phenomenally rapid development still hangs in the air. It will continue to do so until some intrepid historian of uncommon constructive gifts will devote several years of steady comprehensive research exclusively to the earlier half-century. Incidentally, this picture of evolutional continuity in our musical life from Colonial to Cubist times will be welcome for this reason: it may give us that assurance of stock which looks upon accomplishment as something so natural that one need make no noise about it. As a result it may serve to check those who teach the American music lover the manners of parvenus ill-bred enough to bray loudly and publicly of their sudden riches. I also believe that our historians will be able to trace the roots of much that is still objectionable in our musical life to that very period when solid accomplishment, crude experimentation and shrewd charlatanry seem to have crisscrossed at every turn.

What a contrast, for instance, between such a sterling musician as Benjamin Carr, who carried the traditions of the eighteenth century far into the first half of the nineteenth, and Anthony Philip Heinrich! If Benjamin Carr fully merits a biographical monograph, not less so, though for other reasons, our Bohemian adventurer, known to your grandfathers as "Father Heinrich." In no country except ours with its socially still very crude democracy could such a musician have led the weird life he did, a life as fit for a fantastic historical novel as was that of Abt Vogler. But it must not be imagined that Anthony Philip Heinrich was a faker. After one of his returns to Europe he almost wrested from no less a composer than Franz Lachner the prize for a symphony. Was it perhaps his symphony "To the spirit of Beethoven," one of about seventy works ranging from a mere song to "grand" oratorios which he listed in 1845 under the title of "Presentazioni musicali from a Bohemian in America," and which often employ an orchestra approaching that of Richard Strauss? Knowing such facts, one hesitates to laugh at the antics of the composer of "The dawning of music in Kentucky," "The Western Minstrel," and other such works with their bombastic, charlatanic phraseology, and their, of course, by now antiquated music, though an English critic recently declared it not inferior to Bishop's.

Whatever the merits of Heinrich's music, his first mentioned volume is at any rate the bulkiest and most ambitious venture in music publishing in America up to that time (1820) and for a good many years later.[1]

Observations like these forced themselves lately on me at the Library of Congress, where we had begun to catalogue the sheet music deposited for copyright in America between 1820 and 1860. More and more I received the impression that the first half of the nineteenth century and no longer the eighteenth century is the mysterious period in our musical past and, apart from its total pregnant importance for the future, so full of historical trifles that it is a veritable source for the historical short story.

What led in those days, for instance, music publishers of secular music to copyright rather sparingly their sheet music, whereas every compiler of hymn-books rushed to cover, to an extent that in certain Districts musical copyrights were out of all proportion to other publications? Does the history of copyright in America offer an explanation—perhaps the fact that for half a century the word "music" did not figure in our copyright laws, that music publishers had merely their choice between "a book" and "a print," and did not find sufficient protection behind these two categories? Again, what accounts for the evident craze for dance-music in the forties? Valses, polkas, redovas, galops by the hundred almost every year, such worthies as John Conrad Viereck, Charles Grobe, and others supplying the demand with rapid pen. The phenomenon offers no puzzle, once one discovers in it a reflex of Lanner and Strauss and the fascinating Fanny Elsler. But the public was rapidly acquiring a taste for Italian operas also, particularly (it seems) those by Donizetti and Verdi, surpassed only by its interest in the ever fresh "Bohemian Girl"; and our publishers were not

[1] By an extraordinary stroke of good fortune recently the "musical estate" of Anthony Philip Heinrich passed into the possession of the Library of Congress: it comprises many of his most ambitious works in the original manuscript!

slow to cater to both tastes simultaneously by issuing galops, etc., based on favorite operatic airs and choruses. But they also took into account the fact that just then negro minstrel music of the Christy type was rapidly forging ahead in public favor, that the sentimental parlor-ballad, whose chief exponent Foster was to be, had taken hold of our people, and that then as in all times music was a ready vehicle for the expression of patriotic or political sentiments. How original a study could be made of the musical tributes paid to political and military notables or to the Presidents of our country! The music seldom amounts to much artistically, but at least it mirrors the political or patriotic sympathies of each period, as for instance, when the Whig party with Henry Clay for some reason appear to have been extremely popular with our musicians, or when the Mexican War broke out. And what is true of that war, is a hundred times true of our Civil War. A musical historian studying its vast song-literature could throw side-lights on the passions aroused by that mighty strife which would add color to general political history. But not merely the historian of American music, the historian of American caricature as well. For there are hidden in the mass of thousands and thousands of pieces and songs of that period caricatures and cartoons of not less bitter or pathetic a character than those issued through other channels. That fact is not known to musicians, but it is coming to be known to print collectors. Such a piece of music may not be worth ten cents to-day to a collector of music, but it may be worth several dollars to a collector of prints on account of its historical title-page.

If this is narrowing musical history down to a very narrow front, I can only repeat that the interests of a historian of music and musical life are not and ought not to remain confined to matters of musical esthetics or technique. If we can but seldom take pride in such music as music, then at least let us rejoice in the fact that quite often its pictorial title-pages—a fashion probably imported from France—give esthetic satisfaction or afford instructive glimpses into olden times. Once famous steamships pass before our eyes, gorgeous uniforms galore attract the attention, as do exquisite views of historic American buildings, or romantic (and more or less artistic) landscapes or scenes illustrating social life, or grotesque cartoons of negro minstrels, or many a portrait not only of celebrated musicians, but of statesmen and generals, including one of Henry Clay that is a veritable gem of portraiture.

These are but a few of the suggestions for study that I might offer. They will suffice, since it cannot be my irrational intention to draw up an inventory of every conceivable subject, from a history of "the wreckage in the wake of musical journalism in America" to a history of the weird proposals to improve our musical notation or of the movement for a national conservatory, or of the propaganda for more "Americanism" in our musical life, or of musical unionism and its effects, or of music's function in Washington's social life, or of the American temperance song, or of the American impresario in his unique twin capacity of pioneer and peddler, and so forth. My object could only be to suggest that he who seeks interesting subjects (many of them peculiar to our country) will find them as have others, whose ideas of history-writing were blessed with unconventionality and were stimulated by the truism that the general historian, and be he a walking encyclopedia, can never dispense with the explorations of the specialist. Generally speakng, then, the subjects available are just as numerous as are States and cities (musical or not) or individuals who in their day or way contributed their share (or not) in winning for our country the position which it holds in the world of music to-day. The endless variety of subjects will keep pace with our growth as a musical nation and with the endless variety of tastes and preferences of investigators, whether the subject chosen taxes their power of research for a week, a month, a year or ten years. Ample work for all of us lies on the surface or deep under the surface. No subject can be patented or copyrighted. Not one of us has a monopoly on any given subject, and least of all a man who, like myself, has wandered off into other fields and feels as if, by offering these few suggestions, he were reading a valedictory.